UNDERSTANDING AND HEALING
THE HURTS OF CHILDHOOD

UNDERSTANDING AND HEALING THE HURTS OF CHILDHOOD

JIM O'SHEA

FURZE PUBLICATIONS

CONTENTS

Acknowledgements and Permissions

I WANT TO THANK MY FAMILY for their patience and encouragement as I struggled with this book. It was truly a struggle, because as humans we are extremely complex and my hope was to show in such a small book how an insecure attachment can largely dictate how our adulthood will be. Originally I titled the book as *Fear* but quickly realised that it was about attachment issues. It would take many volumes to illustrate this complex issue so I hope I will whet your appetite to learn more about this fascinating formative reality. I used some case studies to illustrate the negative impact of attachment problems. I would like to thank all those who allowed me to use their experiences. I am especially grateful to Jason who compiled a long account of the distresses he suffered in life. Nancy was generous in allowing me to illustrate her intense fear of abandonment, James who was strong enough to show his vulnerability, and Peter who courageously demonstrated his strong fear of death.

I am very grateful to all those who have written so extensively on the various themes in the book. I hope

I have given them full credit for their writings from which I have learned much. I also want to acknowledge specific authors who gave me permission to reproduce some of their work. Robbie Dunton allowed me to list his compilation of the negative and positive beliefs/cognitions which have been used from time immemorial in EMDR therapy. I am very grateful to my trainer, Dr Michael Paterson, who helped me define the essence of EMDR therapy and who is always patient and kind. I thank Fr Brian McKevitt for allowing me to adapt the piece *How to Fight a Fair Fight* published in the *Alive* newspaper in March 2007. I wish to thank Moody publishers for permitting me to introduce the Five Love Languages of Gary Chapman. I am grateful to SPCK Publishing for letting me quote from Paul Hauck's book *Jealousy. Why it happens and how to overcome it* (Sheldon Press). My thanks also to David Leisner for giving me permission to list his Golden Rules.

Finally I want to thank my grandson, Martin, for helping me using his great technological knowledge in getting this book published.

Introduction

IT IS DIFFICULT TO BELIEVE THAT childhood largely dictates how our adult life will be. The seeds are sown from very early childhood before conscious memory begins, and, therefore, in a counselling setting it can take months for the adult to make the connections between childhood and adulthood. It can be challenging to realise that what determines how we will be later in life is the nature of the attachment we have to our parents or caregivers from birth onwards. Attachment is a psychological term, and a *secure* attachment is an intense and unique relationship that forms a lifelong bond. The person that the child forms the bond with is known as the attachment figure. An *insecure* attachment, on the other hand, is the opposite, where no bond or a very weak one is formed, and from that comes many of the painful issues that beset us in adulthood. *This book examines some of these wounds and shows how we can heal them.* It explores fear, anger and jealousy and many other stresses related to these, which are outlined in Appendix 1. The different types of fear looked at are toxic or pathological and are different to normal fear, an emotion that is hardwired in the limbic system of our brains for our protection. Similarly the book examines toxic or core jealousy and anger. Core means something that is in the heart of self, part your being, etched on your neural pathways at a threat to your survival at a very young and dependent age. It entered your core in those early years, because of your fear that your emotional or physical survival was under threat. This book is not meant to be a criticism of parent or caregivers. We do our best as parents, but we must face the reality that our best is not always enough. We are human, but our most important role in life is to properly nurture our children. We don't have to be award winning parents, we only need to be good enough. Unfortunately some may fail to be good enough.

I have referred to many books throughout this book, so that if you are particularly interested in any theme you can read about it in more depth. I have also used several case studies including an extensive one on Jason, who suffered intense fear and many of its shackling offspring, but fortunately did not experience core anger or jealousy. These real life stories show how devastating a childhood insecure attachment can be. You will also see how Jason, in particular, overcame most of his issues, and is beginning to live a happy and fulfilled life.

The names used in these case studies are not the real names of those involved.

Chapter 1

Fear of Abandonment

TOXIC FEAR IS A WIDESPREAD REALITY and is a chronic condition that fills you with constant negativity, and, as Peg Hanafin writes in her book, *Thoughts for your Journey*, it is destructive and paralysing. Moreover, it is bad for your heart and blood pressure. Frequent fear pumps the steroid hormone, cortisol, through your system and damages your health. We need cortisol for our wellbeing, but it becomes harmful when released frequently. Interestingly, facial expressions of fear on your face is a good indicator of cortisol and blood pressure elevation. When Jennifer Lerner (Harvard Kennedy School of Government) was conducting her study of facial expression of fear, anyone taking heart medicine was excluded. The facial expression of fear is shown by raised upper eyelids, brows drawn together, the lips stretched and widened eyes. The widened eyes take in details more rapidly, enabling the brain to assess any danger that might exist. You may like to read Allan Schore on infant facial expressions and the development of the brain.

As you know, the brain is immensely complex, but did you know that it consists of three brains all inter-acting, the reptilian brain, the mammalian brain and the cortex, which is the upper part of the brain and is what makes us human? Sometimes we mistakenly refer to the latter as grey matter. In 2014 Cold Spring Harbor Laboratory discovered a new neural circuit that directly links the key site of fear memory, the amygdala, to the brain stem (reptilian brain). The amygdala is almond shaped mass of grey matter located inside both of the two brain hemispheres.

Technically, fear has been described by Julia Layton as a chain reaction in the brain that starts with a stress-ful event and ends with the release of chemicals that cause a racing heart, fast breathing and energized muscles, resembling in some ways a panic attack. This reaction is known as the fight or flight response. Normal fear is an emotion aroused by danger and is an evolutionary survival response. It is present in humans and research shows that animals, too, have specific, emotional, responses, including fear. A dog, for example, exhibits fear in specific ways by drooling, trembling, losing control of its bladder, cowering, or tucking its tail between its legs. The hair on its back bristles when it is fearful and it often becomes aggres-sive. If not aggressive, it stands with its head lower than its back and avoids eye contact.

BEFORE EXAMINING FEAR IN MORE DETAIL it might be helpful to understand the difference between emotion and feeling, because this book is about feeling rather than emotion. From the primary emotions spring secondary feelings. For example, shame and embarrassment can come from sadness, and jealousy can come from anger or fear. Although we cannot eliminate primary emotions, we can alleviate secondary feelings. So, fear being a primary *emotion*, cannot be eradicated, but negative experiences and harmful relationships creating *feelings* of fear, can be dealt with through various therapies that rewire the brain with more positive neural pathways. Emotions, therefore, are innate, deeply rooted and hardwired in the Limbic System of the brain, while feelings originate in the malleable neural cortex and are reactions and interpretations of emotions. Feelings are influenced by thoughts, memories and images linked to any emotion, and are more complex than emotions, but can be changed as reactions against your circumstances. In other words the cortex is plastic, and this enables changes through therapy.

We are told that there are five basic fears – fear of extinction, mutilation, loss of autonomy, ego-death and fear of abandonment. Fear of abandonment is related to fear of ego-death, which is about the false self that we loath and which will be mentioned throughout this book in the context of the issues outlined in Appendix 1. At this early stage it is well to understand what the different selves are, as this will help you to make better sense of yourself. Partly through reading the great theorist Carl Rogers, I became aware that we have three selves – the real self, the false self, and the invented self. The real self (authentic self) is how you are when you are born, the false self is how you are formed through your childhood environment (your home, school etc.), and the invented self is how you present to the world. The latter is a valuable self insofar as it allows you to interact and to live a relatively functional life. The false self is the one that contains all the negativity picked up in childhood – fear, shame, anger, self-loathing, perfectionism, placating, lack of assertiveness, anger and a whole host of other shackling symptoms. You never want anyone to see this self, but you often think they do and that increases your fear and your shame. How sad it is to live a life where you hate and are ashamed yourself, and have a poor opinion of others! It is the false self that we open up in therapy. The self that we have never shared with anyone, but now have the courage to explore it with a therapist.

We rarely think about fear of abandonment, yet it underlies many of our psychological problems. It is the core of an insecure attachment, breeding the negative belief *I am not good enough*. It is a spectrum issue, running along a scale from mild to severe. Dealing successfully with fear of abandonment effectively eases many other mental health problems, and generally comes from an exploration of our childhood. It is a deep-rooted but irrational fear of being discarded and replaced and being left alone.

Before exploring the foundations of this fear, let us

see what it is like practice? One of my clients Nancy explains it clearly.

> My husband Michael is a salesman and I just feel awful when he is away, and especially when I am lying in bed alone at night. We have no children and I feel the loneliness but most of all a sickening feeling in the pit of my stomach. This makes me feel so helpless and sometimes so angry. I toss and turn while my mind runs riot. Where is he now? Who is he with? I see him in my mind's eye making love to another woman. I am always tempted, but I have learned not to reach for the phone to seek reassurance, because I can never be reassured. He often threatened to leave me and I would beg him to stay with me, that I would change. Sometimes I sent as many as thirty texts a day and he used get very angry and in the end he wouldn't reply at all and that made me worse. I used be frantic. I always felt lost. I know Michael is a very trustworthy husband, but that does not help me at all. The empty feeling of fear is too powerful, although I have learned that I can feed it by thinking in a negative way. I always think about everything in a negative way and I'm haunted by images of unfaithfulness. All these women that I conjure up in my imagination are a lot more beautiful than me, although Michael keeps telling me that I am lovely and that he loves only me. But

in my mind I can never measure up to these women. I am never good enough. How can I compete against them? The frustrating thing is that I know very well that these lovely women are figments of my imagination. They don't exist at all. But they are very real in my mind. I feel lost at these times, and I dread it when he is going away, when I know that I am going to spend sleepless nights worrying. The fact that he is away a lot keeps me on tenterhooks and my nerves get strung out.

You can easily see in this short passage the impact of fear of abandonment, which in this case is very severe – stomach turning, tortured thinking, a feeling of not being good enough, sleeplessness, low self-esteem, feeling lost, and a tendency to worry, and irrational jealousy, all in this case stemming from childhood emotional neglect, mainly stemming from her emotionally withdrawn mother and an ill-tempered father.

It is clear from what Nancy says that her core issue is low self-esteem. If she had high self-esteem she would not compare herself unfavourably with other women. She would feel good enough and they would not be a threat. You can see that she even conjures up imaginary women, a behaviour that is typical of fear of abandonment where the negative is ever present. Trying to convince Nancy that she is being irrational will not help her. The fear of abandonment lies in the pit of her stomach and sickens her. It is core. By the way, do not confuse self-esteem with self-confidence. Nancy is an extremely competent teacher, who loves her job, so it is possible to be self-confident in doing some specific tasks but have low self-esteem, which prevents you exploring new possibilities because you carry shame, fear, anger and the conviction that you are not good enough. Shame becomes part of the neural wiring from a very early age. You will see the sources of shame mentioned in this book, but one source is how a primary carer's expression appears to the young child. If a mother, for example, looks at her child with contempt, blending disgust and anger, the child will feel intense shame and rage. This, of course, can be part of a parent's efforts to help the child self-regulate, but if it happens on a regular basis over a long period of time, it will negatively impact on the child's brain development, and in turn will breed many other pathological feelings. In brief, if the required empathic expression of the primary caregiver regularly becomes contemptuous and hostile, shame and anger will be the lot of the unfortunate child. Under these circumstances, low self-esteem quickly takes root. Controlling parents seem to be unable to connect to their children, because narcissism is the heart of control. Narcissistic or controlling people are unable to feel empathy, even for their own children. This makes the child feel unloved and defective, which breeds shame. Shame and fear of abandonment are compatible bedfellows.

Shame is discussed at length in this book. If you

become shame based from the behaviour of a shamed parent, you will be burned by criticism and take everything personally. When I was about thirteen I began to feel its burning touch. At that age I had no idea what shame was as I entered early adolescence, but the discomfort was distressing. It manifested itself in a painful way one summer when I was going to the *Gaeltacht* (Gaelic speaking area) in West Cork in the late 1950s. I sat beside a Christian Brother on the train, who happened to be going to that *Gaeltacht*. We became friends for over forty years, but on that first meeting he kindly enquired about my father's job. When I heard that unexpected question I could feel my face burning. I absolutely refused to tell him about the shameful job my father had. My whole system was seized with toxic shame and fear. I shrank at the idea that he would judge me by my father's job. I was defined by shame. My father was storekeeper in the local colliery!

My counsellor challenged me to find a creative way to deal with my shame, and I now realise that creativity is a powerful way to highlight and heal shame. This can take the form of art, writing, poetry or whatever type of creativity suits you. I found poetry was most appropriate for me. When my counsellor made the challenge I immediately saw a huge orb filling the room and almost overwhelming me. I left that evening with that image in my mind and so powerful was the urge to describe it, that I pulled in my car and wrote a poem. It only took a few minutes, but you will be at your most creative when you are in distress. The following is what flowed from me –

> *Monstrous Orb,*
> *Devouring me.*
> *Begotten of Evil,*
> *Crimson of the Darkness,*
> *Invader of my soul,*
> *Distilling shame into my heart*
> *For Long years.*
> *How I loathe you,*
> *Hate your taste on my Being*
> *Detest your fiery kiss,*
> *Abhor the foulness of your breath.*
> *Thief of my youth,*
> *Destroyer of my trust,*
> *Murderer of my passion,*
> *Killer of my young love.*
> *Insidiously silky serpent,*
> *Soft petalled deceiver*
> *In your sly invasion.*
> *By my hatred of your fiery embrace,*
> *I cast you forth into the darkness,*
> *From whence you came*
> *That time of innocence*

The quality of the poem, art or piece of writing is irrelevant. What is important is how you can see your shame, reject it, and find some element of control over it. There is nothing more effective in stifling your creativity and willingness to learn and experiment than the inner critical, shaming, voice being reinforced in real life. Like the servant in the scripture, you will bury your talent. This is what happened to 35 year old Jason, a highly intelligent individual. But, intelligence does not counteract fear. His behaviours are typical of those who suffer from this fear. He was acutely conscious of the severity of his fear of being away from home and the loneliness that it fostered. Home was, in short, the only place where he felt comfortable, just like a child with an insecure attachment on his first week in school. The insecure inner child did not feel safe anywhere else.

> Separation from home has always been an issue for me. I never felt comfortable living anywhere but home. I longed to head home when in college and would get the last bus to college on a Monday night and the first home on a Friday. I was so lonely that one night, my father brought me to the bus stop and even though I didn't really talk to him, I told him that I really didn't want to go back. I couldn't face it. He sensed my fear and took me home to my mother and said that the bus didn't turn up. After a sleepless night, I went the following day. I would lie to my mother about my timetable and tell her I had nothing on a Monday, so I could stay at home. As a result of all this, I was missing most of my hours in college. But, thankfully, one of my friends gave me the lecture notes. The

fact that I passed my exams masked how I felt about college, and I put on the impression that I loved it. I think my mother could see through me, but like a lot of things she didn't like to push me on it. It is strange that I longed to get out of the house, but have always found it very difficult to live away from home. Even when living away from home in later life I always felt a pull to go back. This is the main reason why I never travelled. My friends and brothers and sisters all headed on J1 visas, but I never did. I always made up excuses of not having enough money, but deep down I was too afraid. I just couldn't see myself working on a building site away in another part of the world.

Unless properly treated, fear of abandonment will be with you all your life. If Jason thought that becoming qualified and finding a job would end this fear, he was greatly mistaken. Initially this did not seem to be the case when he moved to live with some friends, who represented home and for him normality.

The only time I enjoyed living away from home was when I got my first job after college and I was living with 3 guys I knew really well. I suppose they provided the familiarity I needed – an extension of my family home, maybe. Still, I would come home every weekend. My home was my safe place, it could protect me from my fears and anxieties. At home I could briefly forgot my insecurities. I thought I had cured the anxiety of living away from home, when I lived with my friends after college. I was comfortable in the house and was finally beginning to enjoy living away from home. That changed when I moved jobs to Dublin, when fear and loneliness returned with a vengeance.

Since Jason needed familiarity to cope, he managed to come up with a solution that allowed him to work in Dublin and live at home. He took the train to work every morning, a long journey from the south of Ireland to the city, which left him exhausted and aroused the ire of a bullying manager.

Taking the train would mean moving home and a 2 hour commute each morning and back again in the evening. The lads thought I was crazy travelling this distance. I said I was waiting for the room to come up in Paul's house. Outwardly I told them that this was an awful inconvenience for me, but deep down I was delighted to have moved home. I was comfortable and safe there and I didn't have to hide in my room. The effects the travel had on me and my work were not so good. I was up each morning at 6.10 and the earliest I would be home would be after 7. It put huge stress on my mind and body, but I didn't care. The alternative was moving back to Dublin, which I didn't see as an alternative. My whole life seemed to be a constant rush. Rushing for the train, rushing to work, rushing to the Luas in the evening, rushing to the train again, rushing to training once I came home. I was literally just getting up, going to work and most evening crashing on the couch, when I got home. My energy levels were low and I was often in bad form. It put huge strain on my relationships at work too. I had an awkward assistant manager always looking for confrontation. He thought I should be staying on later each day. I maintained that I had worked hard during the day and got my work done so I was entitled to leave on time. I also put it to him that if I didn't go on time I would miss my train, which would mean me getting home between 8 and 9 o clock. The assistant manager would often arrive at my desk just as I was about to leave and ask me to do some ridiculous task. He would say that it would only take 10 mins. This really pissed me off. He knew I'd miss my train, but to me it was like he was doing this on purpose. Sometimes I would do the task and head off to the train steaming, but other times I would leave. He found this provocative and our relationship was deteriorating fast. The root of this problem was my fear of living with strangers in Dublin.

The late John Bowlby, one time Director of the children's department at the Tavistock Clinic, was one of the first to look at fear of abandonment in detail. He proposed the theory of attachment, already briefly mentioned, as a fundamental part of child development. It is underlies fear and all the issues outlined in Appendix 1, so in reality this book is about attachment. Bowlby also examined the mother's emotional mind-set towards the child, which he saw as determining the long term emotional relationship or bond between mother (or substitute mother) and child. Mistakenly, he did not place the same emphasis on the father as a nurturer. Bowlby's theory is one of the most significant contributions to the understanding of human development and was tested and expanded by Mary Ainsworth, who worked with him for some time in the Tavistock Clinic.

Mark Grant, author of *Pain Control with EMDR* (EMDR is explained in more detail in the last chapter of this book) shows that it is now recognised that the attachment system is a central organizing system in the brain by which infants use their parents for regulating their inner states, until their own psychoneurobiology develops. Initially, the attachment process is confined to non-verbal communication and gestures, when the child begins to mimic the primary caregiver and pays particular attention to her facial expressions. Soon the child will be able to see the difference between a smile and a scowl. The smile bodes well for a secure attachment, but frequent scowling may indicate the opposite. Unfortunately, not every parent is able to create the proper emotional environment to enable the child to acquire a healthy emotional life, and from Bowlby's studies on both humans and primates came the concept of secure and insecure attachment. Allan Schore explores attachment in his studies on the brain.

Bowlby's theories were later developed and refined by the research of other psychologists, which is currently well documented. A broad understanding of these studies will help you to recognise the essence of good parenting in the developmental area, and thus to prevent the formation of core fear, and its accompanying distressing conditions, in your children. I have seen parents change due to counselling challenge with gratifying beneficial results for their children. Sometimes this can be only a matter of awareness to bring about a change of behaviour.

Attachment types can be seen in a child's behaviour. Some years ago RTE Television presented a programme on attachment involving a large group of children, who were scrutinised by a psychologist, where the type of attachment of each child was clearly evident. Bowlby divided attachment into three types, secure, fearful and dismissive. These have been further refined by subsequent theorists, who suggest that there are three types of insecure attachment i.e. ambivalent (anxious-resistant/fearful/preoccupied), anxious-avoidant (dismissive) and, worst of all, disorganised (disoriented). Children with *ambivalent attachment* experience the most distressing fear when separated from their parents and are most likely to suffer fear of abandonment and possible core anger in adult life. Their fear can often be seen during the first week in school, when they are unable to settle and spend a lot of time in distress, wanting to return home. It seems strange that a child wishes to return to a home that is emotionally unsafe, but for the child that home is familiar, and this familiarity is probably the key to the desire to remain there. These fearful children experience inconsistent parenting. Their parents are sometimes nurturing and sometimes punitive. Because of this they have conflicted feelings about one or both of their parents. It has been suggested that children with this insecure-resistant attachment will be narcissistic in adulthood.

Children with *avoidant attachment* behave in a dismissive or aloof way. They rarely show emotion and unlike those with a secure attachment will not seek the comfort of a parent. Usually their parents are aloof and emotionally remote. They separate impassively and return equally impassively, effectively ignoring the caregiver. But they are inwardly distressed. *Disorganised attachment* is particularly difficult to define because it contains elements of the other two, but is close to ambivalent attachment. It is profoundly pathological. Children afflicted with this attachment usually have parents who are abusive and seem life-threatening. These parents can also be withdrawn through stress, anxiety or depression. In such cases children are often confused, fearful and angry. Whatever the reason for the emotional abandonment, their children suffer all their lives as a result.

Some adults who have suffered such distress as a child often say they feel they were adopted. How sad is that! It should be mentioned that adults have corresponding attachment or personality types, which are labelled secure, anxious-preoccupied, dismissive-avoidant and fearful-avoidant. Research shows that about 40% of adults have insecure attachment to a greater or lesser extent, which helps to explain the myriad of relationship difficulties counsellors come across. The anxious-preoccupied people (ambivalent anxious as children) are overly needy, insecure in their relationship and constantly checking that their partner loves them, and may be jealous. They feel worthwhile and worthless alternately, and this ambivalence dictates their lives, for example when they feel worthwhile they like to meet other people and when they fell worthless they dislike meeting others. The dismissive-avoidant people (avoidant as children) are unlikely to have access to feelings, and see themselves as independent and perhaps ruthless, a weakness that they mistakenly regard as a strength. They remain constantly hurt because they cannot connect and often see connection as weakness. Fearful avoidant people (possibly disorganised as children) have some desire for intimacy, but then feel uncomfortable with the intimacy and opt out, harbouring an intense fear of rejection. They then become lonely and opt in, thus creating confusion and uncertainty in relationships. This becomes a tormenting cycle for the lover and the beloved. John Bradshaw in his book *Home Coming* explains this as a person moving between fear of abandonment and fear of engulfment. It can also mean that in intimacy traumatic feelings buried during childhood and hidden in their subconscious are disturbed resulting in a withdrawal. The main characteristic of fearful avoidant people is anger and shame, and they are likely to use violence as a way of control.

By and large, those with an insecure attachment learn to relate in what Mark Grant describes as instrumental ways, able to express love but not feeling it, catering for the other's *material* needs, trying to please others and stressing achievements in their spousal or parental relationships. When the emotional content is not available, however, the result is devastating to all concerned.

I hope you find these definitions helpful in making sense of yourself. If not do not worry. I find it difficult to define my own insecure attachment style. I believe that insecure attachment types have common facets and are not fully individually fenced. In real life it is the insecurity and what it does to you that matters, not the particular type that theorists struggle to define. What all the insecure attachments types have in common is that they create fear and the child creates a shell (psychic numbing or dissociation) to survive. The child represses an overwhelming fear of not surviving. Biologically, this may mean that the primitive brain and the amygdala block any overpowering emotion from trauma, such as the prolonged trauma of childhood mistreatment. If you wish for deeper information in how the brain deals with trauma you might like to consult Babette Rothschild's works. She is one of the world's leading experts on trauma. Because the child is unable to process the pain or to integrate the experience, it is blocked in the brain forever, unless properly treated. Very often it emerges in late teenage years or in adulthood as severe anxiety or depression, which is difficult to shift because the adult cannot connect these complaints to the protracted childhood trauma. In other words it is difficult for the adult to make sense of the unpleasant body sensations of the anxiety, because they are disconnected from the long drawn out trauma of neglect in childhood. Obviously it is easy to connect anxiety to a single trauma which can be recalled in detail. Again, much depends on the severity of the trauma, and it is worthwhile understanding that what is not a trauma from the adult point of view may be traumatic for the child.

While numbing or repression as an automatic defence mechanism is necessary for the child's emotional survival, it is counterproductive in adulthood rendering the adult unamenable to healthy emotional contact. Many relationships have foundered on the rock of this 'coldness'. It is very understandable that an adult may wish to avoid breaking that shell and experiencing the pain that was frozen so long ago. But unless that pain is experienced some adults will not only suffer from fear and inner turmoil, but may also become controlling and the controlling personality is driven not so much by anger, but by fear of abandonment and the shame that accompanies it. This is clearly argued in Donald Dutton's books, which explore the concept of attachment and its negative consequences.

We cannot discuss attachment without looking at the concept of separation. John Bowlby was one of the first to show that they are closely related. In other words, if a child is securely attached to a consistently reliable parent, it has the foundation to explore its world and ultimately leave and live independently, always possessing core security, a spirit of autonomy and the ability to love and trust. Separation, therefore, is a psychological term denoting an emotional process tending towards independence, bearing in mind that all very young children are wary and dislike being separated from their mothers. Those of you with small children will see that they love meeting their grandparents, but any suggestion of a stay over will bring on resistance, anxiety and tantrums until they leave toddler stage. Separation, therefore, is about your instinct for safety. Essentially it is about survival and fear of not surviving, either physically or emotionally. For those with fear of abandonment the world is a very unsafe place. Basically if you cannot trust your parents to meet your needs, who can you trust? Jason's distress in relation to his father is a good indication of this.

Psychiatrists have specific benchmarks in diagnosing the child's anxiety when they are separated from their parents (called attachment figures in psychological terminology). When three or more of the following criteria (at the time of writing) are present (plus some other conditions) they label it as a 'disorder' –

1. Recurrent excessive distress when separation from home or major attachment figures occurs or is anticipated.
2. Persistent and excessive worry about losing or about possible harm befalling major attachment figures.
3. Persistent and excessive worry that an untoward event will lead to separation from a major attachment figure (e.g. being lost or being kidnapped).
4. Persistent reluctance or refusal to go anywhere because of fear of separation.
5. Persistently and excessively fearful or reluctant to be alone or without major attachment figures at home or without significant adults in other settings.
6. Persistent reluctance or refusal to go to sleep without being near a major attachment figure or to sleep away from home.
7. Repeated nightmares involving the theme of separation.
8. Repeated complaints of physical symptoms, such as headaches, stomach aches nausea or vomiting, when separation from major attachment figures occurs or is anticipated.

If less than three of these criteria is not present, then the child may not be labelled as having a disorder, but is probably suffering from separation anxiety. According to Dr Ivor Browne the death of a parent, when the child is young, may intensify the relationship with the remaining parent and lead to separation difficulties in adult life. In many ways, life is about separation and is based upon independence, the building of good boundaries and a sense of self, (boundaries are explained in more detail in the final chapter of this book). Proper separation brings self-esteem (feeling good enough), the capacity to self-soothe and a sense of meaning in your life. The opposite of separation is over involvement, possible enmeshment, feeling over-whelmed, fear and anger.

As you can see, attachment and separation are very complex issues because the nature and the quality of the attachment (and hence separation) depends upon how parents respond on a regular basis to meet the child's needs, and how they frequently attune themselves to the child's emotional state in its attempts to feel secure and safe. It is about connection or disconnection, depending on the type of attachment.

The actual level of connection or disconnection has a profound effect on how our brain (neo-cortex) is wired and much research has been carried out to show that the neural pathways laid in childhood are strongly influenced by the type of attachment to our primary caregiver. In other words, the type of emotional relationship the very young child has with the primary caregiver, helps to wire its brain, and the brain structures made by the experiences and relationships in those early months dictate how we will behave and relate all our lives, and when we explore our feelings and behaviours in adult life, we must remember that these early patterns are in our subconscious. It follows that a negative environment and negative relationships at that young age lays the foundation of distress in later life.

Linda Graham gives and excellent description of attachment and the brain in her article *The Neuroscience of Attachment*, which you can find on the internet. As already mentioned, Allan Schore is an expert on brain formation and emotional development. He is a neurobiologist in the Department of Psychiatry and Biobehavioral Sciences, UCLA, and uses brain scans and thousands of studies to prove the connection between brain development and attachment. His major work, *Affect Regulation and the Origin of the Self. The Neurobiology of Emotional Development*, is a complex work, offering the most detailed examination and explanation of the brain in this context.

In their book, *Born for Love*, Maia Szalavitz and Bruce Perry also give a fascinating, but less detailed account, of how the brain installs the attachment in the infant's malleable brain, bearing in mind that ninety percent of brain growth occurs prior to puberty, much of it in the earlier years. When the caregiver nurtures and comforts the child on a frequent basis three neurotransmitters (the 'chemical messengers' dopamine, serotonin and oxytocin) are released, and over time these create the psychological bond between child and parent, bringing calmness and comfort to both. Oxytocin is particularly important in mothering. Farmers sometimes inject young heifers with it to stimulate the flow of milk for the new calf. It is noteworthy, too, that dopamine is also released when a mother's face looks joyful and stimulates the infant. Such mirroring is essential for human emotional development.

The bond of love that grows from maternal warmth is the best and most natural antidote to fear. If, however, the parent is withdrawn or punitive these chemicals are not activated, and an emotional void exists between the child and the parent. It is an awful coldness that withers the emotional development of the child and has undesirable long-term consequences. Bruce Perry and Maia Szalavitz put it another way in their explanation that a failure to stimulate the lower areas of the brain by affection in the early years means that the human has to use cognitive ways to make connections. In such cases people often say they are numb. Their behaviour mimics autism, but is not autism. It is nothing more that frozen feelings, one of my own sad experiences for decades. But, the repercussions can be far worse than mere numbness, because it is now known that children can waste away and die if they live in a world devoid of empathy, with little emotional nourishment.

At first sight this may be difficult to believe, until we examine the behaviour of children in some continental orphanages, where until recently the initial stress and ultimate disconnection of children was clear to see. This was often followed by early child death in these establishments, where there was no environment for secure attachment, and where, as Dr Ivor Browne states, 'the cold heavy hand of meaningless discipline' is frequent. John Bowlby had already noticed this when observing children in institutions from the late 1940s. Research shows that children, even as young as one year old, adopted by American couples from Romanian orphanages, suffered mental health problems years later. Romania is now rectifying this horrifying situation in different ways, but the evidence shows that no matter how comfortable an orphanage is, the consistent warmth by a particular caregiver is essential for emotional growth. If orphanage staff members are warm and kind that is helpful, but it is not enough. Studies show, for example, that children living in prison fare far better, simply because they are with their mothers.

Anne Thurston, Associate Professor in John Hopkins University and Director of the Grassroots China Initiative, visited a Chinese orphanage in the 1990s and found the children there lying silent, withdrawn and immobile. She gives a chilling description of the orphanage and of the 'dying' room attached to it. The child wants to live, it is born to live and will do anything to live. Survival is a primal instinct, but the child is dependent on the adult for this survival. Further, if she receives consistent emotional support and affection she is able to love and have empathy later on in life with fundamental positive consequences for

25

herself and for her descendants. Allan Schore points out that brain studies have shown that as early as eighteen months the human is capable of empathy for others. Empathy, therefore, is innate and embroidered on the neural circuit, but it can be obliterated if the child is not emotionally nurtured.

We always understood that the child's first attachment-separation experience occurs at birth, when it leaves the warm comforting womb. But, is the womb always comforting and can the prenate experience fear of abandonment? Ivor Browne writes about the awareness and sensitivity of the foetus, and the psychologist Carista Luminare-Rosenin in her book, *Parenting Begins Before Conception,* holds that the mother can create an emotionally enriching womb environment that has a psychologically positive effect on the foetus. In other words, the mother and child already have a relationship before birth, and that bond is created early in the pregnancy. The father contributes to this by treating his partner with love and kindness and it is known that massaging the pregnant belly is very beneficial for the parents and the child. The baby is a social creature and that begins in the womb, where it seeks stimulation. There is evidence that it can establish some kind of bond with the father by recognising his voice, if the father speaks to it sufficiently often. It is one way for the father to come into contact with the foetus and is a way to bond with it, as he feels it responding and kicking in the womb.

If a negative womb environment is created, however, the foetus will be less secure and the assertion of the Vietnamese Buddhist monk, Thich Nhat Hanh, that fear is generated at birth and that we experience nine months safety in the womb is untrue. One study with a sample of 2891 women came to the conclusion that there was an association between prenatal depression and emotional and behavioural problems of children in mid to late childhood. Research shows that the foetus can experience a wide range of emotions including fear. It would seem that even when its eyes are fused (up to week 24), it has extra sensory perception and there are suggestions that it can even sense if it is not wanted, and subsequently has more psychological issues later in life. These include school problems. Other evidence suggests that people who have negative experiences in the womb grow into adulthood feeling unwanted and unlovable, two of the major hallmarks of adult fear of abandonment.

The foetus is unprotected from external negative stimuli, such as any traumatic event or experience to which the mother is exposed. When we realise that constant rowing between parents is as traumatic for a child as a serious road accident or a natural disaster for an adult, how much more traumatic and fearful is such conflict for the foetus, helpless and trapped in the womb! Frequent angry shouting is extremely disturbing for the unborn child.

It is also true that the child in the womb remembers experiences, thus reinforcing fear and probably keeping it in the subconscious for its entire life. This is known as cellular memory, where the memories are encoded in cells. Prenatal memories are very important, because they are the first memories of the child's environment. We know, for example, that a mother with emotional distress from stressful experiences (e.g. depression) two years before birth can find it difficult to bond with the child. The foetus can experience similar problems, since a traumatic prenatal life makes bonding more difficult following the birth. It seems that it can numb, just as the child suffering parental neglect, and can develop feelings of deep mistrust. It is not difficult to imagine the impact on the child's future emotional life, if the fear in the womb is aggravated by an unloving childhood following birth! There is every reason to believe that the foetus reacts emotionally to the mother's use of alcohol or medication, and this reaction may be fear because it is helpless. Experiments also show that foetuses react to loud noises by emptying their bladders, a clear sign of fear. As a young child I saw children urinating in fear, as we stood by the blackboard in the small school I attended.

Fear is now seen as one of the prominent emotions experienced by the foetus. Modern research also suggests that an anxious child has a larger amygdala (fear centre) than others, and while this does appear to be true of prenates, increased cortisol (stress hormone) in the mother also affects the structure and organisation of the foetal amygdala. There is some evidence, too, that a foetus at sixteen weeks can experience aggression, which is closely related to fear. Perhaps this is because it can hear at sixteen weeks. It can also cry with distress in the second half of its womb life and at an early stage the foetus experiences pain through its sensory systems, because it does not yet have the nerve pathways to soothe pain.

Perhaps the best works on prenatal life have been done by the late Dr David Chamberlain. His recent book *Windows to the Womb: Revealing the Conscious Baby from Conception to Birth* is fascinating. Chamberlain, who was President of the Association for Prenatal and Perinatal Psychology and Health, offers credible evidence of foetal emotions and behaviour in the womb. The case studies he offers in one section of book from hypnosis should perhaps be treated with caution, because false memories can be created by hypnosis. This is not to say, however, that this is the case with the examples given by him.

The relationship between child and adult as the crucial factor in fear of abandonment begins, therefore, long before the child is born. Without realising it, the mother, as primary nurturer (in the great majority of cases), continues the process of nurturing (or the opposite) when the baby is born. Her maternal task is to make the child feel secure immediately after birth. Some books on parenting, perhaps, go too far in stressing the degree of nurturing a child needs. An over loved child may have as many problems in later life as an under loved one. It is important not to over-compensate for deficiencies in our own childhood by smothering our children.

If a secure attachment is badly disrupted similar problems follow. This can occur, for example, if a caregiver gets depression or is sporadically unwell, or dies. The consequences of this can be serious in terms of the emotional development of the child and many of the psychological and emotional ills outlined in Appendix 1 may follow into adult life. We must understand that an insecure attachment is a serious core trauma that renders the sufferer incapable of self-soothing and hence fosters the growth of fear and its distressing companions in later life. If parents are extremely cross and if the child is so fearful that he has not a voice this may later show itself in the adult as severe anxiety, which is difficult to heal. As an adult you will always know if you have had an insecure attachment with a parent. If such is the case you will not feel an emotional bond with the parent simply because he or she did not create it in pre-puberty childhood. In my experience as a counsellor it cannot be created in adulthood unless the parent undergoes significant change through professional help. If that happens, a warm bond can then be established with the adult child, who also needs parental love.

Unfortunately, however, very few parents, who, for whatever reasons, cause childhood distress, seek to change and the bond is never created. This is one of the very sad realities of many parent adult-child relationships. What often surprises me is that I occasionally meet people who have insecure attachment to their parents and had extremely abusive childhoods, but are warm and empathic. I normally presumed that there was someone in their lives who loved them, but that is not always the case. I cannot explain this, but what is clear is that the great majority of people who have an insecure attachment suffer long term negative consequences to a greater or lesser degree. While mothers are vital to the emotional nourishment of small children and have a long term impact on the emotional life of the child, it is clear that male children gradually incline towards their fathers as role models from whom they seek approval. The importance of a father is only lately being recognised. A seriously insecure attachment of the male child to his father has disastrous consequences later on in life. The role and emotional influence of the father in relation to female children should not, however, be underestimated either.

You have seen how one of Jason's issues was fear of abandonment, and the following excerpt shows how significant his insecure attachment to his father was, and how it impacted on him, breeding shame, hurt, jealousy, discord, fear, depression, low self-esteem, poor self-confidence, and a stubborn desire for his father's approval.

> We are a very sporting family with rugby being the passion. My father was a really good player as a young man and would be very well respected in the community. My relationship with him

has always been pretty much non-existent for as long as I can remember. I can remember times when I was young asking him to come and play with me and my younger brother, but he never would. My mother would always encourage him, but he didn't have any interest. On the odd time he would come out, it would be for only a few minutes. I would plead with him to stay out for longer but he never would. I would often visit my best friend's house. We would have big games of soccer or rugby and his father would play with us, encouraging us and really getting involved. Often we would still be out playing in the dark. Even though he might have finished a hard day's work, he would never disappoint us and always played enthusiastically. I never had that with my father, I would play with my brothers but that was it. As my father was a decent rugby player himself, it was natural that we, his sons, would play. He got involved in my older brother's teams, but never in mine or my younger brother's. My older brother and father seemed to have had a close relationship always; so it was, I suppose, natural for him to get involved in his teams. He had high hopes for him. I was a little bit younger, but I was also togging out with my brother. My father would never pick me on the team, even though I felt I was better than some of the lads starting. My mother often used to ask my father to push for me, when picking the team. He never listened. I felt very low about this and felt like I was an embarrassment to him. My feeling was that he thought I was useless and eventually I started thinking this way myself. Sometimes if there was a row at home between him and me, he would often remark that I was useless on the rugby field. This cut deeply as I loved rugby and a lot of our identity at home was based around rugby and how well you could play it. What made it worse at the time was that my younger brother was rapidly improving and was clearly going to be better than me. This I found very difficult and jealously would kick in. I would often pick on him and resented him for being better. I think the only time I remember my father being proud was when the 3 of us played on an underage team together and won a competition. Myself and my older brother held key positions on the team, while my younger brother was the star. As he was a good player himself, there was always pressure on me and my brothers to be decent players. I often resented this pressure, but this was one of the times I was proud to have the family name. Unfortunately, I have always played with very low self-confidence. I do my bit for the team, but I never put myself out there to receive the ball. I am terrified of making a mistake and people accusing me of losing a game. So I sell myself short. I know I could be a lot better player than I am and have ability, but I just can't force myself to demand the ball. I am transfixed by fear. I could see that the management could see leadership qualities in me, but I just couldn't see them in myself. Self-doubt would fill me and I was never comfortable in a leadership role. I liked soccer as well as rugby, but my lack of self-confidence was making me hate playing it. I have often been asked for trials for higher teams, but I just couldn't make myself go. I convinced myself that I wasn't as good as all these other players, and I would make up some lame excuse not to go. I have no doubt that all this stems from not getting any encouragement from my father. I always felt belittled and useless around him.

Things got worse as I got older. We stopped talking to each other almost completely. I could never sit in the same room as him so I got a T.V. into the other living room and spent all my time there. I just couldn't talk to him and I know he felt the same way. It was just too awkward for both of us, so we would avoid each other. Car journeys were the worst. I never looked for him to take me anywhere and always looked for my mother. Sometimes needs must, and he was the only person there to drop me to training or wherever. Even the shortest of trips would be painful. We would try talk about rugby, but it was always forced, and mostly it would just fall into a deafening silence. Even today as an adult, there is still the awkwardness between us. As I got older and started drinking I would head out most nights, a lot of times to escape the house.

The insecure attachment Jason had with his father not only affected his relationship with him, but impacted on his ability to live. It was so detrimental that he ultimately decided to give up soccer, a game he liked. He was unable to enjoy the game, because every time he went on the field the thought of pleasing his father was uppermost in his mind. Failure to do so resulted in unbearable shame. For those of you with secure attachment it is difficult for you to understand how childhood can affect an adult to this extent. Jason's thinking is clear in this extract, when he contemplates the decision he made in May 2015.

Today I cried uncontrollably, and it is rarely I cried in childhood. I can no longer handle the stress of playing soccer. One evening last week I turned up for a match looking disinterested. This was a front for being terrified. I hid during the match. I tried not to get on the ball for fear of making a mistake. At one stage in the first half, my hands were shaking. All that was going through my head was how useless people in the stand would think I am. It was a horrible feeling. I never felt so alone. I then got on a few balls and made mistakes. I just couldn't handle this anymore. I considered walking off the field but instead I hid for the rest of the match. I got a ball at one stage and drove it over the side line. In my frustration I gave the guy I was marking a dig in the ribs. He was only a young lad and did nothing wrong. By the end of the game all that was in my head was that this is the last game of soccer I will play. I played one more game. I togged in, cracking jokes with the lads but deep down I was in bits. I could no longer keep the show on the road. Why was I playing? Why was I doing this to myself? I drove around town and my head was spinning with all these questions. When I got home there was nobody there. I parked in the driveway and broke down. I sobbed uncontrollably. I got into the house and I went to the sitting room and I still couldn't stop. I then went to my bedroom and the tears just flowed. I lay on my bed and let it all out. This was the tipping point for me. I just kept asking myself why I am doing something that makes me so unhappy. Then I decided that it was time to be brave. I decided that I would give up soccer for good. I never played for myself or my own enjoyment. It was always to please someone else, usually my family, or because my friends were playing. Secretly it was to please my father.

When you consider that sad situation and the issues it bred in Jason, you might think that his mother would be able to compensate for it. But that was not the case, showing how vital the father is for the boy in terms of attachment and ultimate happiness. Yet, his mother had a positive formative influence on him in other ways, because Jason is a warm, kind person lacking any controlling impulse, although as an adult he finds it impossible to form an intimate relationship or make a date, currently the major issue in his counselling. It is unlikely that he would have this kindness, if his mother had been a remote figure.

> My mother and I have always been close. I can remember in my childhood being very attached to her and often crying my eyes out if she had to go somewhere or was tending to my younger brother and not me. I always felt, unlike my father, that I could talk to her. There was never anything awkward or forced about our relationship and we could talk easily and randomly. She always encouraged me and showed she cared. Unfortunately, I became too reliant on my mother. She was so good to me and she would do anything for me. Even the smallest things I would get her to do for me and I never stood on my own two feet. She was too soft on me and let me away with too much.

So, the most important aspect of parenting is to create a secure environment in the home for the child to emotionally thrive. This must be consistent and ongoing, at least until the time of puberty, when the brain begins to undergo significant change and development, and the process of separation accelerates. If the mother is unable to do this, then the father can do it, or anyone else who has frequent contact with the child. All we need is for someone to show us love on a consistent basis. Secure attachment means that there is a close warm bond or connection between the child and one or both parents, who are attuned to the child's feelings and needs. It is better if the child has a secure attachment to both parents. A child with a secure attachment will grow into an adult with strong self-esteem and a strong sense of independence, a willingness to explore the environment, and will never have to carry emotional or psychological distresses. People with secure attachment are comfortable in their skin, have good judgement, are loving and are capable of forming loving relationships, intimate or otherwise. Biologically it means the creation of the balanced development of the left and right hemispheres of the brain. Creating this secure attachment is the most important task a parent has, and until recently it was advocated that it must begin immediately after birth. We now know differently.

If good enough parenting determines the creation of a secure attachment, obviously it is crucial to understand how this happens on a practical basis. In theory this is very easy, although, judging from the extent of attachment problems, it may not always be so simple to do. Good enough parenting involves understanding and meeting the dependency needs of your children. That is the secret of a happiness when they reach adulthood. It is about how to create an optimum emotional environment for the child.

Psychologists propose different types of needs that a child requires for lasting emotional nourishment. Don Carter in his iceberg series (*Thaw, Thawing*) lists four childhood dependency needs –love, approval, worth, and competence; indispensable foundation stones for adult life. These needs combine to make a child feel loved and lovable, feelings that endure for an entire lifetime, irrespective of circumstances and fate. Feeling lovable is the essence of self-esteem, which is ultimately unquenchable. Our primary relationship is with ourselves and if that is not right we cannot relate to others. Low self-esteem can spell anger, self-loathing, negative self-analysis, envy, jealousy, suspicion, hardness and fear, to name but a few. It is important for parents to understand self-esteem, and Robert Kelsey has a small but informative section on it in his book *What's Stopping You.* In the final analysis, the important thing is that even if such parenting is alien to you, you can choose to meet these needs of your children. Needs must be met or the lifelong negative consequences listed above are inevitable.

But, how are these needs met? In the first instance, if you choose to spend *time* with your children then they will feel regarded, special and loved. This might seem simple, but in many cases does not always happen and leaves the child bereft. It is not the amount of time that matters but the quality of that time. So, time equals love. Children think in black or white terms – you love me or you don't. There is no in-between. Saying the words 'I love you' to the child is not enough. Jasmin Lee Cori in her book *The Emotionally Absent Mother*, makes the point that love is best expressed in nonverbal ways, such as touch and this means taking the time to be physically and warmly close to the child. You have already seen what happened to children in orphanages, where there was a sterile emotional environment.

Touch is the heart of *affection*, and that is how you make the child feel a sense of approval, the second need. Alice Miller, the great Polish psychiatrist, advocated that the first year of the child is the most important one. This is the time when the child should be hugged and nurtured with affection. Miller argued that warm maternal body contact is of incalculable value in the formation of a child's development, while Allan Schore shows that affection has a profound effect on the development of the brain's amygdala, where memories of emotional events are stored. Professor Jane Simington also argues that touch is essential for psychological and physical development and the maintenance of life. She writes that touch is the earliest form of communication for the human, when the uterine waters soothe the skin of the foetus. It is now known that skin to skin contacts have benefits for both baby and mothers, who have the ability to thermoregulate (maintain homeostasis or internal core temperature) for the baby. So important is touch and affection that it appears to affect the IQ of the human and their capacity to learn. It certainly affects their concentration levels. Recent research has shown that tender stroking helps premature infants to thrive both physically and cognitively.

All the years up to the age of puberty are important for the human, but the younger years, particularly at the toddler stage, especially so. Children shown kindness and affection feel special, feel accepted and loved. As adults they will not be seeking approval, will not see it as imperative to be always nice, and will have good boundaries. Recently I bought a small book called the *Little Book of Hugs. A gift to bring comfort and Joy*, by Lois Blyth, which I recommend and which I think you will greatly enjoy. A hug is a non-verbal sign of love and protection. A hug is worth a thousand words. You can give your child a hug even if you feel apathetic about it, or even if it is alien to you because you never experienced it in your childhood. You can choose your behaviour.

Affection and love needs are obviously closely linked, and all of the dependency needs overlap into a holistic parental behaviour sending out positive messages to your child, which in adult life increases his capacity to give affection and love in the best sense of the word. The third need is making the child feel worthwhile. We do this by *attending* to her. Essentially it means showing an interest in the child, praising them, asking how they are, what they are doing, how they are feeling and so on. When a child is attended to in this way they feel worthwhile, and will not grow into adulthood seeking attention or feeling dependent on another for their happiness or self-esteem. If this need is not met in childhood the adulthood seeking attention will never cease. As Amy Lew and Betty Lou Bettner wrote, it is like a cup with a hole in the bottom that can never be filled.

The fourth need is showing a child what to do; giving them *direction*. It is easy to dismiss this need as less important than the others, but it is a vital component of human development. It is hard to believe that we have to be shown everything. Children carefully observe how parents do things and learn in that way also. Parents are role models and it is incredible how children learn by observing and then by doing. The great Irish poet, Seán Ó Ríordáin, once wrote that the mind of the poet is like the mind of the child, always exploring, learning, and experiencing the immediate environment. Failing to meet the direction need in the child will instil feelings of incompetency (the condition of being incompetent). This will be looked at in more detail in the chapter on fear of failure.

Failure by his father to help him meet his dependency needs was resented by Jason, who as an adult felt inept. He defined himself by how his father treated him.

> My dad would never show me how to do anything, whether it was mending a puncture on my bike or latterly changing a wheel on the car. Just simple things that a father would show

his son. I was too embarrassed and ashamed to ask him how to do any of these tasks. Anytime there was work to do around the house he would never ask me to help him. I just knew he was thinking I was lazy and useless. I would work very hard for my uncle and he would always compliment me to my mother. She would say it to my father to ask me to help, but he would just say that I wouldn't do anything if I wasn't being paid for it. This wasn't true and I would have gladly helped him, but he would never ask. He would ask my older brother to help him, but never me. It really made me feel useless and good for nothing. As a result, I began to resent him for it. I would rebel a bit and try wind him up. It often ended in a blazing row with me sprinting out the door away from his clutches. If he had caught me I would have been beaten.

Parental failure to meet dependency needs is, in effect, traumatic for the child, and inflicts what is called an emotional or soul wound, which is too painful to experience. The result in teenage years, especially around the age of sixteen, is a severe lack of concentration in school, where the child's psychic energy is diverted to protect this emotional wound. Children who have very low levels of concentration carry a severe wound and their behaviour consists of either disturbing the class, fantasising, doodling, or all three. This behaviour does not require any concentration and their class time is almost exclusively focussed on the wound to soothe the emotional pain. This is a core defence mechanism to avoid the pain of rejection and is subconscious. Of course, with the arrival of the digital age all young humans are now in danger of losing the ability to concentrate for long periods. The famous neuroscientist, Susan Greenfield, explores themes such as this in her interesting book, *Mind Change. How digital technologies are leaving their mark on our brains.*

Children with a severe wound generally drop out of school around fifteen or sixteen. Unfortunately, the wounded inner child remains throughout adult life and the concentration levels do not change, except in activities that the individuals enjoy. My clinical experience repeatedly shows this and clients confirm that the theory is correct. In the initial counselling session I normally ask about the level of concentration at the age of sixteen, and from this I get a general impression of the client's childhood. In my long experience as a teacher I have also seen the behaviour of wounded children many times, and misjudged it as impertinence or sheer bad manners. In those years I was unaware of dependency needs and insecure attachment. Educating teachers, especially those at primary level, on this aspect of formation would be very beneficial, and prevent some stress in the classroom.

To sum up, therefore, failure to meet dependency needs can be equated to childhood emotional neglect that leads to attachment problems, which in turn breed fear of abandonment and its many toxic offspring. Children can suffer emotional starvation in many ways and it is by no means always a deliberate act by parents. Most parents want the best for their children and would never dream of harming them, but it is not the good intentions of parents that matter, but what happens in the practical situation of child rearing; for example, addicted parents find it very difficult or even impossible to make emotional contact with their children. Parents who are ill, looking after their own aged parents, or nursing soul wounds from their own childhood, are likely to be diverted from their parenting task and generally fail to meet the emotional needs of their children. Severe and constant depression and its dark world make the creation of an emotional bond almost impossible. Bruce Perry tells a story about a depressed mother who used television as a means of occupying her only son. In effect the child was 'reared' by the television, learning most of his language from this machine that incessantly babbled from the corner, unresponsive to his needs. The effect on the child was disastrous, and probably long lasting.

As you can see, many circumstances preventing adequate parenting are simply unavoidable. One of the most familiar cases in my experience is that of having a large family, where parents struggle to find time to meet the needs of their children. Frequently, in such cases clusters of children form within the family some with maternal figures taking care of younger siblings. Due to modern life and financial necessity, increasingly either one or both parents have no option but to work long hours and are reluctantly absent from their children's lives. Despite the pressure of time, it is, nonetheless, vital to make time for children and most parents strive to do this.

We must, however, recognise that not all circumstances are unavoidable. While we appreciate that parents do the best they can for their children, we also have to accept that there are parents who deliberately harm them. This may be cultural in some societies where human development is poorly understood or there is a misplaced idea of what parenting is. This is most evident in subsistence economies, where corporal punishment is seen as the optimum way to bring about obedience to ensure the survival of the family.

Unfortunately, childhood neglect may also be due to abusive parenting in so-called enlightened societies. It is quite prevalent in modern well-developed countries. Have you ever, for example, wondered why Adolf Hitler behaved in such a monstrous way and was responsible for the deaths of millions, or why Stalin had millions murdered without any shred of remorse? These are extreme cases, of course, but they illustrate a point. Alice Miller in her book, *For Your Own Good. The Roots of Violence in Child-rearing*, paints an interesting portrait of Hitler. He was a dutiful child, who had a very distressing childhood. Instead of being emotionally nurtured, he was from a very young age, frequently humiliated and beaten by his father, Alois. He was eighteen when his mother, Klara, died from breast cancer, and by that stage would have permanently benefitted from any emotional maternal warmth she might have given him. But, his father's savagery was so consistent that she could never lessen to any significant extent the psychological damage inflicted on him. But, there may also have been maternal shortcomings. Alice Miller challenges the idea that Hitler was loved by his mother, but perhaps was spoiled, an ultimately devastating experience in itself. Many parents confuse spoiling with love, but it is a trauma which comes to fruition in adult life. That, however, was the least of Hitler's worries as he endured the cruelty of his father. As in almost all cases of childhood abuse there was a transgenerational factor involved. Hitler's father was born outside of wedlock into poverty and was separated from his mother, Maria Anna Schicklgruber, when he was five years old. There is also the possibility that Alois's father was partly Jewish. Hitler was aware of this and uncertainty about one's ancestry can cause anxiety in itself and the possibility of a Jewish ancestry enraged him. Hence, six million Jewish people perished.

Hitler suffered severe fear of abandonment as an adult, even when he was Fuhrer. There is plenty of evidence of his nightmares, cries of terror and shrieks in the night at the image of his long dead father, even when at the pinnacle of his power. He feared the Jews, he feared medicine (even though he allowed his doctor to heavily medicate him as he got older and more stressed), he feared heights, he feared being poisoned and had a food taster, and he feared death, although he committed suicide.

It is more than likely that Hitler suffered from Post-Traumatic Stress Disorder as a result of his childhood. Certainly he has some of the symptoms of PTSD, which is an intense anxiety reaction caused by adverse circumstances including childhood neglect. For example, the mistreatment by his father was beyond the norm of suffering, and Hitler became emotionally dissociated from others, apart from his terrifying dreams, he suffered from insomnia and was subjected to mood swings, he had poor concentration, he was devoid of emotions apart from rage and anger and he frequently relived the emotional trauma of childhood as he tried to sleep. Laurence Rees in his book, *The Dark Charisma of Adolf Hitler*, rightly states that his main characteristic was his 'capacity to hate.' Hitler's description in *Mein Kampf* of a three year old child witnessing the brutal behaviour of the father against the mother undoubtedly refers to his own experience. A battered mother, filled with fear, cannot protect her child from a brutal father. Ultimately the massive childhood trauma, stored in his psyche as a child, eventually emerged and as Alice Miller puts it 'the child who was once persecuted now becomes the persecutor.' And millions died.

From this chapter I hope you now understand fear of abandonment coming from insecure attachment. Equally important, if you are a parent, especially of young children, you will realise how you can ensure (or choose to ensure) their mental health and mental wellbeing by meeting their dependency needs of love, affection, attention and direction. I do not believe that there can be a more invaluable contribution to the mental health of your descendants than this. Further I would add that if you are the child of controlling parent(s) you may have inherited some controlling tendencies that accompany your fear of abandonment. Acknowledge this and take steps to heal it so that you will more easily be able to meet the dependency needs of your children. The final chapter in this book looks in some detail at how to heal issues that come from an insecure attachment, including fear of abandonment.

Chapter 2

Anger Coming from an Insecure Attachment

MANY PEOPLE WHO HAD AN INSECURE attachment in childhood carry anger as adults, some of it intensely evident and some latent. I have, however, met people who suffered neglect in childhood, who assured me that they did not feel anger and I believed them. Sometimes during a counselling session the anger emerges, but not always. Generally, I have found that children who suffered physical abuse show anger in adulthood.

Before looking at the nature of anger, its management and healing, it is worth considering that anger is strongly influenced by culture. It should be noted that culture affects all the themes in this book and it also dictates how people are socialised. For example, women may feel as angry as men, but it may be culturally forbidden for them to show the anger and they have to hide it beneath a meek and obedient façade. Similarly they may be socialised to show a soft and gentle nature that conceals a different inner emotional state. This is true in societies where males exercise dominance.

Apart from the existence of such abusive societies, we now live in an increasingly multicultural world where we travel widely and intermarry with other races, so failure to understand what provokes the emotional reactions of other cultures can cause misunderstandings, confusion and sometimes conflict, particularly in relation to anger triggers. Likewise, emotional reactions taken from Irish culture may come across as deviant to other cultures. The Japanese psychologist Junko Tanaka-Matsumi offers some interesting research on anger in a cross-cultural context. Basically different cultures, particularly in Eastern countries and among Eastern immigrants and refugees, cluster different words associated with anger. In the United States anger is clustered with such words as fury, wrath, hostility, and resentment. In Spanish culture there are precise words for different levels of anger.

Some studies have found that in various European countries personal and intimate relationships were the major source of anger. This was followed by being treated unjustly and poor behaviour by strangers in a locality. In Japan, however, interacting with strangers was the principal reason for anger, possibly because of the hierarchical nature of relationships there. Some people, such as the Japanese and the Utku Eskimos, forbid expressions of negative emotions such as anger, especially in public, lest they disrupt social harmony. Facial expressions, which are often used as gauging the presence of anger, also differ from culture to culture.

At one time Ireland brought a religio-cultural dimension to anger. Older Irish people up to the 1970s learned from their catechism that anger was a sin, and not just a sin, but one of the seven capital or deadly sins. This became ingrained in us. Although I attended school in the 1940s I still remember the seven deadly sins – pride, covetousness, lust, anger, gluttony, envy and sloth. They were called deadly because they were seen as the sources of all sin. The question is how can a feeling be a sin? Unfortunately, categorising anger as a sin has created psychological difficulties for people, especially older people, who may have passed on the belief that anger is wrong to their children. My experience as a counsellor is that many people, young and old, see anger as 'wrong' and confuse the feeling and the sensation of anger with angry behaviour. Because we may feel that it is improper to feel angry we sometimes use other names for it, such as frustrated, disappointed, irritated, indignant, displeased, offended, or upset.

Irrespective of culture, anger is complex and can be broadly classed as healthy and unhealthy or toxic. As with all human feelings and behaviours, it is a feeling that we experience in individual ways. Some brood in silence, some react strongly and vocally, some have finely tuned anger antennae. Stacey Milescu in her pamphlet *Anger Management. Self Help Guide for Controlling Your Anger*, lists twenty four reasons why we get angry. These include grieving, tiredness, rudeness, pain, injustice, embarrassment, being bullied or humiliated, failure, and money problems.

Healthy anger is an *emotion* hardwired in the limbic system of the brain and is necessary for our survival, while toxic anger is a *feeling* in the cortex that therefore can be changed. It motivates you to find solutions to problems. Most people have a sense of justice and fairness, and when they see injustice and unfairness they may experience anger, which drives them to do something about it. Millions of people in Europe were outraged following the banking collapse and the Eurozone debt crisis in 2008-2009, when they were forced to suffer wage cuts, unemployment, cuts to services, investment loss, and inability to pay mortgages or rents leading in some cases to homelessness. This widespread rage is expressed in many ways through mass demonstrations, conversations, letters to newspapers, interviews on radio and television, and through the voting system, so that future governments may be more careful in preserving integrity in every area where they exercise influence. If we see injustice in society our anger can drive us to bring about reform. Examples of this would be the impact of Nelson Mandela on South Africa. We can also look at women's rights movements as expressions of anger at how women were exploited and treated unfairly in societies, especially in the area of employment, income and promotion.

Anger, therefore, is a protection mechanism. It can protect us from being exploited or harmed. Marcia Cannon, in her book, *The Gift of Anger* describes it as a power boost that enables us to stand up for ourselves in certain situations where we are in danger, to be assertive and to achieve our goals. She sets a short exercise, which will help you to see appropriate anger as a power boost in your life. So if you can think of a time when you were moderately angry, examine it, write it down and think about what caused you to be angry. Did the power boost you experienced help you to take a stand, to use your boundaries, to do something? How did that feel when it was over? Did you feel your courage rise? Did you feel yourself becoming more determined? Did you feel better about yourself? Did your anger get you what you were looking for? If not what happened? Mike Fisher, who has written several books on anger, also examines it as a positive force which alerts others that we are serious in what we say. He points out that anger facilitates getting things done quickly and gives us a feeling of power and control in our own lives (not over others). Healthy anger also helps us combat fear and depression. The motto better be mad than sad has a lot of merit. Fisher also makes the valid point that healthy anger helps us leave abusive situations and relieve our frustrations.

Situational anger arises from incidents that provoke our resentment. It is a response to a particular situation. So, for example, if somebody disrespects you it is highly likely that you will feel angry. Linda Andrews, a writer on health and psychological issues from Albuquerque in New Mexico, reveals that 1.7 million people are assaulted in the workplace in the United States each year. Some of this is a reaction to a stressful situation, and there is probably a great reservoir of anger among people caught in a deadly daily grind of cut-throat competition. We hear about employees being driven to the detriment of their family life, mergers or take-overs, unrealistic targets, bullying behaviour, lack of security of tenure, and the absence of loyalty by either company or employee. Being used and abused is a strong breeding ground for anger.

There are also involuntary situations that provoke healthy anger, which is, for example, one of the most important feelings in the grief process. It is more likely that older people suffer bereavement and these are the very ones who may regard anger as sinful, especially if it is directed at God. I think we must give God more credit for recognising a feeling and seeing it as such. In the second year of grieving the death of my youngest child, Cathal, I applied for a job as Principal of a second level school. In the months preparing for the interview I pushed my grief away, compartmentalised it and did a successful interview. Later, as I happily drove home, my grief suddenly came crashing onto me and I was forced to park my car at the roadside. The anger I felt at God surged and almost overwhelmed me. It is probably true that the more religious we are, the angrier we become at God, feeling that he has failed to protect us or somehow betrayed us or treated us unfairly. After all, our perception is that God is almighty and has the power to divert tragedy from us.

I swore at God in the car that day for allowing my child to be taken from me and causing pain and chaos in my family. I remember catching the steering wheel and trying to wrench it from its moorings as I shouted at Him. Gary Chapman, a well-known relationship therapist, labels our anger at God as distorted because He has done us no wrong. God was not responsible for the death of my child. He would not have wished this misfortune on me or my family, but, we often project anger at other people, so God is no exception. If you are a believer and a religious person Chapman advises that you take your anger to God rather than being angry with Him. Sometimes we can pray in our rage and I believe that prayers are always answered, although it sometimes takes a long time, perhaps many years. I also believe that God works through people so I am never waiting for miracles. In a way I believe that it is a miracle when a person with toxic or core rage faces it and seeks help to heal.

The human is born with hope, curiosity and love, but when an infant's dependency needs are not met these turn to ashes, and toxic or core anger is one of the external signs of fear of abandonment. Initially, the faces of angry infants are contorted and crimson as they rage, but if the emotional (or physical) neglect continues they withdraw and the faces register sadness and resignation. The anger turns inward and becomes toxic, to emerge in adulthood as chronic rage, when it is sometimes used as a control mechanism. This anger is an instinct to allay the fear of the inner abandoned child. Healthy anger is an energetic and normally short-lived response to hurt, but toxic anger is chronic, long-lasting, and devastating. Some writers have described toxic anger as similar to post-traumatic stress, i.e. the stress following a trauma. The trauma in this case is the loss of a childhood, which is a prolonged emotional experience that is extremely difficult to process. This emotional neglect is the greatest killer of the human spirit, but it is not the only way that children are infused with toxic anger.

It is said that when we are born we only know how to survive in the wilderness. Everything else is learned. There is, therefore, the possibility that children, who are constantly exposed to anger, may eventually learn it. Anger is seen by them as a way of communication, because their parents can only communicate in an angry way. In other words, for such children angry communication is normal because that is all they see. They also recognise that an angry parent gets what he or she wants, and may form a belief that anger is power to dominate others. This behaviour may be carried on in adult life. It is essential for parents to be aware of their own anger and how they express and use it. They should strongly consider how they deal with it, although this presumes a level of awareness that they may not have.

As you have seen, childhood can be lost in various ways. Sometimes a parent's own feelings may be so frozen that the children are unused to seeing the expression of emotion, or they may be forbidden to express their own feelings. This is a tragedy. If they feel sad they must put on a 'smiley face.' Even crying can be forbidden and this is the greatest tragedy because our tears are inbuilt ways of releasing tension and expressing sadness and empathy. Children are often afraid to express their anger because they might make matters worse or because they feel that their parents might not understand. When children are emotionally muzzled in this way they suffer a deep loss, and anger may emerge in adolescence or early adulthood.

While we can explain the creation of toxic anger and see it as a burden, we must also realise how harmful it is to those who bear the brunt of it. It is the engine which drives abuse of all kinds – verbal, psychological, physical, sexual, or financial. Abuse may be about power and control, but it is fuelled by anger and shame. In a sense anger and shame are in opposite camps. Anger gives a sense of power, but shame cripples us. Toxic anger destroys peace and tranquillity, creating fear, hostility, a sour atmosphere, the death of love, the destruction of relationships, and creates many psychological and emotional problems for children that eventually blight their adulthood.

I see toxic anger as having a three stage cycle. The first stage is one of calmness. The next is of rising anger, where sourness and bad humour is evident. The third phase is the explosion, the venting of the anger on the unfortunate victims, adults and children. When this aggression is vented, the calm phase returns and on it goes, keeping the victims hypervigilant. Those who are victims of this cycle generally use the same phrases – walking on eggshells or being on tenter-hooks. Sometimes there is no explosion but a sullen withdrawing which has an even worse impact on the other. An angry silence is a powerful way to control.

People with toxic anger express it in different ways, referred to as five anger styles by Mike Fisher. He describes the first one as the intimidator, whose threat-ening behaviour brings compliance through fear. The second anger style is interrogation. The interrogator is manipulative and questions the victims to make them feel small and ashamed. It is often supported by a powerful, persuasive but irrational logic. Thirdly we have the victim anger style. The 'poor me' type seeks to make us feel guilty for not meeting their needs. It is the 'look at all I have done for you and there is no thanks for it, would you blame me for being angry with you' type of mentality. It can be quite crushing if practised on people who have a strong caring or rescuing streak because the 'poor me' person always needs rescuing. The fourth anger style is distancing or withdrawing, which makes the other person wonder what is going on, although they will always sense the anger in the distancer. The distancer will rarely get into a conflict and generally will minimise their feelings, or intellectualise them i.e. they will always give a thought when asked about a feeling. The fifth anger style is winding-up. The 'winder upper' controls people by jocosity, teasing and making little of others in a witty way. They are disliked and avoided and the knife they sink in you is just as sharp as that of the violent controller. Seeing other people angry somehow meets a perverse need of the 'winder upper', who is unable to express his own anger and somehow sees it expressed through other people's anger. It is projection and a way of avoiding their own anger. Winding up can be learned in childhood when the child is showered with shame and is a distinct sign that a parent is incapable of loving or cherishing.

Anger can also be categorised as explosive or implosive and someone who is constantly angry without good reason, carries the burden of toxic anger. Explosive anger is a violent outburst and can also vary in intensity, ranging from mild annoyance to a very strong feeling of rage, where it is expressed by shouting, banging things, throwing objects, sulking, glaring, gritting the teeth, shaking the head, waving fists, looking away, making sour comments and hitting or punching some unfortunate person. If you are chronically angry you should realise that it not only damages other people, but is destructive to yourself. Silent or implosive anger is as destructive, if not more so, than the explosive type. One is like a bomb blowing up around you, and the other is like a bomb blowing up inside you. Implosive anger is never digested and burns on.

Why, you might ask, do people keep a lid on their anger and keep it hidden? Partly because they have a fear of offending others, partly because they want to be liked and partly because their self-esteem is low. There is evidence of the damage done by suppressing anger in the context of employees, who have to stifle anger rather than confront customers, whereby their company would lose business. Research on types of work where showing anger would lose custom is very insightful. A study of flight attendants brought up some interesting results. This was carried out by David Kemper a specialist in human emotions. Flight attendants have no option but to remain calm and suppress any anger or irritations when confronted by the offensive behaviour of some passengers. The study showed that the attendants reported feeling numb and came to have considerable emotional problems. We can assume that the same happens to others, who have to please the public or their customers. The basic lesson is that suppressing our anger leads to mental and physical health issues. The problem is made greater if their anger is toxic.

If you wish to get a deeper insight into the damaging impact of anger on your body, you might like to consult Garry Chapman's book, *Anger. Handling a Powerful Emotion in a Healthy Way*. He explains that as the angry feeling emerges and intensifies, the heart pumps faster and drives adrenaline through your body. The adrenal glands produce two hormones that in turn affect your heart rate and blood pressure. Anger has similar physiological symptoms to panic attacks as adrenaline is released and courses through your body. Normally adrenaline in the system serves a useful purpose, but chronic (toxic) anger keeps the adrenaline activated and the body in high alert. What happens is that a neurotransmitter or hormone called acetylcholine ceases to be effective. This hormone is a mechanism with many functions in your nervous system, one of which is to ease the effects of adrenaline. If that is disabled your health is in danger, because the body's major systems such as the heart, the nervous system and breathing functions are affected as ongoing anger keeps our bodies in constant arousal and disrupts its proper functioning. Toxic Anger can lead to liver and kidney damage and increased cholesterol, as well as mental health issues such as anxiety and depression. Studies show that those with the highest level of anger have twice the risk of heart disease and three times the risk of heart attack. Anger arousal affects the sympathetic nervous system, which mobilises the flight or fight response and affects most of the body's internal organs. Other illnesses that may arise from chronic anger are type 2 diabetes, lowering of the immune system, premenstrual syndrome, erectile dysfunction, lowered libido, headaches, backaches, allergies, asthma, arthritis, colitis, irritable bowel syndrome, being prone to infection, slower wound healing, ulcers, migraine and high risk of a stroke.

It is relatively rare for a person with implosive anger to become explosive, but if they do they can unleash torrents of anger for all the years they have swallowed their rage and turned it in on themselves. Some psychologists tend to label implosive anger as passive aggressive anger and others view it as covert psychological control. Passive aggressive anger leaves the targeted

ANGER COMING FROM AN INSECURE ATTACHMENT

person confused, feeling guilty, wondering what is going on, and sometimes irritated. Passive aggressive people may not even realise that they are showing anger, but they are beset by troubled personalities, and are irritable, sarcastic, quarrelsome, cranky, embittered and moody. They may not even understand what anger is. They possibly learned it as children in a home where a controlling parent would not allow others to express their feelings or their anger, sometimes seeing it as disobedience or a threat to their control. The lethal result of such control is that the anger becomes contained internally and expresses itself in a masked way. While passive aggressive people may seem pleasant and greet you with a smile, their anger flows beneath, and they put the knife into you in an indirect way. It has been described as sugar-coated hostility. Mike Fisher calls it the velvet dagger. Passive aggressive people are often 'winder-uppers' and provoke anger in others by their sarcasm. One writer describes them as harbouring vindictive intent beneath a seductive veneer. Passive aggressive people are neither able to show aggression nor assertiveness openly, but cannot always conceal their burning anger.

It is helpful to know at least some of the behaviours of people with passive aggressive anger. They use long periods of silence, where communication is replaced by sourness, withdrawal and angry expressions. They are frequently uncooperative in helping with household chores causing irritation in partners and creating an atmosphere of tension, which is detrimental to children.

They can be deliberately forgetful and even apologise for this, causing doubt and confusion in others. Being deliberately late is sometimes used. This gives them a sense of control over others and points to the irresponsibility of passive aggressors, who prefer to blame other people for their own mistakes. They have an unerring instinct to press the most sensitive buttons arousing rage in others. Many are manipulative, devious, co-dependent, insincere, gossipy, dishonest and false. This is only a brief summary of passive aggressive behaviours, which are dealt with in more detail by Cathy Meyer and Mike Fisher.

Passive aggressive anger is often seen in the workplace, where work expectations and requirements are undermined on a regular basis. Sometimes it is reactive and healthy and sometimes ancient and toxic. An employee, boiling inside, may subtly thwart the efforts of co-workers, especially managers, to advance a company or an organisation. Let us take Jason as a good example of someone using passive aggressive anger against his bosses. His passive aggression was not toxic or core, but was a reaction to the bullying of his superiors, who tried to overwork him and sought to thwart his efforts to get an appropriately early train home. This is how he describes dealing with a toxic workplace.

> My trainer still really intimidated me and I
> hated when he corrected my work. Because I
> was afraid to ask him questions, I would take

risks with my work. I would be sick with worry, hoping that it would work out for me. On the days when things weren't going well for me he would often come over and ask me for my work. It was code for hurry up, in my book. It just made things worse and in my rush to get things done, I would make mistakes. It destroyed me when he would call me over. I knew there was something wrong and I'd dread making the walk to his desk. He would ask me questions about the work, knowing that I wouldn't know the answer. It was soul destroying saying I didn't know as he looked in disgust at me. At the time I just thought it was all part of the job and it was all my fault. But as I grew more confident and competent with the work, I realised he was a bully.

I was under immense pressure one day when the Assistant Supervisor put me looking for meaningless ad hoc reports. I told her I was too busy with the daily stuff and they would have to wait. She said she didn't care and ordered me to get them done. I told her that this wasn't possible and reminded her of my timetable. There was 1 or 2 sick (probably due to the stress of the job) so I was doing 3 people's work. She told me to talk to my manager if I wasn't happy with the workload to start staying later. This angered me as we didn't get paid for overtime and I felt I was giving too much of myself already. I wanted to tell her to back off, grab my coat and head for home. Again my natural instinct was to always to head home in times of stress. I went to management for a meeting and told them my grievances. They backed her up and maintained that I had to stay later to finish work if that's what it took. I told them if they distributed the work more evenly that I would be able get the work done. I was adamant that because I was good at my job, I was getting punished with huge workloads. I would have been better off being no good I maintained, because such workers were given little work or responsibility. They eased my workload for a few weeks but things went back to the same story again. This wasn't good for my mental health. As well as the fears and anxieties I already had, stress and pressure were being added to the mix. The final straw was when I was due a wage increase, but this wasn't given to me as they maintained there was a freeze across the company on increases.

Initially, I saw Jason's behaviour as assertiveness, which it was, so there may be an underlying connection between assertiveness and healthy passive aggression, although I think it is better, if possible, to openly state your anger. He also had the cushion of his decision to pursue a profession in a different area. What follows after such intense and sustained provocation is a clear cut and excellent example of reactive passive aggression.

> My attitude towards work completely changed. I pretty much gave management the two fingers. I decided I wouldn't give a toss about work and just concentrate on preparing for my new direction. This was going to be my career, and not just a job like in the building society. I would go to work each day and do my work and head home. I wouldn't get involved in anything that wasn't to do with my immediate work and do the bare minimum. If I was loaded with a heavy timetable I would tell management that there must be some mistake, that surely I couldn't possibly be expected to do so much work. If they said I was, I would just say that's fine but expect things to be late. Things that I mostly knew how to do, I now looked for proper training, or told them I didn't know how to do that work because I was not trained in it. This created a bad relationship between me and management, but I didn't care. I had given them my all before and I felt it was thrown back in my face, so this was my new tactic. I took a back seat in areas where I was the leader before; tasks that I had a sound knowledge of. I would do my bit and help some of the lads, but that would be it. At one stage, one of the girls on the same level as me, who was anxious for promotion, was

asked by a new Assistant Supervisor to train the rest of us on a few tasks. Months earlier I had trained her on these, but I just sat there, not even hiding my disinterest as she tried to teach me things that I had done many times before. I didn't give a toss and made my disinterest and displeasure towards work known with my body language. It came to a stage where management were nearly afraid to ask me to do work, which suited me just fine. Because I was still one of the strongest members of the team, they couldn't get rid of me, especially as others on the team had made a few high profile mistakes. In fact they tried to accommodate me more, as long as I worked harder. I told them I would, but continued my laissez faire approach to work. This continued for months with my distain for management clear…. I had the odd meeting about my attitude and not doing enough, but my response was always that I was still doing more than everyone on the team and my standard of work was good. They couldn't argue with this so there was a stalemate. It suited me fine because it was just a wage to me now. The lads would slap me saying I was the enfant terrible of the office, but I didn't mind.

In some cases passive aggressive employees in key positions withhold particular expertise from management, who are normally unaware of what may be happening. Occasionally employees may use a so-called illness to express passive aggressive anger in the workplace, and can, for example, refuse to attend meetings because of a particular 'illness'. But, managers or proprietors are more likely to subject others to passive aggressive anger, because they have power.

If those who are on the receiving end of passive aggression understand how it operates they can somehow distance themselves from the person who is causing them discomfort, perhaps even feel sadness for them, although this is not easily done. I find that some people who are subjected to passive aggressive behaviour often step into the child's shoes and operate from there, becoming fearful or angry, confused and uncomfortable.

You can imagine how this type of insidious anger can be very damaging to the employees. It creates a very unpleasant environment where co-operation and friendliness are damaged. Communication becomes hostile and the atmosphere is soured. One of my clients, Olive, wrote an unsent letter to her boss who was guilty of explosive and passive aggressive anger. This letter is in my book on abuse in the chapter on workplace bullying and is worth reading to see how a passive aggressive individual operates. This girl, who was college educated, had to ask permission to go to the toilet, and was fearful of taking her lunch break. She was afraid to take sick days and her life was a misery until she wisely decided to leave. It was a question of her health or her job. The office where she worked was filled with fear, favouritism, hypocrisy, and unspoken resentment. Friendliness, when it was shown, was false and soon turned to hostility. Psychologists argue that hostility is not necessarily the same as anger. Anger is an emotion, but hostility is a frame of mind, a rational or thinking concept that harbours enmity, blame, a desire to punish, and ill-will. Psychologists make the point that hostile people are capable of torturing others in a cold calculated way without any apparent feeling of anger. But, Olive's boss was deeply angry, yet his hostile intention of getting rid of her to make way for a friend was cold and calculated.

It is easy to see that anger can degenerate into hatred. There is no satisfactory explanation of the difference between anger and hatred. Hatred is depicted as an intense, long lasting and overwhelming anger. Some researchers maintain that anger does not last as long as hatred, but chronic anger lasts for a lifetime and may never degenerate into hatred. Neurobiologists have discovered that part of the hate neuro-circuit is connected to aggression and the desire to destroy. This is clearly an unwanted and dangerous trait, and applies as much to women as to men, although aggression by males is generally more lethal. Psychologists tend to differentiate between anger and aggression. Some argue that aggression is a behaviour in response to anger. Research shows that anger is only followed by aggression about ten percent of the time. It is probably more true to say that being really angry brings on thoughts of aggression and violence, but that these thoughts are not generally followed through. One of the similarities between toxic anger and aggression is that they exclude empathy, which has been stifled at a very young age through neglect.

Not all aggression is direct (striking or attacking another person). Indirect aggression might include damaging a person's property. This would, for example, include breaking the windows of someone's house, stealing property in retaliation for some slight or insult, or perhaps, stealing and deliberately crashing someone's car. There are many examples of indirect aggression, which should also be distinguished from verbal anger.

While normally quiet, well-adjusted, people can behave aggressively if sufficiently provoked, aggression can be expected from those with toxic anger. It is also part of domestic violence. In the criminal world aggression is used inspire fear. Even the elderly are not spared in violent burglaries and the results are seen in the wounds and bruises of these unfortunate victims. Researchers call this instrumental aggression as against emotional aggression, and some suggest that such violence can be done without anger. Perhaps so, but there is little doubt that such criminals are by and large angry people. We sometimes read about families being held prisoner as a way of robbing an institution. These tiger kidnappings are well planned and seem cold and calculated without any anger. We can portray them as motivated by greed for money and a determination to get it, but I have little doubt that these perpetrators are angry individuals, because they show little compassion in their behaviour and are willing to hurt and terrify others. We may not always see the anger in such criminals, but, surely it would be a contradiction for a non-angry person to deliberately inflict pain on another, even under serious provocation. If we look at people who behave in a criminal and violent way, and if we look at their background we will generally see the seeds from which the anger and the aggression were bred. Childhood!

Frequently, prior to the aggressive act of injuring another the culprit indulges in verbal aggression or loud threats. Emotional aggression is a different subtype and can also be part of the criminal outlook. It normally occurs when anger reaches such a level that the individual will react aggressively, irrespective of the cost in terms of prosecution. Again, some researchers suggest that this subtype can occur without anger, and may be perpetrated from boredom or for a thrill or from a sense of adventure. My belief is that aggression is always cushioned in anger.

It is easy to see that aggression is almost a way of living for some criminals in their mutual relationships. It is part of a subculture with the 'strongest' at the top of the hierarchy retaining control over others. Unfortunately, they must maintain their aggression to remain there and to 'prove' themselves. Violent ways of resolving conflict through aggression are probably valued and respected in such a subculture, where expressions of anger and aggression are constantly reinforced. But, we don't even have to go to a criminal subculture to witness this. There are families where aggression is the main way to resolve conflict and where the physically strongest may be the most admired. In such families aggression may be passed down and learned for generations, each generation breeding a new set of violent individuals, so that aggression becomes inbuilt. It is ineffably sad to imagine that innocent children from a very young age are brainwashed and go on to live a life of violence in their teenage and adult years. Firstly it becomes a habit, then a way of being, a way of self-definition and finally an addiction. If we really want to see aggression and anger as an addiction, we only have to consider serial killers. Research has shown that aggressive behaviour helps them meet a basic need. They may put forward reasons for killing others, such as sex workers, as protecting society from immorality, but the killing gives them relief from whatever inner stresses that torment them. When the relief wears off they kill again and again.

Many people confuse the feeling of anger with angry behaviour. We are not responsible for our feelings, but we must own our behaviour. Yet, some people see angry behaviour as an advantage and refuse to give it up. This is seen in the household, in the workplace and in society. Parents may see angry behaviour as necessary to discipline their children. They feel that anger 'persuades' their children to do as they are told and to obey household rules. Unfortunately this is a very misplaced and irrational belief. All that they are doing is teaching their children that anger is the best way to communicate and to have control. Such a belief can then be carried on for generations within a family system.

Others feel that anger is somehow genetic and point to anger in the wider family. The old saying 'Like father like son' may be true, but can be misinterpreted. An angry father may create an angry son, but the angry father will have been formed by an angry, neglectful parent, and so on back through generations. Creating a loving bond with our children will have major implications for society. If you look at the violence that is perpetrated on others by violent people you will invariably find that such perpetrators never experienced love or affection in their childhood. This can become a vicious circle as they abuse their children who may in turn become adult abusers. It is more likely that anger is either learned or generated in the core, but it may be part of temperament which is inherited.

Toxic anger may be seen as part of a personality disorder, which is a broad term for personality types who are emotionally unstable, impulsive and who find it difficult to relate to other people. Some personality disorders are labelled as paranoid, schizoid, anti-social, borderline and narcissistic. Anger is viewed as only a small part of the larger personality problem, but it is easy to see that narcissistic people with a blaming mind-set, who see themselves as superior to others, could easily be aroused to anger. A small trigger can provoke a strong angry outburst. Such people tend to be rigid, inflexible and have black and white thinking and find it difficult to deal with the changes and challenges of life. They are dysfunctional and see anger as outside of themselves, so it is unlikely that they will make much of an effort to change. Their irrational and irresponsible mantra is 'you made me angry' or 'only for you I would not be angry'.

Those who carry the burden of toxic anger and are driven by the controlling impulse are also inclined to have a poor view of their victims. As narcissists, they occupy a very high perch in their own eyes and tend to look down on others and therefore assume that others are deserving targets of their anger. There is an inherent irony in this, because anger is often driven by shame, a burning feeling that is about the self and about feeling flawed or defective. So the reality is that a shamed person who does not feel good enough makes himself feel better by spraying it on others. Shame is chronic and permeates all other feelings, utterly preventing any type of happiness. It has been described as the annihilation of the self. Shame and anger are, however, very different. Shame is debilitating and anger energising, but they are comfortable bedfellows. The greater the shame the greater the anger it generates. It is possible to fully experience rage, but shame is so burning that it is impossible to feel it fully. John Bradshaw's book, *Healing the Shame That Binds You* is worth reading for an insightful exploration of toxic shame.

Anger is also associated with other types of personality, which, unlike personality disorders, are not pathological, but they might help you to make better sense of yourself. The theory of Type A and Type B personalities was first proposed by two cardiologists, Meyer Friedman and Ray Rosenman, and aroused much debate among psychologists. While there is plenty of scope for disagreement, there is much to be said in support of their theory in the context of anger. We need not be concerned about Type B personalities, who are less stressed and less inclined to anger than Type A. The Type A personality is not necessarily a narcissistic disorder although many narcissists are type A. Neither is it a psychological disorder, but simply points to particular characteristics some people have. In my clinical experience, they have one common factor in that they have childhood attachment problems. Type As are probably over organised, task orientated, and obsessed with time management. They are always in a hurry and always feeling that time is running out. They are generally high achievers and addicted to work and busyness. They are driven and always have deadlines and hate delays or obstructions. They face challenges head on and are creative in finding solutions. Above all, Type A personalities are very competitive and hate losing. They are often pessimistic, hostile and aggressive. They are continuously on a treadmill that brings constant stress and is a serious threat to health.

Type A personalities also seem to share another unwanted trait – impatience, which is related to anger (and anxiety). Generally people are unaware of the latent hostility which drives impatience and the damage it does to their mental and probably physical health. Unfortunately, it was once one of my main characteristics. I always rushed whenever I was doing a task and normally had to redo it several times before I got it right. That was all very well until I became a Principal, responsible for a big school, when my impatience sometimes landed me in trouble because of my mistakes. My writing was illegible because of my haste. When, as a young man, I worked in an oil company, I could code twice as many sales dockets as my colleagues. But, I made twice as many mistakes. When I learned to type I became a very fast and inaccurate typist because I rushed when learning.

Impatience, which drives us to achieve a goal, is actually self-defeating because patient practice and behaviour enables us to be more efficient, to think things out and find the best solution to a problem. This exasperating trait also keeps anxiety levels consistently high and feeds a low level of anger on the treadmill of constant pressure. If you are impatient you probably have set very high standards and unrealistic expectations. Impatient people can be like spoiled children, needing instant gratification and suffering frustration if thwarted. One of the biggest issues with impatience is that it interferes with good listening and understanding of others, because impatient individuals are constantly distracted thinking about what is next on their to-do list. On the other hand impatient people can also be sensitive about themselves and find it difficult to process feedback.

There are other theories about impatience. One is that it is based on fear, such as fear of missing out or a fear based craving to get something done. Professors Chen-Bo Zhong and Sanford DeVoe of Toronto University came up with novel research, claiming that fast food promotes impatience. Their research proposes that even thinking about fast food increases our desire for time-saving products and their actual consumption allows people to fill their stomach quickly and move on to other things.

Finally, in looking at anger and its ancillary feelings, you should distinguish between anger and bitterness. There are many differences between normal anger and bitterness. There are, however, many common characteristics between toxic anger and bitterness. They are both long lasting, although toxic anger lasts a lifetime, while you can let go of bitterness and resentment. Both also carry an element of vengeance, although it is stronger in bitterness. They are both harmful and constant silent companions. As you will see in the following section anger, even toxic anger can be managed, but bitterness can be all – consuming. Unlike toxic anger, bitterness is not bred in you as a child, but arises because of some real or imagined injustice done to you as an adult, where it is akin to resentment, a feeling that shares some of the characteristics of anger. Resentment can be the vehicle of anger, but has the core of bitterness. Those who have toxic anger are more vulnerable to bitterness, because they are sensitive and never forget a slight.

Unless you let go of the memory of the injustice, bitterness will persist and become like a second skin to you. If you are bitter you feel like a victim, whereas toxic anger makes you feel powerful, although it is bred from being a victim of childhood neglect. Both are bad for your health, so you should try and find empathy for yourself and let your bitterness go. Forgiveness is the best antidote for bitterness, but it is not easy to access, because, as shown above, it is a feeling that may or may not arrive, in which case you may have to rely on some type of cognitive forgiveness. In practice this would mean letting go of vengeance.

Anger Management for Adults

YOU ARE NOW AWARE OF THE nature and types of anger, and the destructive impact it can have on your health. This can be avoided if you learn how to manage it properly. Anger management is not about healing, but management and healing work in tandem and are closely interlinked. Some techniques for anger management also lead to healing.

Anger management is what it says – a way of helping people to control the anger, process it safely and acquire communication skills. Those who have learned that aggression is the only way to communicate have to be re-educated on communication skills and how to handle the various crises they will meet during their life. Crucially, the person in an anger management programme or with a counsellor must be willing to change. It is my experience that people who are sent by the courts to do anger management only come because they are forced to, and it is more likely that this intervention will fail. There are two types of anger management. One is consistent and frequent management using a wide variety of techniques to soothe and soften the anger, the other is the immediate application of techniques in any situation where anger arises.

Anger management is an ongoing process that brings temporary relief, giving you space to work on your anger and ultimately to heal it. There are some problematic issues in the context of anger management. If the anger is toxic reflecting childhood trauma, it may be compounded by other complaints such as addiction, drug abuse, depression, anxiety, and a whole host of debilitating issues outlined in Appendix 1. Anger management, therefore, is a temporary technique until the sources of the anger have been dealt with and it is no longer needed.

Cognitive Restructuring

Cognitive restructuring is part of Cognitive Behaviour Therapy (CBT) and is helpful as an anger management tool. It is a technique where you learn to identify and dispute irrational or defective thoughts or distortions, such as all or nothing thinking and over-generalisations. It has long been understood that distorted thoughts fuel anger, and by understanding them and changing them you can soften the anger. According to Albert

Ellis, one of the founders of cognitive theory, there are four irrational core beliefs or thoughts that lead to anger. Ellis obviously had a sense of humour, and the first type of thought he labelled 'awfulising' or 'catastrophising'. So, for example, if someone crashes into your car you might say 'this is awful, this is a catastrophe.' The next thought that arises is what he calls 'I can't stand it itis'. That might sound something like this, 'I can't put up with this. This is simply intolerable.' This is generally followed by a 'should' or an 'ought', which Ellis calls 'musturbation'. The thought here might be 'that driver should have been more careful, he ought to have concentrated more.' The next thought is a labelling one. 'That guy is a right idiot.'

So how do you restructure these anger provoking thoughts? You might say something like this. 'This is very unfortunate, but it could be worse. I might have been hurt. I can get the car fixed on his insurance. It would have saved a lot of hassle if that driver had been paying attention, but I suppose we all make mistakes.' If you manage to do this you will slow down your anger and replace it by mild irritation or annoyance. It is also compatible with the five steps for managing anger mentioned later on.

Cognitive restructuring also includes challenging what psychologists call overestimation and underestimation. What this means is that angry people tend to anticipate the worst outcomes and underestimate their own abilities to deal with problems. It is about standing back and making a more balanced, accurate and optimistic estimation of what is going on and what realistically might happen. It prevents personalised conclusions and reasoning, which stoke anger. It also helps you to communicate better and in a calmer manner.

Anger Journal

An anger journal is one of the most important ways to understand your anger and is an excellent anger management technique, because it gives you time to examine your thoughts with greater accuracy and to see your stress triggers. You can work out your own headings for the journal or diary, but they should include the circumstances that aroused your anger, the physical, mental and emotional cues that accompanied the anger, its intensity level and duration, and any other feelings that accompanied it. An anger journal will show you how you express anger, for example, are you an exploder or an imploder, or do you use passive aggressive anger? When you examine your anger journal you have time to realise that the issue may not always be the external factor that is the problem, but how you define it. In other words, the problem may lie with yourself, how you think, your beliefs, expectations, and your judgement. When you can access whether the level of your anger is justified or whether it is due to your own thinking or beliefs, you are in a better position to manage it. The journal would help you to readjust your thinking and your beliefs. One of the positive things about anger is that it makes you examine your beliefs. You can hold them up to the light, consider where and when you formed them and if they are rational or irrational. You will see your own particular patterns and in this way come to understand your anger, and this will make it easier to control it in future. It might also be useful to see if some of the circumstances listed were similar to those that made you angry as a child.

By standing back from your anger using a journal, you become almost an external observer. Writing slows you down, while anger sweeps you away. You could extend the idea of including an unsent letter in your journal as a way of expanding it by writing in more detail about what happened and more importantly what happened to you. Marcia Cannon makes the useful suggestion that you could write a letter to yourself as if you were writing to a best friend and make sure you put every single detail into it. You can pour all your thoughts and feelings into the letter and feel empathy for yourself. This could be further enhanced by using inner childwork, when you use your non-dominant hand to write the letter, and where the extent of old losses and distresses becomes apparent.

If you keep doing your anger journal over a long period you will begin to notice how you are changing and you will be encouraged to continue to change. You will notice that circumstances and behaviours that made you angry previously may no longer do so.

An Anger Contract

Whenever you write stuff down it gives you a better opportunity to understand it, and an anger contract is a technique used by many counsellors to help those tormented by toxic anger. It is very compatible with keeping an anger journal. It gives clients a sense of control before the anger erupts and is a very simple and brief contract that they must sign. It might run like this –

> *I will take responsibility for my behaviour and promise that I will vent my anger appropriately. This includes non-violent and non-hurtful ways of expressing my anger. I will tell people that I am angry rather than berating them. I will take every opportunity of properly communicating with my partner or with others to prevent an outpouring of anger. I recognise that I may need help from those I trust to help me overcome the anger that binds me.*

Communicating Anger

You have already seen how some children learn that anger is the only way to communicate, and bring this into adulthood with disastrous consequences for a calm relationship. If both parties can stand back, check their thinking, and are willing to sit down and look at their relationship, they can find a way to safely process the anger. Gary Chapman suggests six ways of processing anger. He suggests that the first step is to acknowledge the presence of anger and not to condemn yourself for experiencing it. The next step is a vital one, i.e. letting you partner know that you feel angry, rather than suppressing it, leading to passive aggressive, silent rage. There must also be some kind of acceptance by both that it is not right to vent anger on the other. Such venting will invite retaliation and ongoing conflict, so having a discussion on the source of the anger may help to alleviate it. Recognising the source is important and may call for an apology from one partner. When the anger has dissolved, try and return to loving ways. There is a caveat, however. If your partner has a high controlling impulse there is little you can do to remove the anger from the relationship, and you will have to deal with your own retaliatory anger.

Understanding the Difference between Aggression and Assertiveness

Before you learn how to properly communicate anger, it is worthwhile exploring the difference between aggression and assertiveness. Managing anger is about replacing aggression with assertiveness. Assertiveness is very different from aggression, and is part of healthy, protective anger. People who are assertive are normally kind, responsible, good listeners, empathic, and non-violent, unlike aggressive individuals who take out their anger on others. Aggression rides roughshod over the rights of others, while assertiveness recognises the rights of both sides. Assertiveness underlies good self-esteem, while, more often than not, aggressive people have low self-esteem. To put it simply, if we feel worthwhile we will not allow anyone to walk on us and we will not inflict pain on others. It is a matter of respecting boundaries, those essential safeguards which are discussed in several sections of this book. But, apart from working on boundaries, you can also practise assertiveness. It is difficult to do it on your own and the assistance of a professional is advisable. In such cases you will give some examples of where you have been aggressive and the counsellor will help you to find assertive ways of responding. As with boundaries you will have to practise this until it becomes a normal way of responding. What happens in such cases is that the brain creates a new program to facilitate assertive responses.

Problem solving is also an effective way of converting aggression to assertiveness. In problem solving you come up with solutions, where you examine various situations of aggressive behaviour. You can analyse the consequences of this behaviour, and come up with other responses you might have made and the consequences of these. So, for example, if you shouted at your boss and threatened him, the consequences might be suspension or firing, but if you walked away you might be at most reprimanded. If you decided that it would be best to request a meeting at a later stage, the consequences might be a much better outcome because you will then have a voice – an assertive or a rational voice, rather than an aggressive and irrational voice. All of this is a learned behaviour and it can be done with time and patience and making mistakes.

Relaxation Techniques

Since anger is an emotion charged with energy, relaxation techniques can help relieve the stress it causes you. Progressive muscle relaxation is particularly successful as an anger management tool. It is also one of the easiest to practise. It involves the tensing and relaxing of each of the 16 different muscles groups in your body. Tense each muscle hard enough for about ten seconds and then suddenly relax the muscle for fifteen seconds. The whole exercise could take up to half an hour. As you release each muscle imagine the anger or stress seeping away. Begin with your fists, then your biceps (muscles on the upper arm), then your triceps (muscles underneath the arm). Raise your eyebrows to tighten the forehead muscles and tense the muscles at the back of your head, close your eyelids tightly, open your mouth wide and stretch your jaw, then go to the back of your neck, tense your shoulders, push your shoulder blades back, breathe deeply to tighten the stomach muscles, arch your back, clench your buttocks, tighten your thigh muscles, pull up your toes, tighten your calf muscles, curl your toes and tense your feet. If this is done properly it will greatly relax your body and weaken your anger.

How to Vent Anger Successfully

There is a lot of debate about how to discharge anger safely. Some research suggests that venting anger explosively causes more harm than good, while some writers contend that suppressing it is equally harmful. Because anger is full of energy, therapists once believed that an energetic venting (e.g. using a punch bag) was the best, but research now shows that this is detrimental to our health and causes as much damage as an outburst of anger. Current theory also holds that explosively venting anger merely nurtures volatility. Finding gentle ways to process it is recommended, for example, listening to gentle music or water flowing in a stream. When you are taking a shower you can imagine the anger flowing away with the water. These gentle anger management techniques will help you to ease your stress and take better care of yourself. As the stress eases so does the chronic vigilance that keeps the fire of anger smouldering.

The Unsent Letter

The unsent letter, mentioned above, is one of the best ways to vent your anger. In this you can express exactly how you feel, using any type of language you like, while showing in detail the reasons for your anger. You can use the letter to deal with normal or with toxic anger. The letter is for your healing and to give you a voice. If the letter is to heal toxic anger, it is about reclaiming your power, and expressing your anger at being neglected in childhood. When your power is taken as a child you feel fearful as an adult, and a letter to those who sowed that fear can help to release you from its grip. It does not matter if the person, who caused you this distress, is alive or dead. The letter should be worded strongly, using the non-dominant hand to access the feelings of the inner child, and should express not only your anger but any other feeling you have suffered as a result of neglectful parenting. When you have finished you could read it aloud to a therapist or a close friend and then tear it up or burn it. This is a symbol of freedom because you are now having a voice and tearing down the power of the person who hurt you. If you burn the letter you will see their ancient power vanishing in smoke.

Abdominal or Diaphragmatic Breathing

Abdominal breathing is one of the best ways to ease the stress of anger. Most people breathe through their chests (probably an evolutionary behaviour to take in more oxygen when the world was more danger-ous millennia ago) so they have to learn abdominal breathing. It can take up to three months of daily practice to master this. Ten minutes practice per day is sufficient. This routine should be rigorously followed and it is equally good for anxiety and panic attacks. The usual way is to sit in a chair, put a book on your abdomen and attempt to lift the book with each breath.

You breathe in through your nose and your abdomen expands and rises the book, then you breathe out and your abdomen falls. Initially when you are practising you will find that your chest expands and your abdomen stubbornly refuses to rise. Don't be discouraged, because with constant practice you will master this way of breathing. Gradually only your abdomen will expand and your chest will not move. When you have mastered this, it will become your normal way of breathing and you can easily slip into deep breathing when the occasion demands. Abdominal breathing calms your body and brings your mind and body together. It is a technique that works whether you like it or not. It is a technique I learned over fifty years ago, and I know that you can master it, if you persevere.

The Four Steps and the Golden Rules of Mike Fisher

Mike Fisher outlines four steps and some 'golden' rules that are easy to implement, if you accept responsibility for how you vent your anger. The first step is an awareness of the primary source of your anger – perhaps unmet needs. This second step is about taking responsibility for yourself and acquiring key communications skills such as attentive listening, hearing and understanding rather than trying to win an argument. The third step is to become the external observer, seeing the big picture, and recognising what you are responsible for in a particular conflict. The final step is to expect a reaction from others who might wish to see you remain as you are, and to be aware of your own resistance to change. His 'golden' rules include having empathy for the other person, looking at the other's point of view, respecting the opinions of others, having anger buddies and a support network, being aware of internalised shame and lowering your expectations of others. These are valuable suggestions and will certainly work with healthy anger.

Road Rage

Road rage is a common feature of today's life, but can be relatively easily managed. Some writers argue that it is mislabelled as rage, and is anger. That is not always the case, because people are frequently assaulted by a driver in a fit of rage. Any driver can become angry, but if a person has core anger it can quickly and easily degenerate into rage. Research shows that controlling people are more likely to suffer from road rage than others, and that means there are many people subject to it. Narcissistic people think that they own the road. They find it difficult to soothe their rage, but like all others they can become aware and change. Alas! This seldom happens.

To prevent or ease road rage, learn how to stay in the moment, pause to think, and postpone judgement. Perhaps you are in a hurry and a car in front of you is moving slowly and you find your irritation and anger rising by the minute. If you can access your empathy for the driver it will soothe your anger.

For example, the driver may be elderly and fearful or over-careful. Self-talk is always good in these situations. You could say to yourself that someday you, too, will be elderly and perhaps fearful, when you would appreciate sympathy and understanding for elderly drivers. Remind yourself that you are no better than others, that they have paid their road tax and are entitled to use the road. More thought and more understanding brings calm and prevents unwarranted anger.

Mike Fisher makes some practical suggestions for avoiding road rage, such as making the interior of your car comfortable and putting on soothing music. Another way of avoiding irritation is to leave early for your destination and drive at a leisurely pace. The AA route finder or Sat Nav. are useful in giving distance, which allows you to manage your time and avoid stress. Putting in the destination on the Sat Nav. the previous night reduces stress also. Practising courtesy on the roads and making allowances for others will give you a good feeling about yourself, and will makes you feel in control. The car is a very obedient companion. If you have cruise control use it. It might save you some penalty points at least, but it will help you avoid competitiveness and anger. Positive self-talk and mindfulness are as helpful in avoiding the stress of road rage as any other type of anger. Be content in the world you have created – a clean car interior, soothing music and adequate time to reach your destination.

Dealing with Immediate Anger

Much of what has been written so far involves a long term and continuous approach to managing anger and relieving distress, and it takes some time before it comes into effect. In the meantime you have to find some means to deal with on the spot anger, when a confrontation is imminent. There are two practical ways you can immediately manage your anger in a conflict, and both work very well. The first is simply to tell the offending person how you feel and why. There is no blame in this method and it will not invite retaliation. In practice it would be something like this – 'I feel angry because I feel disrespected.' Do not underestimate the power of this statement. It is more powerful and more effective than shouting at someone or blaming them. You are only saying how you feel. You are entitled to say how you feel. No one can say how you should feel. Yet this is a much more difficult anger management technique than you realise. It is particularly difficult for those with poor boundaries, who are afraid of challenging others, wanting perhaps their approval.

The other technique involves a five step procedure, which can be carried out in a few seconds. You must bear in mind that you only have a very brief opportunity to control your anger. The amygdala, that part of your brain that processes emotion, allows only a quarter of a second to respond to an event that triggers it. While this almost instant response is happening the increased blood flow goes to the frontal lobe of your brain that controls your reasoning and this takes two seconds to react. This brief window allows you to create more time to process the anger, using the five step technique. These steps must be followed in order and is an internal processing of the rising anger.

1. Be aware of body cues which tell you that you are about to become angry. The cue may be in your head (ache), in your chest (tightness), in your stomach (tightness), in your fists (clenching).
2. Awareness – be aware that the anger is about to arrive – you could use the following words – 'I can feel anger coming'.
3. Acknowledgement – acknowledge the fact that you are angry and getting angrier – 'I am really angry now'.
4. Have an internal conversation with yourself. The longer the conversation the better. The idea is to talk down and dilute the anger. Your internal conversation might be like this. – 'I am really raging right now. Look at the state of the place. The children scatter their toys all over the floor, and my husband/wife just leaves them there. This is driving me mad especially because I am always telling them to clean up. Why don't they listen to me? They have no respect for me.'
5. Finally try and find some empathy (understanding) for the person causing the offence. Empathy is indispensable and without it the technique

will fail. You only need a tiny element of it, and it is easier if you know the person who is the source of your anger. But, it is equally essential if you are angry with a stranger. Empathy looks like this – 'My wife is a very kind person. She is a very good mother. She loves me and loves the children. I can't expect her to keep picking up after the children. Children need to play. I also have a responsibility to show them what to do.'

I hope that at least some of these techniques help you not only to manage or control your anger, but help you to heal as well. Ultimately, you are not responsible for your angry feelings, but you have a choice about how to process and express your anger. You can choose to hesitate, to give yourself space, not to vent your anger on someone, and not to blame or criticise them. This may be hard, but you have a choice. Even in your worst moments you have a choice. I can never accept it when someone says to me that they are unable to control their anger. Many show admirable self-control in external circumstance, but not so much in their own home. The books on anger in the bibliography are worth reading if you have an anger issue.

Anger Management for Children

MANY PARENTS COMPLAIN THAT THEIR CHILDREN are angry and disruptive. This is a serious source of worry and anxiety to them, so it is just as important to help children manage and heal anger as it is for adults. The sooner the anger is dealt with in a person's life the better, because it prevents much distress in adulthood, both on a personal and relationship level. There are some books that might help you as a parent or teacher to deal with such anger. Elaine Whitehouse and Warwick Pudney have written a small worthwhile book, *A Volcano in my Tummy. Helping Children to handle Anger*, which contains 25 lessons on anger that can be built into the school curriculum. My only concern is that the book deals with children from six to fifteen years of age. Because of brain changes over that span, it is more difficult to eradicate toxic anger from a fifteen year old than the anger of a six year old. With kinder parenting and understanding teachers, the harm done to a younger child can be undone, but the neural wiring that takes place during life stages six and seven (13 to 19 years of age – the life stages will be looked at in the final chapter) is much harder to change. Bearing that in mind, Whitehouse and Pudney's book sets about creating a framework for helping your children to become aware of the initial feeling of anger and then of making choices about what to do with it. In that way they learn about the differences between the angry feeling and the angry behaviour. When you show your children how to process their anger, you have to be aware of how you as a parents vent yours. Small children learn all the time, and they learn how their parents and others, such as their teachers, express their anger. They need to know that angry feelings are acceptable, but violence towards others is not. As a parent you must allow your children to feel anger. It is very damaging to make them suppress it, and if that happens there is every possibility that they may experience many psychological difficulties, including depression, when they grow into adulthood.

If you understand the other feelings that lie behind anger, you will be in a much better position to help your children process it. There are numerous other feelings masked by anger. These include hurt, fear, shame, feelings of abandonment and rejection, vulnerability, feeling unloved and unlovable. Very often hurt is the main feeling behind anger, and if you talk to your children about that hurt, you will have a healing effect on them. Sometimes with younger children fear is the feeling that triggers anger. Fear is about survival and being in danger ultimately provokes anger. There are many fears that a child may harbour and hence many reasons for their anger. Anger is very quick to fill a vacuum, and it can readily fill the emptiness in an unloved child. Children who have not experienced love, will not know why they are angry, the parent or parents who are unable to give love will be puzzled and possibly blame the child. How often do we label our children without pausing to consider why they are as they are? Let us not label them as angry children. Let us look at ourselves as parents and take responsibility for forming them this way. Children need unconditional love, and those who get it will thrive and never suffer core anger. Anger will also fill the vacuum in a child who feels a failure, feels powerless, unwanted, is hungry, is in danger of being hurt, is deprived of something essential, is not liked by other children, or is confused.

There are many quick decisions to take when you are faced with an angry child, but basically you should not retaliate inappropriately. Always remain in your adult shoes. It is not uncommon for adults to regress into their childhood shoes when dealing with certain situations, including dealing with an angry child. When this happens we can end up with two angry children in confrontation – the angry child and the angry inner child of the adult. By staying in the adult's shoes you can remain calm and show the child how to deal with anger. If you show control and calmness in an angry situation they too will learn this behaviour.

It is also beneficial for the child if you reflect and acknowledge the anger that he is showing. Allowing him to express the reasons for the anger helps to allay it. Perhaps you might ask yourself the questions posed by Whitehouse and Pudney – have your children the opportunity to express their anger at home (or in school)? Can they take it for granted that they can express their feelings, or are you as a parent too fearful of anger to allow it to be vented by them? If so why? You may have to look back at your own childhood to find the reason. You could also check if you are more comfortable with giving boys the space to express their anger, but not the girls. Your belief might be that it is more acceptable for boys to express anger than girls, that it is a sign of masculinity, a testosterone fuelled feeling! Overall, therefore, listening to your children is of the utmost importance, and listening means hearing what they have to say, acknowledging it and taking it seriously. That does not mean giving in to a child's demands, but giving her respect and time, and letting her see that what she has to say is important.

The adolescent life stage is a particularly difficult one for the human. That stage stretches from about thirteen to nineteen years, or even later. Early and mid-adolescence bring painful challenges. Teenagers in that stage are dealing with profound physical changes and emotional upheaval. Their emotional responses become more intense, heightened and easily triggered. Parents can be bewildered by the startling changes they see in their children as their brain develops in an extraordinary and complex way. Teenagers themselves may become equally bewildered and troubled at the intensity of their feelings, including their anger.

I have researched several works on teenage anger and I recommend Nick Luxmoore's book, *Working with Anger and Young People*. Nick is an English psychotherapist and school counsellor, and he highlights many issues that provoke anger in teens. The most prominent ones are body image problems, feeling left out, being hurt by negative comments from parents, being disrespected, disregarded, run down, criticised, losing a relationship, being bullied, bereaved, suffering loneliness and, above all, experiencing abandonment. Anger can be seen as a defence against all of these, masking the hurt and the fear. The feeling of anger must be allowed and acknowledged and then the pain, hurt and fear explored. That does not mean allowing teenagers to inflict their anger on others, including a parent or teacher.

What is really problematic in dealing with teenagers is trying to help those who are unable to properly express their anger, who have been 'taught' at home that anger is not a nice feeling, that good children do not get angry, or, on the contrary, that anger is the only way to communicate. There is also the question of how comfortable a teenager feels in second level school. Some therapists use the word attachment for this and see schools as unconsciously offering a mothering experience. That is a thought that might make teachers, who rightly wish to keep boundaries clear, uncomfortable. It is probably more relevant at primary school level. I recall that as a young child we always addressed a married female teacher as 'mam'! It is possible to be warm and nurturing and yet keep appropriate boundaries.

Because of the huge numbers involved, the pressure cooker atmosphere from nine o'clock to four, and the dynamic of so many relationships, school is a place where anger can suddenly blow up and create very difficult situations. When I look back on my life as a school Principal, I realise that some of the many issues that came to my door involved feelings of intense anger. Teachers would arrive frustrated at the behaviour of some students, who disrupted their classes, abused them, or refused to do their homework. Students would erupt because they may have felt they were being treated unfairly. Additionally, some teachers and some students brought an ancient anger with them, and when a particular trigger was pulled or a particular button pressed the anger emerged. My job was to try to defuse the anger both of the teacher and the respective students. I now realise that I also had to deal with my own anger as well. There were certain things that angered me and fuelled the childhood anger that I carried. My anger was over-provoked by the very idea that a student would disrupt a class, or had drawn graffiti on a wall, or misbehaved in the town at lunchtime. When I explored it later during my counselling sessions I realised that behind my anger lay fear; fear that I was losing control or that students did not respect me or were not afraid of me. Perhaps my greatest fear was that the school would get a bad name and reflect poorly on me. I personalised all this through my own shame and subconsciously focussed on my own shortcomings. When I look back at my time as a teacher, I can see that I did not always control my anger and I regret it. It was based on the treadmill of fear, a fertile ground for chronic anxiety. So, as teachers or Principals we focus on the behaviour, because that is our job, as counsellors, however, we look for the hurt, and in that we may discover our own wounds.

Professionals dealing with teenagers, in particular, are vulnerable to burn out from the impact of constant exposure to anger. Students may express this anger in different ways, such as avoidance of doing their tasks, procrastinating, being forgetful, being sarcastic, or, unfortunately, using abusive language. Some writers use the phrase projective identification, whereby one person (a teacher) absorbs the anger of another (the student) and acts out the other's anger. Teachers have many sources of frustration. Sometimes the job seems impossible and despite very hard work they are open to criticism because they cannot cater for the educational needs of the wide variety of students they deal with. I think that students nowadays feel much freer in expressing their anger. In my school days we would not dare show it and the result was buried anger and fear. The lesson to be learned from the past is that anger is a feeling and its expression is important, but such venting must be within proper boundaries.

There is a workbook entitled *The Anger Workbook for Teens. Activities to help you deal with anger and frustration*, which is a practical and useful tool for school staff to help angry teenagers explore their anger. Compiled by Raychelle Lohmann, a professional school counsellor in North Carolina, this workbook contains thirty-six activities and advises that two or three is the maximum that should be done each week. Some of the most important sections deal with keeping an anger log, recognising anger buttons, understanding family dynamics, physical symptoms of anger, burying emotions, using anger positively, relaxation techniques, an anger contract, taking responsibility for one's own actions, stages of anger, coping with conflict, good listening, clear communication, assertiveness and change. Photocopies can be made of each section, for example, the anger log or family anger pattern (a type of genogram looking at anger in the wider family).

One of the hidden ingredients that foment anger in school is rarely mentioned – being shamed. Shame sometimes forms part of the anger jigsaw, and hierarchical institutions are breeding grounds for it. I have observed this poisonous ingredient as a teacher and Principal for over thirty years, and as a primary school pupil long ago, when the school ethos was based more on power and inequality. There is a strange, almost subconscious, contradiction in school relationships, because while school is a place of formation and extraordinary hard work, shame can sometimes discolour that development. This was more evident in my childhood, and indeed for many years afterwards. Society itself was shame based in those days, and a culture saturated with shame was passed from generation to generation in many aspects of life. Poor people were obvious targets. As a historian researching the Poor Law, I was taken aback at Minute Book headings such 'No. of lunatics/ bastards in the workhouse'. You can imagine how people and children labelled in this shameful way were treated!

In my own small, rural school as a young child, I remember rows of dunce's hats peering down from the tops of presses and small children standing in corners wearing these shaming badges. I recall shaming remarks made to children which would not be tolerated today. Yet, I doubt if shame has been eradicated from our schools. There is no reason to assume that teachers are no more or no less shame based than others, and their sarcastic and belittling remarks, especially in primary school, where children are most vulnerable, are particularly detrimental. Like parents, teachers make negative remarks to small children and, no more than parents, do not realise the damage that this causes. It is the great killer of creativity, creating doubt and confusion that ultimately may hold us in a barren place. The infant is the most creative of all people, mainly because she has not yet been exposed to a shaming environment.

Shaming remarks made to children under twelve have a more drastic and permanent impact that can become core because, like parents, teachers spend a lot of time with them, and the *frequency* of these remarks is a key element in laying the crop of shame. A combination of parental and teaching shaming is particularly damaging and reinforces the sense of not being good enough in the child. We can choose not to shame any child. Education is not just about intellectual or cognitive development, it must include emotional nourishment as well, which is facilitated by praise and allowing children the space to interact with each other. So, I will leave this chapter with a simple poem by an unknown poet on the practical difference between shame and praise –

"I've got 2 A's" the small boy cried,
His voice was filled with glee
His father very bluntly asked
"Why did you not get three?"

"I've mowed the grass" the tall boy said
"And put the mower away".
His father asked him with a shrug,
"Did you clean off the clay?

"Mom, I've got the dishes done,"
The girl called from the door.
Her mother very calmly said
"And did you sweep the floor?"

The children in the house next door
Seemed happy and content.
The same things happened over there,
But this is how it went:

"I've got 2 A's the small boy cried,
His voice was filled with glee.
His father very proudly said
"That's great! I'm glad you live with me."

"I've mowed the grass," the tall boy said
"And put the mower away,"
His father answered with much joy,
"You've made my happy day"

"Mom, I've got the dishes done"
The girl called from the door.
Her mother smiled and softly said,
"Each day I love you more."

Children need encouragement
For tasks they're asked to do
If they're to lead a happy life,
So much depends on you.

Chapter 3

Toxic Jealousy Stemming from an insecure childhood attachment.

IN MY EXPERIENCE TOXIC JEALOUSY IS one of the most painful wounds of childhood and is worth understanding. It is related to envy, but is not the same. Envy is a coveting of something another has, such as wealth, achievement, or fame, while jealousy is a fear of being replaced by another person. Jealousy can be about a sense of unfairness, sibling rivalry, fear of being betrayed and above all can be found in romantic relationships. It is, therefore, about relationships and has been in existence for as long as human kind. Toxic or pathological jealousy is one of the most excruciating realities you can come across. Not only is it extremely painful, but is very difficult to heal. It applies to all races and civilizations; although in cultural terms, research shows that there are high jealousy and low jealousy societies. In societies where male dominance is the norm, jealousy is more evident.

Jealousy has been described by Hildegard Baumgart as a relational conflict and a response to the provocative behaviour of a partner. Such provocation would, for example, include blatant flirting at one end and infidelity at the other. This type of jealousy is normal and not toxic. It could be seen as reactive jealousy.

You can find plenty of references to jealousy in the Old Testament, and a good example of toxic jealousy is in the story of Cain and Abel, the sons of Adam and Eve, which does not say much about the latter's parenting! Abel drew the jealous wrath of Cain because his offering was favoured by the Lord, and he paid for it with his life. The God of the Old Testament is also portrayed as a jealous God, although this is interpreted as a loving God, who wishes to save us. Likewise, it is a frequent theme in films and literature. Shakespeare used jealousy as the fatal weakness in his flawed hero, Othello.

There is always a triadic relationship when jealousy arises, and it is evident in all gender orientations. I have, for example, come across intense toxic jealousy in homosexual relationships. In the Old Testament there is God, his people and rival gods. In Shakespearean drama you have Othello, his wife (Desdemona), and Cassio. In reality there is no relationship between Cassio and Desdemona. Either Othello was gullible when he was deceived by the ploys of the cunning Iago, or he had toxic jealousy! In toxic jealousy the third person in the relationship is generally a figment of the jealous person's imagination. Sometimes, and in what seems to be a contradiction, the fictional third party is used by the jealous person as an excuse to abandon a relationship, ironically because of fear of abandonment. Nancy Friday sums it up well when she wrote that she treacherously dreamt of her partner's next lover. Nancy's unfortunate and unsuspecting successor will soon become the target, and on it goes destroying relationship after relationship. Generally speaking, it is not the rival, but the partner, who attracts the ire of the jealous person, although a rival by his or her flirtatious behaviour can do so. This can be the case in both normal and toxic jealousy.

Toxic or core jealousy is the great destroyer of relationships, where so much fruitless energy goes into driving a partner away and sometimes those afflicted with toxic jealousy can be jealous of their own children. Jealousy of one's children is often unconscious, but I have heard mothers voice it clearly. It is one of the most self-defeating and self-destructive traits known, where even threats of suicide are used to control and isolate the victim. There is plenty of evidence that such threats may also be real, because the pain of jealousy can generate suicidal thoughts, and suicide can on rare occasions be a futile act of jealous revenge. It is generally accompanied by all or nothing thinking. Jealousy at first excites the lover, who feels flattered at such intense attention. She thinks she is being adored rather than trapped, but that soon changes with the emotional strangulation. Yet despite the torture suffered by this asphyxiation, the sad fact is that faithfulness rather than betrayal is the norm in most relationships. I have seldom seen a case even in an abusive relationship, where the victim does not strive to save the relationship in the face of all odds. This is a sad and ironic reality.

Toxic Jealousy is complex and obsessional. Any obsession is consuming. When we are obsessed we cannot interact properly with others and we certainly cannot make any emotional connection with them. It stifles our creativity and our spirituality, kills our souls and fills us with paranoia and depressive thoughts. Obsessional thinking brings us into a world of negativity and distress. Morbid jealousy is a close relative of toxic jealousy and seems to be based upon other underlying pathological conditions such as paranoia or Emotionally Unstable Personality Disorder (Borderline Personality Disorder). Irrespective of how we label it, the destructive power toxic jealousy wields over an individual can be overwhelming.

Jack came to me some years ago distraught at the breakdown of his marriage. He had been with his wife, Lynn, for eight years and they had two children. Initially Jack had been an attentive and loving boyfriend, whom she regarded as a soulmate. But, within a month of getting married she noticed a change in him. He became more and more possessive. Initially, she had been flattered and misunderstood his possessiveness and jealousy for love. When they went out at the week-end he continuously watched her and noted if she seemed to be admiring other men. After some years, however, she felt smothered and became alarmed when Jack grew more threatening, as she tried to preserve her independence within the relationship. Lynn was a faithful and loyal wife, but his toxic jealousy accompanied by anger destroyed her happiness and left him bereft. I felt saddened by his haunted face as he began his story.

> My wife, Lynn, left me a month ago and on no account will come back to me. I manage to see my children every week end, but my heart is broken. I miss the three of them so much and I can't get a wink of sleep. I normally wake up at 3 or 4 o'clock and that's it. I lie awake for hours waiting for the clock to go off. What's killing me is that she begged me two years ago to go for counselling but I refused point blank. I know now that I did wrong but I could not bear the thought of her being with another man. Not indeed that I knew that she was seeing someone else. She told me I was being ridiculous. I could feel my anger rising when she came in from a night out and my imagination went into over-drive. The more I thought about it the more I fantasised about her being with another man and the madder I became, until one night I pushed her. I wanted to hit her hard, to hurt her, to make her feel my pain. Why should I suffer while she was gallivanting all over the country? I can even feel my anger coming on now when I think about it, even though I know she was

only out with her friends, except that I know there was one fella in the group who fancied her, because she is a beautiful woman. I used demand to see her text messages and made sure I checked her Facebook. When she closed me out of her Facebook I became paranoid. I just was not able to trust her. Whenever we were in the pub I watched her to see who she was looking at and could feel my stomach turn. I could feel myself turning sour and worked myself up so that we always fought, when we got home. Eventually we stopped going out together and she moved into another room. The next day I always said I was sorry, but in the end she got fed up of it and took the children and went home to her mother. She is now living in another house that she rents.

That is only a small part of Jack's story and although he worked hard his relationship never rekindled. You can probably see echoes of Nancy's story, told earlier. Toxic jealousy is the angry cutting edge of fear of abandonment. It is the essence of this fear. The relationship counsellor, Lynda Bevin, also concurs that fear of abandonment is a main source of jealousy. Altogether, she lists thirteen fears associated with it, such as fear of being betrayed, of losing face, of being criticised or rejected because of body image problems and feeling inadequate. Toxic jealousy is, therefore, complex and multifaceted. It is an irrational but profound feeling of anticipated loss that keeps the sufferer on a treadmill of hyper vigilance. Mired in suspicion, he is driven to endless questioning of his partner, checking her phone, phone bills, text messages, Facebook activity, bank statements, and speedometer, to name but a few. It is intrusive in every sense and torments both partners. Jealousy powered by the need to control extends into almost every aspect of a relationship, sometimes, as with Jack and Lynn, inflicting fatal damage to it.

There is some disagreement among researchers about the triggers that spark jealousy from a gender perspective. Some sociobiologists, such as David Buss, theorise that jealousy is about male anger at the likelihood of losing the prospect to procreate if a female partner threatens to leave, and in his opinion it is an evolutionary reaction. Men also face uncertainty in terms of parenthood in the face of a real threat (unlike toxic jealousy where the threat is usually delusional). The woman knows she is the mother of the child, but the father cannot be certain, particularly if there is infidelity on the woman's part. Buss calls it paternity uncertainty and Nancy Friday opines that a jealous man is protecting his self-esteem. These feelings and thoughts are magnified a thousand fold by toxic jealousy. Her work, *Jealousy*, is one of the most interesting books you can find, where she chronicles the constant struggle with the intensity of her feelings. She is, however, able to stand back and view her jealousy with some humour and irony.

The evolutionary exponents agree that men of all cultures are more likely to react jealously to sexual infidelity, while women are more affected by emotional infidelity because their investment in the relationship is more emotional. Others feel that female jealousy is inspired by feared loss of economic and other resources such as time, energy, wealth, emotional investment in children, responsibility, and loyalty provided by the male partner. The switching of emotional commitment to another male may be an indicator of this. Rebecca Allen, in a limited study, argues that while women are significantly more affected by emotional infidelity, they are also affected by sexual infidelity. She shows that culture has some impact on research outcome as well. This sounds more realistic, because some of the confusion arises from a failure by researchers to distinguish between healthy and toxic jealousy. If we accept that toxic jealousy is the progeny of fear of abandonment and therefore of neural origin, we have to accept that women are as jealous as men. In other words, females are just as likely as men to suffer fear of abandonment because of insecure attachment issues. There is now some attention being paid to jealousy in the context of attachment, and it is recognised that an insecure attachment sharpens the tooth of jealousy. I believe that it is at the core of jealousy.

Irrespective of gender, there is a whole amalgam of other feelings and sensations that accompany toxic jealousy. These include fear, loneliness, bitterness, anger, terror, feeling lost, stomach churning and despair.

Many of the symptoms surrounding jealousy are similar to post-traumatic stress – sleeplessness, hypervigilance, irritability and suicidal thinking. It is so irrational and the loneliness so core, that people with core jealousy will remain with their partners, even if they do not love them; anything but seeing them in the arms of another! I remember as a teenager being in love with a beautiful girl. At that time I had decided that I would enter the priesthood, but my fear of abandonment and my jealousy were so great that I clung to her until the last moment, when she broke off our relationship. Seeing this young girl in the arms of another teenager was heart-breaking at the time. I still remember the awful turning in my stomach when I first saw them together. That was over fifty years ago and in subsequent years I discovered how difficult it is to break the stranglehold of jealousy, one of the most painful offspring of an insecure attachment.

From Friday's book you can see that jealousy is part of control. Normal jealousy makes for vigilance from the evolutionary point of view, but toxic jealousy sets up a system of surveillance to keep constant watch on a partner. In that sense it is a specific and powerful control mechanism and possibly the primary control mechanism in a relationship. It stems from a feeling of inferiority and still-born self-esteem, which Dr Paul Hauck call 'an inferiority complex of mammoth pro-portions.' When both partners suffer from jealousy they use their knowledge as a way of mutual control and they live in a co-dependent state, feeding off each other's jealousy. Ironically, while jealous people put on a show of strength as part of their invented self, it is easy to control them because of their internal distress.

As with fear of abandonment the cancer of toxic jealousy remains for an entire lifetime, because unlike healthy jealousy it is not just influenced by sex, but by control. If sex was the main cause of the jealousy it might ease with age, but toxic jealousy is equally intense as a control mechanism irrespective of age. I have known older people cursed with the impulse to control, harbouring intense jealousy. Indeed, the controlling impulse can often increase with age.

Donald Dutton refers to toxic jealousy in an intimate relationship as conjugal paranoia, as the would-be perpetrator boils with anger and fear and incessantly ruminates about the partner, entering a negative fear-filled world that sometimes culminates in violence and perhaps suicide. The thought of losing the partner becomes unbearable and the ability to control the impulse to kill is sometimes lost. It is estimated that at least a quarter of all murders involve a jealous partner. Dutton makes the point that such jealous perpetrators are split between the violent and the remorseful parts of themselves. Two very different selves, two opposite selves joined by the glue of the hidden fear of being abandoned. The angry self is terrorised at the thought of losing the partner, and the repentant self pleads to prevent the separation.

When there is fear of abandonment, there is no ease, but always an elaborately constructed, negative and torturous imaginary world containing imaginary rivals. Unless you have experienced it, it is difficult to understand the terror that arises in the fear-filled person at the thought of these imaginary rivals. Suspicion corrodes the soul and the very sense of self is threatened by the threat of abandonment.

It is appalling to think that the jealous person is not capable of properly loving another, but more of attaching to them. This always shocks those who hear it, partly because they are unaware of the internal conflicts of the jealous person. Love is difficult to define, but it certainly involves allowing the other space to develop and socially relate. Love frees us, and takes joy in the freedom of the other. It is about fulfilment by having our intimacy and emotional needs met. Jealous people, with the controlling impulse, operate in the very opposite way, stifling and restricting victims. They only love themselves and expect partners and children to meet their needs, as they view the world from their narcissistic thrones.

In striving to control his partner, the jealous person keeps her in a prison of possessiveness. There is a distinction between jealousy and possessiveness, although Dr Helen Ford, a holistic practitioner working in Stourbridge, puts it well when she writes about possessive jealousy and destructive jealousy. I suppose toxic jealousy is the parent of possessiveness, but for convenience and because they are so intertwined, I will occasionally use them interchangeably here. In my experience, the possessive person is also a jealous person. If jealousy is a destructive feeling, possessiveness is a destructive behaviour driven by it.

Possessiveness is an obsessional behaviour, and is about isolation and keeping a partner solely for yourself from as many people as possible. The victim is always deliberately isolated whether through violence or through other controlling means, and frequently submits for the sake of safety or a quiet life. Initially the presence of possessiveness seems to indicate love. 'He loves me so much that he keeps me for himself', might be how the partner thinks. But, possessiveness is obviously the very opposite of love. It is an emotional prison that sucks the life out of you and leaves you feeling empty and confused. The controlling person is more often than not a charmer and the victim is smitten, misinterpreting the possessiveness and delighting in the fact that he or she has found a soulmate.

Yet, without the imprisoned partner the jealous person's definition of himself falls apart, because he defines himself as a worthwhile person only if he feels he is loved. It is a strange kind of 'love' when you find yourself being confined in almost every part of your life– how you dress, where you go, what you do, being held suffocatingly close, being detached from your friends, hearing your family being criticised or even being isolated from them. Jealousy is always behind these behaviours. Unhappily, possessiveness can extend to the victim even when the relationship has ended, and can cause endless torment. I have seen cases where separated fathers were prevented from seeing their children, or where grandparents were prevented from seeing their grandchildren, because of the jealousy of some mothers. This is not to say that mothers are more jealous than fathers, but in most cases the mother is given custody of the children and she has to power to exclude the father, if she so wishes. The psychological concept of the abusive and jealous personality is not normally considered by the court, unless there are obvious and proven cases of physical abuse.

Jealousy can also be a symptom of Adult Separation Anxiety Disorder (ASAD). Research shows that about one third of children who suffer from separation anxiety as a disorder go on to be afflicted by it in adulthood. This means that in two thirds of cases it is developed in adulthood. Furthermore, a higher percentage of adults than children suffer from it, although this is not surprising considering the extent of attachment issues among people. Research done by Katherine Shear, Professor of Psychiatry in Columbia University, shows that it is early onset, usually beginning in the late teens, and it afflicts more women than men. It can also develop in tandem with complicated or long drawn out grief. Those who have it are also likely to have social fear, suffer from panic attacks or agoraphobia and are vulnerable to drug addictions. This means that those who suffer from ASAD are more likely to be treated for the comorbid complaint and their separation anxiety is left untouched.

Yet, while jealousy is frequently a symptom of ASAD, I frequently meet people who have significant separation anxiety, but do not suffer from jealousy. Despite their painful anxiety they choose not to restrict their partners' freedom in an angry or jealous fashion, but cause them constant stress by pestering them with incessant text messages or phone calls about where they are, who they are with, what they are doing and when will they be home. One client, Richard, told me that his wife bombarded him with texts when he was at work, until he eventually turned off his phone during the day, thus ironically increasing her anxiety. It is a vicious circle, but clearly it is very difficult to live with someone suffering from ASAD, because of their unrelenting and intrusive demands. People, whose partners are anxious in this way, always refer to them as needy, a label that points to a childhood where their dependency needs were not met.

As you can now see, jealousy like any feeling is complex. You can experience different types and levels of it, and it is one of the most difficult burdens to shed. Extreme toxic jealousy is almost unbearable. It is a feeling you do not want. You hate having it and it seems to take on a life of its own, effectively ruining your peace of mind. It is frustrating that despite all your efforts it refuses to go away. No one technique will ease the trauma of jealousy, but the final chapter of this book will provide many techniques to help you deal with the issues arising from an insecure attachment, including jealousy. There are also techniques that directly target jealousy outlined in the remainder of this chapter.

What do you do if you want to rid yourself of Toxic Jealousy?

UNDERSTANDING FEAR OF ABANDONMENT AND ATTACH-MENT issues is *fundamental* to dealing with jealousy. You need to know the roots of this painful condition, why you feel inferior and why you see others as superior to you. You need to realise that it comes from an early feeling of not experiencing love and a failure by a parent of making an emotional bond through meeting your dependency needs. Any individual who feels bonded to a parent will never experience toxic jealousy in adulthood. It is not possible. Further this tormenting body sensation that is jealousy can manifest itself as a host of other negative feelings such as anger, fear, anxiety, sadness, rage, and shame.

Since jealousy is a major controlling mechanism it is not possible to understand it, unless you understand the concept of control and the controlling personality. You must lay bare that personality by understanding its traits and realise that the narcissistic creation is just a show, and behind all the bluster is a vulnerable child struggling in adult shoes. That is not an easy thing to do, because narcissism is a failure to recognise your personal deficiencies and a tendency to blame your partner. Failure to do so, however, may allow a period of control, but ultimately will destroy your relationship and leave you struggling with chronic loneliness.

When you understand the controlling personality, looking at the different theories of jealousy will bring you further along the road to healing it, but it is very difficult, if not impossible, to heal it on your own. It is likely you will need a therapist to help you to make sense of your childhood and find the roots of toxic jealousy.

Communication is the key to a good relationship and couple counselling can help to resolve that issue, although, unfortunately, it will not work if one of the partners is controlling. That is my experience, and I have never seen an exception to it. Individual counselling is essential to ensure that the jealousy is permanently eradicated. As I have mentioned this is a very difficult task, and Nancy Friday shows her many failures to find healing, even with effective therapists. I have a feeling that EMDR therapy may be the best way to heal. Therapy should be supplemented by finding the humility to turn to your partner. I have seen people tormented by core jealousy relieve their torment and jealous impulse, when they begin to talk to their partners about their fears. This is particularly effective if the partners are trustworthy and reliable, so it is important to be aware of potential support from them. There is no point in turning to an equally jealous partner, who will only exploit and control you further. If your partner is supportive you have to give them time to become accustomed to dealing with a 'new' you. Turning to a reliable partner will give you a sense of control, because toxic jealousy can make you feel out of control. What is the alternative but to continue to live a life of anger, misery and jealousy, putting the relationship under increasing strain?

As you strive to understand the roots of jealousy, and the importance of good communication with your partner it would be useful to realise that jealousy can be seen as a love addiction, which explains why it is so difficult to eradicate. But, as in any addiction, it is important to recognise and admit that you have a jealous personality, that it has nothing to do with your partner unless he also has toxic jealousy. This admission will be difficult for you because of the nature of jealousy as a control mechanism. Yet, it will also be a relief and the beginning of your rehabilitation, and will help you to take back some the power that the jealousy has taken from you.

Your black and white thinking and sense of entitlement are powerful obstacles to dealing with jealousy. It is important to put this black and white thinking under the microscope and see the fear of being hurt preventing you from reaching out for help. But, you are hurt from childhood, and appearing to be 'strong' will only bind you and imprison you. Remember that vulnerability is a decision, a choice, a behaviour, and you have control over it, just as you have control over jealous behaviour. Vulnerability is essential in the healing of toxic jealousy.

You may be unaware of your jealousy. It is well known that controlling people practise projection i.e. accuse their partners of being controlling. This is a blatant denial of their own condition and a projecting of their own undesirable traits onto their partners. It is a defence mechanism that psychologists sometimes cause externalisation, whereby you blame others for issues rather than admit ownership of them yourself. So become aware, and take this first step of looking in the mirror and taking responsibility for your behaviour rather than blaming your partner. Only you can decide how you will behave, and you can decide you will not behave in a jealous manner even if you feel the pain of jealousy. If you continue to act in a non-jealous manner eventually your brain will make a new program and it will become natural not to behave in this controlling way. This takes much time and work.

Sometimes, we can be carried along by a powerful, destructive emotion, so try and take some time out to think about it. Sit in a quiet place, and think long and seriously about your irrational jealousy, how it controls your happiness and your life, how it destroys your friendships and damages your relationship. Realise that jealousy is a major emotional problem controlling you, just as you try to control your partner. Ask yourself some hard questions. Do you want to spend the rest of your life having frequent sleepless nights, nurturing negative and irrational thoughts, living in a negative fantasy world, experiencing stomach churning sensations? Realise that pathological jealousy is a burden and it will remain with you all of your life, if you don't do something about it. Consider that your relationship may eventually break down and you will be left alone. Realise that your jealousy will rear its ugly head in almost every aspect of your intimate relationships and you will never be happy or make your partner happy. Look back at all the times that you have been eaten by jealousy. Where has it got you? What has it achieved, apart from misery? This awareness is the beginning of your journey for you to do something about this affliction. If you are a controlling person, patience is not one of your virtues, and endurance is difficult for you. But, if you wish to shed this burden you will have to be patient and to endure. Unfortunately, it may take the shock of your partner leaving you, to spur you to seek help. That is my experience as a counsellor.

Having thought long and seriously, begin a written jealousy history going back as far as you can and writing down as many details as possible. Then keep a jealousy diary which will give you some power over this distressing sensation. In the diary write down the behaviours involved in the jealous incidents, and in particular the thoughts which promoted these jealous behaviours and compare them to past jealous behaviours. Write about how your jealousy manifested itself. Was it through anger, rage, or anxiety? When you see something written down it can bring home the irrationality of your jealous thinking and behaviour, and the destruction they are causing. Looking at those other feelings can help you deal with them separately and reduce the bodily sensations brought on by jealousy. You could also look at the triggers that bring on the jealousy and this will help you prepare for them. These triggers might include your 'checking' behaviours; checking your partner's freedom in talking to the opposite sex, checking their Facebook account and checking their time spent shopping. You need to ask yourself what you are getting from such irrational behaviour. It is in your power to change your behaviour. You have a choice.

One of the most important steps you can take is to examine your core values and core beliefs, which are mentioned throughout this book. Remember that your core beliefs are built around your feeling of not being good enough, and ironically these can express themselves as a narcissistic outlook. You are convinced that your partner must meet your needs and you will try to cut out any obstacles to this. Isolation of your partner is your answer to meet this need. See if you have the strength to embrace humility and talk to your partner about your jealousy. *Remind yourself that if you fail your relationship will most likely founder.*

If you want to deal with core jealousy you must examine the false self. Put it under the spotlight. It is in that false self, which grew from an insecure attachment, that jealousy lurks. Jealousy is the core of that self, which was created from emotional neglect. This feeling of being deficient is a most depressing one, giving you a negative outlook on life as well as on yourself. Remember, however, that while you do not have a choice in how you feel, you have one in how you behave. So, if you are unfortunate enough to be afflicted by core jealousy that is not your fault, and you must accept that you are this way right now. Acceptance is an insight and is the key to healing. If, however, you choose to limit the freedom of another person, you must accept responsibility for such behaviour, and realise that this is inexcusable.

You do not have the right to limit the legitimate freedom of others, so it is vital to look at your behaviour. Are you frequently trying to make partners jealous by flirting or passing complimentary comments about others to generate jealousy? Are you playing games with them? Are you shackling them in a suffocating relationship? There is a practice called the **SOS** technique that is ideally suited to help you control your jealousy as well as make you aware of how you are killing your relationship. SOS is an acronym for **Stop, Observe** and **Shift**. It is immediate and powerful and is one of the best techniques to combat negative thinking, one of the drivers of toxic jealousy.

The SOS technique is very easy to use. When the irrational jealous thought arises, say the word **stop** (in your mind) as emphatically as possible. Then '**observe**' what is happening to you, how the jealous thoughts are unhinging you, making you unhappy, depriving you of sleep, and so on. Then **shift** to something positive. It does not really matter what that is, so long as it is positive. You could also change your thinking in a positive direction, for example, realising that your thoughts are irrational, that your partner is faithful and has always been faithful, that you have nothing to worry about, and that your past jealous outbursts have been unjustified. You may have to use this many times during the day.

Frequency is the key word to bring about brain change, so you may need to use the SOS technique first thing in the morning to set a positive tone for the day, not just regarding jealousy but in relation to fear and any negativity that you create through your irrational thinking. That shifting from the negative to the positive brings you an empowering gift that allows you to create the kind of day that nourishes you, rather than one that shrivels your spirit.

Looking at it another way, jealousy is being over-sensitised to your partner's relationships and behaviours with others. Desensitise yourself to this and your jealousy threshold will heighten. Desensitisation is part of exposure therapy, which will be looked at later when dealing with social fear. The more you allow yourself to be exposed to your partners absence or interaction with others the greater the chance you have of blunting your feelings of jealousy. You can control jealous behaviour, and one way to do this is to pretend that you are a non-jealous person and behave as such. Again, frequency is important in installing this behaviour in your brain. This behavioural technique can have the same result as exposure therapy and with practice you will come to see yourself as a non-jealous person. Remember that your partner chose to be with you. She could have chosen someone else, but she is sticking with you despite your painfully possessive behaviour. That shows how much she loves you. Keep reminding yourself that she does not share your opinion that you are not good enough.

We can tell a lot from symbols. There is a technique used by couple counsellors using three circles, which you could use to show the dynamic of your relationship from the jealousy perspective. It is very simple to do and contains clear messages. Draw one circle and fill it with your pastimes and activities, draw another for your partner, and in the third circle put in your mutual activities. If you examine these and find that you generally do a lot together, that your circle is full and your partner's is sparse then you are most likely jealous and controlling. You can use this technique to initiate a discussion that will ultimately ensure that all three spaces are functioning. Try to understand that unless all three spaces are functioning well, the relationship is unhealthy, and unhealthy relationships wither and eventually die.

Finally, you might be interested in some of the techniques suggested by Dr Helen Ford for dealing with toxic jealousy (which she sees as a consequence of frustrated love). Her technique is to write a list of the support, love, appreciation, encouragement, praise, affection, etc. which you see others getting and which you would like for yourself. You can add to these and write a short note on each so that you have a specific understanding of them as they would apply to you. Then spend a few minutes meditating on each of them and imagine having them. Look back through your life and see if you ever had any of them, and how that made you feel. If you have never experienced any of them, then begin the process of self-nurturing and self-empathy and open up to receiving nurturing from another person.

The processes explained above will help heal your toxic jealousy. They may seem easy, but because of the traits of the pathologically jealous person they are difficult. They demand a way of being that is alien to you and they demand a degree of tenacity, knowledge and insight that demands much effort. But, what is the alternative? As already stated, jealousy does not abate with age, but rather increases, and if you choose to suffocate and torment, your toxic jealousy is also a hell that you will have to endure for your entire life. Is that what you want?

What to do if you have an irrationally jealous partner, who refuses to do something about his or her jealousy?

IN THE CASE OF TOXIC JEALOUSY, this will involve a long, difficult and sometimes fruitless struggle that takes patience, knowledge and determination. If you are in a relationship with a jealous partner your life may be constricted depending on the level of jealousy as a control mechanism, and you will well understand the insightful quotation of the writer Gloria Steinem – 'a pedestal is as much a prison as any other small confined place.' You will initially have felt adored and special on that pedestal and then smothered and fearful as the noose of jealousy tightens. Unfortunately, for many the smothering gets worse as the years pass by and the prison door is rarely opened. But, you do not have to remain in that prison. You can free yourself emotionally and even physically if necessary. Your first task is to make sense of why this irrational jealousy exists. To do this you have to educate yourself on the traits of the controlling or abusive personality outlined in the chapter on anger. While this personality is created in childhood and causes many burdens, perpetrators cannot make excuses for inexcusable behaviour caused by jealousy. Whatever their childhood, partners have no right to use it as an excuse for torturing others.

You may need professional help in making sense of abusiveness *per se* in the context of toxic jealousy, and then your next task in coping with a jealous partner is to understand the complexity of jealousy itself and its roots in an insecure attachment. Your bedrock and safeguard is your self-esteem. Good self-esteem is the basis of happiness and a sign of strength. If you have good self-esteem and you have a jealous partner, despite being oppressed you are the one with the power, because jealous people have no self-esteem. You have the inner calmness of feeling loved by parents long ago, and are not tormented by possessiveness. You do not fear abandonment. There is no contest here, although the jealous person may come across as the powerful one as they project an invented self to impress others. The invented self is no match for the true self. You must, however, be aware of this and constantly remind yourself of your inner strength. I have met people who were physically abused by jealous partners, but were aware of their own goodness and strength, and despite feeling fearful of the violence felt an accompanying calm that enabled them to leave the relationship. It was a strange mixture, but understandable, and they needed therapy to deal with the impact of the abuse. I have seen others in a jealous non-violent relationship who were aware that there must be equality in any relationship and fought to establish it in their struggle with the jealous person. Their assertiveness sometimes paid off, but it is not wise to be assertive with a violent jealous partner. Unfortunately, leaving the relationship is the only answer.

It is also helpful to consider the irrational train of thought of your jealous partner and the behaviour that follows from this. You will, for example, notice the irony of how he tries to make you jealous. This comes from his fear of abandonment and this behaviour is one of the key elements of toxic jealousy. Its main purpose is to make him feel better and is rather like how such people dispense shame and spew it onto others. It is an infallible sign of his low self-esteem. For a moment this makes jealous people feel good, they feel that they are loved and good enough. This feeling does not last for long and the provocation continues. It is a continuous probing to test the other, and fits with the tendency of jealous people to ask on a regular basis if their partners love them. Realise, too, that infidelity is often part of the jealous person's arsenal, and unlike others they feel no remorse for it. Many, but not all, are unscrupulous in inflicting hurt. Those who do not inflict hurt are carrying adult separation anxiety, discussed earlier. If your partner is unfaithful you will be angry and jealous. This jealousy is reactive and normal. As you consider the infidelity it is important to erect appropriate boundaries. These boundaries may stretch to leaving the relationship. You may find that mistrust has been created by the infidelity, and if you decide to leave it is important not to bring that to other relationships. While your mistrust is justified and understandable in relation to the ex-partner it can be damaging to new relationships.

When you understand the controlling personality, the complexity of jealousy and the irrationality of your partner trying to make you jealous, you can then consider your options. You have choices. You can remain and be subject to jealous outbursts where your freedom is curtailed and you are walking on eggshells, or you can face your tormentor with assertiveness and try to get some degree of freedom. You can only get freedom if you realise that you cannot placate the jealous person. Do not, for example, allow him to make you wear drab clothes as a way of placating him. He will never be satisfied no matter what you do to please him. Placating will only make matters worse.

Assertiveness is the best way to deal with a non-violent bully, but it is essential to confront the jealous person in a calm way, putting aside any anger you may feel and making it clear that there will be consequences if such conduct continues. This can create a crisis, and sometimes a crisis is the only way to resolve this painful situation. What I have noticed is that most people with a jealous partner are unable to take such a vital step, because they have been so devastated by jealous behaviour and hurtful words. They have lost their self-confidence, their belief in their own worth, and they fear the consequences of creating a crisis. Sometimes the help of a close friend or a professional can help them take the necessary steps.

Assertiveness can also be shown in a practical way. Your controlling partner will be very interested in your social network sites such as Facebook, and his jealousy will prompt him to frequently check your conversations and contacts. You can prevent this by concealing your passwords. This will enflame his suspicions and increase his jealousy, but it will show your strength and independence. Revealing these passwords will not curtail his jealous feelings and the harassment will not abate. You have a right to be private and your behaviour in concealing the passwords is a sign of good boundaries.

While it is not easy for the tormented to confront, it is equally hard for the tormentor to listen. I came across a piece in the newspaper *Alive* in March 2007 entitled *How to Fight a Fair Fight*, which I have adapted as a way of dealing with jealousy. It might even form a contract between you and your jealous partner to ensure some degree of harmony and respect and to highlight the reality of jealousy in your relationship. It is, however, a contract that your partner will find difficult, but admitting to being jealous is essential for healing it. I have adapted it as a way to be assertive and to reject jealousy while offering respect to your partner, but not to his or her behaviour.

We are on the same side. The goal is not for me or you to win, but to solve the scourge of jealousy and to love each other better.

Your feelings matter to me even if they are different from mine. I will try to understand them and your jealousy and I will try to help you to understand mine and the pain your jealousy inflicts on me.

I will not shout, throw or slam anything, but I will oppose jealous control.

If I need space to think or cool off, I will go to another room and find a reasonable response to your jealousy.

I will not ascribe motives to your actions. I cannot read your mind and won't try, but I will let you know that while I understand the roots of jealousy, I will not accept any excuse for jealous behaviour.

I will keep quiet when you talk, and try to understand everything you say, but I will challenge your jealous conduct.

I will allow as much space as is necessary for the discussion and I will help you to make sense of your jealousy in a non-threatening way.

I will not give you the silent treatment. I will do my best to express my thoughts and feelings so that you can understand how

> jealousy affects me. I will not clam up, sulk
> or manipulate because that is the behaviour
> of a jealous person.
>   I will not throw old grudges in your face
> even if they were the result of jealous behaviour.
>   I will apologise quickly if I break any of
> the above rules, and I will try to do better as
> we go along.
>   I will admit when I'm wrong. I will ask for
> your forgiveness.
>   If we can't solve a problem on our own in
> a reasonable amount of time, we will agree to
> outside help to restore our relationship.

There is a technique in couples counselling called the five love languages, which should be useful in helping to heal jealousy, but would not work with violent jealousy. The use of the love languages might slowly diminish and help to heal non-violent toxic jealousy, especially of those suffering from adult separation anxiety. If you wish to learn more about the love languages you might like to consult Gary Chapman's book, *The 5 Love languages*. You can also discover your primary love language by doing the quiz on **www.5lovelanguages.com**. This would help to ease your pain and increase the intimacy that is destroyed by jealousy. Essentially the love languages are a challenge to your jealous partner to meet your needs. People with toxic jealousy are only concerned with their own needs and meeting the needs of their partners would not come easy to them.

The love languages are words of affirmation, acts of service, receiving gifts, quality time and physical touch. Chapman's theory is that all of us have a primary love language, which, if enacted, can enrich a relationship and bring harmony. So, if your partner's primary love language is words of affirmation they will feel loved by your praise and appreciation. If they thrive on acts of service their motto is 'actions speak louder than words' and when you do something for them their emotional response is aroused. Most of us give gifts at particular times of the year such as anniversaries, birthdays and Christmas. Gifts are seen as an expression of love, although not everybody places the same emphasis on them as expressions of love. But, for some it makes them feel loved at a deep level, even if the gift is not expensive. Gifts are seen as a symbol of love to them and draws them closer to their partner. Their motto is 'it's the thought that counts'. Quality time is a love language desired by many in a world that has become increasingly busier and more demanding. It means giving your partner undivided attention, listening, engaging and communicating in an empathic and understanding way. Your jealous partner will find it hard to put down the paper or turn off the television, but doing so will help him mitigate the jealousy that grips him. The importance of touch has already been reflected on earlier as one of the most essential life giving requirements of the young child. When we lovingly touch the skin of the baby he feels loved and secure. Our skin is immensely sensitive to touch. Touch is equally important in adulthood and is the primary love language of many people. If your partner has not experienced affection in childhood he will find it difficult to meet this need, if that is your primary love language. Again, it will be a learning process for him as you challenge his jealousy. In practice it may range from a casual touch of affection to kissing and making love.

The 'Dutch Cow' technique advocated by the psychologist Dr Ayala Pines is an unusual but effective way to challenge a jealous partner, who may be pestering you with texts. It would be especially effective if your partner has Adult Separation Anxiety. Using this technique, you call your partner very frequently and she must tell you where she is, who she is with, what she is doing. Every hour ask her all the questions she pesters you with. Eventually, and hopefully, she will experience the same sort of annoyance that you feel from being hounded, and come to some understanding of her irrationally jealous behaviour.

Similar to the idea of the Dutch Cow technique is that of role change. You take the role of the jealous partner and your partner that of the non-jealous partner. It is an interesting way of exploring jealousy, but can only take place if the jealous partner admits to jealousy and agrees to take part in the experiment. That is not likely with someone suffering from toxic jealousy, but possible with a person carrying adult separation anxiety.

As you can see, dealing with a partner carrying toxic jealousy is difficult and if, despite your best efforts, your partner ignores and continues to torment and distress you, you may as a last resort decide to leave him or her. It is a last resort, because no one wants to see a marriage or a relationship destroyed. But was there ever a real relationship? Were you really loved? Generally people who are toxically jealous are unable to love, but rather attach. This is clearer in the context of fear of abandonment. Leaving, or the threat to leave, will create a crisis and may prompt your jealous partner to seek professional help. This is very common and sometimes, but, not always, the jealous person heals and changes. Leaving a relationship where jealousy breeds violence is essential.

I have met many people in a jealous relationship who seemed determined to leave, but it never happened. It takes considerable courage to leave as you consider the occasional happiness you may experience with the jealous person. By leaving you face grieving the loss of a 'companion', a relationship, a marriage and so on. It also brings fear of the unknown. It is my experience that this fear is magnified, if you, too, have an element of fear of abandonment. Grieving can be severe despite the psychological battering that has been inflicted on you by your jealous partner. You will grieve the charming partner you first met and when that is done you will then see his darker side that kept you enslaved and experience relief and freedom. You have the courage to leave, because you already have shown courage in remaining in a jealous relationship for so long.

Chapter 4

Fear of Failure

FEAR OF FAILURE IS ONE OF the most debilitating types of fear coming from an insecure attachment. Petrúska Clarkson in her book, *The Achilles Syndrome. Overcoming the Secret Fear of Failure*, rightly calls it a secret fear. It is closely related to social fear, although you may notice when a person has social fear, but fear of failure can be hidden behind a confident front. The invented self can conceal it well. It is insidious, because you may not even be aware that you have it, since you are so busy making excuses and dodging good opportunities that you fail to notice your invisible but powerful shackles. Apart from avoidance, this fear operates almost in a subconscious way, although it manifests itself as an irritating reluctance to grasp opportunities, or in everyday life to get things done. Such procrastination is an infallible guide to fear of failure. The procrastinator will put off important tasks and busy himself with other less important things. When I set time for writing I will first tidy my desk, hoover the office, cruise the internet, make a cup of coffee and then reluctantly begin writing. My fear of failure is mild, but it was severe long ago and my procrastination is residual from that time. One of the best ways to deal with procrastination is to make a list of tasks that need to be done. There is always a list on my kitchen table. I might spend a week ignoring it, but eventually it provokes me to act. Crossing off one item gives an impetus to tackle the next job. It is best to make this a priority list. The list is never completed because new tasks continually arise, so the list is a life line for the procrastinator.

Failure in the context of fear is not what it seems to those who are fortunate to have had a secure attachment to parents and, therefore, are blessed with high self-esteem. They see it as no more than negative circumstances from which they learn and move on. It is a well-worn cliché, but nevertheless true, that we learn by mistakes. But in the context of fear, making mistakes or so-called failing creates a secret world of negativity, self-hatred and shame, to a greater or lesser degree. Fear of failure is a chronic core condition that permeates many aspects of your life and sometimes it feels as if the self is a failure. It weakens your resolve to develop yourself and improve your life. It brings on worry about how you interact with others personally and professionally, how you parent, how you learn and how you live. Your fear ceaselessly shadows you and you become very conscious that if you fail, others will think less of you, be disappointed and lose interest. It has also been named as fear of ego-death, which is fear of humiliation and shame whereby your sense of self and identity is threatened, and the sense of self destroyed.

You can either learn this fear or it becomes engendered in you through neglectful parenting. I believe that fear of failure comes from a core feeling of not being good enough, which is turn stems from a child's feeling of being unloved, and perhaps being overtly or covertly criticised. When you are emotionally abandoned you automatically blame yourself. This blame is an instinct in small children, who have neither the experience nor the cognitive ability to understand that the blame does not lie with them. John Bradshaw puts it well when he writes that small children regard their parents as godlike and never wrong. From this idealisation the child's logic points to themselves as the guilty party. Ultimately they feel guilty and ashamed. This internal self-criticism can make your life miserable and cause you many stresses.

This is perfectly understandable to me because I can identify with some of it. Despite my successes and achievements, I can look back now and understand how shackled I was by fear of failure. I will give you two important examples, both in the 1980s, when fear of failure prevented me from moving on in my professional life. At the time I did not realise that I had this fear and I am amazed that it is only in writing this book thirty five years later that this has become clear to me. I have also learned that we must own the fear, but that is difficult when we do not know that we have it, so it is important to bring it to awareness.

Obviously we need someone to articulate it to us and then we can explore it.

I had graduated from University College Cork with a Ph. D in History in 1979 and shortly afterwards a position as a History lecturer in a teacher's training college became available. I knew from a particular source that I had a very good chance of getting the job. When I remember my letter of application I still feel embarrassed. I wish I had it now to publish and you would see how this invisible fear trapped me. In my letter I managed to convey to the College authorities my keen interest in the job as well as my reluctance to take it because I needed to get my Sixth Years through their Irish course that year! I feel sure that they were convinced that I was either a supremely arrogant or an extremely unintelligent person. Is it not interesting that an intelligent person full of fear can come across as arrogant, lacking good judgement and even stupid?

My second experience was shocking. I received a letter giving me the privilege of responding to a lecture (using the Irish language on Land League agitation) by an eminent professor at the Oireachtas of that year. I had published a book on the priests' involvement in politics, and in particular on the land league, so I was well qualified in Irish and was an ideal candidate for this honour that was offered to me. I replied refusing to do so and compounded my refusal by offering to deliver a lecture myself at some future date. On the surface, this was the height of arrogance, but in reality it was the reply from someone bound by fear. The Oireachtas committee must have been appalled at such arrogance, and the professor rightly felt insulted.

One of the links between both these incidents was novelty and unfamiliarity. They were both situations that I had never experienced before, and in that connection fear of failure can be linked to social fear and toxic shame. But, there are also other lessons that can be learned from these two examples, which show that the impact of fear of failure is not always clear cut. This is because it is many layered and can be very specific rather than general in its impact. I have been successful career wise and never lacked drive. I know many people bedevilled with this fear, who are highly motivated and ambitious. Driven by fear they seek power as a mistaken way to get self-esteem and many famous and wealthy people harbour fear of failure behind successful careers. So, research showing that people with fear of failure always expect to fail is not necessarily valid and you should not allow yourself to be labelled as a failure, even if you have this fear.

The reality is that those with fear of failure can be quite driven in some areas, and shackled in others. That contradiction can be partly explained by some peculiar and irrational beliefs that go with this fear. The main one is disbelief at your success. If you are beset by such fear, you will question all your successes. When I got my Ph.D. I felt that the markers were lenient, that I did not deserve such a success. I never gave myself credit for five long years of research and grind. In the early years, whenever I wrote a book I would wonder at how I could have done it. It was surely a fluke! I always made some excuse because I never felt good enough and I was keenly aware of criticism, which would only reinforce my poor opinion of myself. It took decades to work through this core fear and banish it from my life. It is not at all egotistic to give yourself approval and recognise your achievements, accepting and appreciating the praise of others. In truth, fear of failure can be defined by the large difference in other people's appreciation of your talents and your own poor opinion of them, hidden behind the invented self.

If we examine the fear of failure that Jason harboured, you will see that his was paralysing. Unlike my fear, it was evident and palpable and clearly in his awareness as he prepared for two interviews in preparation for his professional training. He found a tutor who helped bolster his confidence and helped lower his fear of failure somewhat. This is how he described his psychological struggle, his negative thinking, his unhealthy, undermining behaviour and the positive impact of exposure, in dealing with fear.

> I was extremely nervous going down to the first interview. It was a complete disaster. Anxiety consumed me and I didn't understand many of the questions. Coming out of the interview I was drenched in sweat, bright red in the face and a feeling of sickness in the pit of my stomach. My heart was still racing as I drove home. The

second interview went better. I felt the experience of the first one had helped and I wasn't as nervous. I was quietly satisfied coming out of that interview. The results came a few weeks later, but doubt and fear came rushing back. Negative thoughts consumed me. I wasn't good enough to get into the college, I was miles off the standard and I hadn't a hope qualifying. I started comparing myself to others negatively. I was now back in work feeling very sorry for myself. I decided that I would do my usual thing and give up. I didn't bother with the Irish study for a few weeks. As it was Christmas I consoled myself by going out with friends and consuming large amounts of alcohol. I fell back into a rut and was considering giving up the idea of becoming a professional. . After a few weeks, something clicked with me. I suppose through the encouragement from my family, in particular my mother, and from my Irish tutor, I came back around again. I decided that I would study hard for the next six weeks and see where that took me. I started to think more positively. By the time the interview came around I was more confident. My level of Irish had improved greatly and the experience of the 2 previous interviews had helped to ease my worry. The English part of the interview went extremely well. The Irish went ok and no more. I conversed well but didn't understand one question he had asked. When I came out of the interview, I was drained. Again I concentrated on the negatives. Even though most of the interview had been a success, the Irish question I missed was all I could think of. I told my family that I didn't think I would get in. A few weeks later, I got the news that I had been accepted. This was great but I wasn't overjoyed. I took the view that they must have been finding the places hard to fill. Again I was running myself down. Even in a great moment for myself I found the negative.

The course started and, unfortunately, old habits started to rear their head again when preparatory course assignments started. I started to skip some of the work that we were to do, and contributed nothing. I was lucky that the workload was small for the first few months otherwise the course could have gotten away from me very quickly. All the work thus far in the course had been done online so I didn't have to meet any of my classmates. The induction day was on a Wednesday and I was terrified thinking about it. I could hardly sleep for a week before it. I was so worried about going back into a lecture hall full of people and not knowing anyone. I was very close to not going, but the fear of messing up this college course won out. When I was half way to the college, I considered turning around. Again I pushed through. I got to the college and

I had a pain in my stomach from anxiety. My luck seemed to be in, however. While looking for the hall, I met another student who was lost. We hit it off straight away. We had lots in common and I had someone to pal around with for the day. Unfortunately, he wasn't going to be in my group that day. I decided that I would join his group anyway. The day went well and I had made a friend. I still left early though. I just couldn't wait to get home and back to where I felt safe. I definitely didn't feel safe among hundreds of students. I never dawned on me that they might be nervous too on the first day. I just berated myself for being such a wreck on day one. Our next day was going to be in our groups and not the whole year together. This would be how our course worked. We would be in a class of 30 people for all our subjects and my deficiencies would be shown up.

These are a few examples to show how fear of failure operates. To help you in further understanding this more fully, let us go back to the dependency needs and recall how the inner child can contaminate the views and beliefs of the adult. The scripts you learned as a child map your adult life, and if they are negative your adulthood is like a house built on sand. If you look at the experiences that Jason and I had, the relevant question is what had we to fear? He had a degree and some experience in the commercial world. I was highly educated and I was well qualified to be a good lecturer in History or to deliver a response to the professor's lecture at the Oireachtas. The adults may have been well qualified, but the poor inner children were fearful, because their dependency needs were not properly met at the appropriate time. Counsellors rightly tend to emphasise the importance of the first three needs (love, affection and attention), but the fourth one, direction, is the most relevant in the case of fear of failure.

If you are not shown how to do things you may feel defective and a fraud, even if your achievements are noteworthy. The uninformed inner child binds you and you become afraid of change, avoiding new opportunities to enrich and give more meaning to your life. Petrúska Clarkson, who writes about what she calls pseudocompetency, was amazed when some of the very intelligent and highly achieving clients she treated felt flawed in terms of competency and felt as if they were imposters. She uses the term Achilles Syndrome to describe people who look like winners but feel like losers. When writing about her highly achieving clients, she noted that 'there was always a worm in the apple of their success.'

Robert Kelsey, an eminently successful businessman, describes himself as 'technically inept' in his work as a banker, and admits to having an early negative childhood and leaving school early. His invented self was of a confident negotiator and his false self a fearful, shamed inner child. In his case leaving school early, and no doubt having a serious attention deficit because of his childhood, would have created a feeling of incompetency. That feeling is secret, core and ever present. In my own life I discovered that feeling incompetent was not always about the failure of parents to give direction, but can also be caused by a rushed education. I skipped at least four years of primary and secondary school, and the inner child in me sabotaged any feeling of well-being and confidence that I should have felt from successful third level achievements. I was puzzled by the contradiction between my educational achievements and my feelings of failure. All the outward circumstances would point to success. It was only when I read about incompetency that I finally made sense of this aspect of my personality. I found that understanding this was of immense help in banishing the feeling of failure that I had carried for decades. Knowledge can sometimes heal.

Since parents are responsible for their children's formation, including educational development, there is a lesson to be learned from this to ensure that the direction need is met. Most children must develop slowly in terms of learning, otherwise there is always a sense of unfinished business and not being good enough. The child loves learning and proper learning teaches competency. You can see the satisfaction in children's faces as they become more competent and master increasingly difficult tasks as they get older. Education is like an edifice, where you need a good foundation and every storey must be carefully constructed. There is also a message here for teachers, who have the responsibility of delivering their subject areas as thoroughly as possible. Every effort should be made to ensure that all students understand the topics under discussion and that no student is left behind. This is no easy task considering the dynamics of the classroom today in terms of absenteeism, the pressure of examinations, teacher competence and enthusiasm, and the concentration level of students. You have already seen that lack of concentration comes from a parent's failure to meet the child's dependency needs. If a child daydreams constantly, he is in effect absent, and how can you teach someone who is effectively absent? The teacher cannot force a student to concentrate because it runs contrary to his neural wiring.

If you suffer from a fear of failure, an exploration of your childhood role in the family might point to another root. Sometimes there is a natural order in these roles. Generally speaking, every member of a family has particular roles. The eldest child is normally the star or the hero, the one who always wants to do the right thing, the good child. The second cannot be the star and becomes the opposite, not exactly the villain but the rebel, very often drawing the fire of parents and testing their patience. Frequently the third child is the quiet one, and the youngest is the comedian or entertainer. Within large families there are groups who associate with each other and form small 'families' within the larger one. I examined my own family of five children and the role theory fitted exactly, but it is not always true of every family. The child adopts a role to have a voice perhaps, or even to survive. That is all very well, but when a role is imposed on a child, the whole parenting dynamic of the family changes and the developmental process of that child is interrupted. Sometimes, circumstances dictate that giving a child an adult role may be necessary. I have met adults whose mothers died, or were ill or depressed, and as children they took on the role of parent. From my experience the psychological damage suffered varies, but in cases where a child is forced by dysfunctional parents to be their caretaker, the consequences can result in chronic distress later in life for that child. A child given an adult role is bound to fail. There is every chance that such a child will reach adulthood with a core feeling of failure and incompetency. I have seen such victims in a very conflicted state, feeling proud, angry, anxious, confused and fearful.

Worst of all, it has been shown that feeling incompetent is one of the drivers for power and control, the basis for bullying. As the carrier of shame and a feeling of defectiveness, it drives the human to present a capable front as a means of avoiding criticism and gaining praise. Whatever its roots, becoming aware of your incompetency and understanding it are the initial steps in healing its impact and lessening your fear of failure. There is little enough written on it, but your understanding will be increased by reading the books of Clarkson and Kelsey. Your awareness and knowledge will allow you to admit that you are incompetent in some areas and proficient in others. This admission will come as a relief to you because you will be able to make sense of yourself and change. Trying to hide incompetency only increases the shame and the fear of being found out. Admitting that you cannot do something takes courage, but it means you are being real and it opens the door to learning and the more you learn and understand the more you grow and develop as a human being, and the less likely you will succumb to fear of failure. You will step out of the child's shoes and see failure as a valuable lesson or a learning experience.

There is an ironic component of incompetency that you also need to be aware of, which has been well addressed in the literature. Since this secret world harbours a deep sense of shame, it also brings the curse of pathological perfectionism. Research shows that a high level of perfectionism is strongly linked with fear of failure. Pathological perfectionism is not about doing your best or striving for excellence, but about making unrealistic goals; of setting the bar so high that you will never clear it and then feeling ashamed for failing. Perfectionism is a way of thinking and of being, which includes constant negative comparison with others that relentlessly drive it.

If you practise perfectionism you hope to get approval, one of the dependency needs absent from your childhood. If you 'fail' and sense disapproval, avoidance will become your normal behaviour. It is a murderous never-ending treadmill where you keep trying and failing. Any treadmill that you cannot get off is like an addiction. You agonise about making a mistake, or saying or doing the wrong thing. Pathological perfectionism is just as much a prison as fear of failure is. It feeds into it and is probably more shackling because it is how you define yourself – 'I am only ok if I never make a mistake'. It provokes self-criticism and more than likely a low level of chronic depression. Adults who bring perfectionism from childhood suffer intensely as they try to nurture an invented self that can never be nurtured. They may suffer not only fear, but anxiety, worry, depression, anger, fatigue and health problems. They never feel good enough.

This subconscious desire to be good enough is a parallel, but connected, treadmill to perfectionism promoting fear of failure. It has many roots, and the behaviour is a never ending drive to please others. The greater your fear of failure the more approval you seek. The need for approval is one of the greatest forces driving the perfectionist. You will never say no because your boundaries are flawed and apart from fearing that you might hurt others by a refusal, you crave to be liked. You will always be obliging to others to help you feel better. You might say that it is a good thing to be nice, to be helpful. It is important that you define yourself by your kindness, but, that is different from defining yourself as being nice to get approval. That definition of the self is fatal. What happens if for some reason, for example, illness, you do not get the opportunity to be nice to others? You will feel empty. You will feel the nothingness of fear. Being kind is an intrinsic trait not a behaviour. If you define yourself by this intrinsic trait you will never feel empty because no matter what happens it will be there in your core.

I was driven by the need for approval. As a Principal, I needed approval from the students, the staff, the parents, the Board of Management, the Department of Education, the townspeople and the trustees! And my perfectionism was murderous. I took responsibility for every brick in the building, every mark on the walls. I constantly felt under scrutiny. It is no wonder that I retired at fifty-eight and for three months lay on a couch exhausted, until I found the motivation to complete the final part of my counselling course. This was the result of spending years on that treadmill, being hard on myself, driving myself, worrying, lacking self-empathy and fearing failure. The upshot of all of this striving was that I was rightly regarded as a good Principal. It was, however, to the detriment of my health. My perfectionistic thinking and my inability to properly delegate were my downfall. This type of thinking is well explored in the second edition of *When Perfect Isn't Good Enough* by Martin Antony and Richard Swinson. They identify perfectionistic thoughts and provide exercises to help change such thoughts. Some of the common characteristics of perfectionistic thinking is the intense focus it has on yourself and the possibility of intense anger and shame. I wanted everything to be perfect in my school – the quality of the teaching, the behaviour of the students, the quality of the school building. That is all very well, but the fact that I took personal responsibility for all of these pointed to perfectionistic thinking. If there is a mark on a wall, it is my fault. If a child misbehaves during lunch break, it is my fault. If a teacher is underperforming, it is my fault. Each one of these is a monkey, and as the monkeys accumulate on your shoulder exhaustion and stress will eventually come.

Antony and Swinson (2009) detail many strategies and exercises for dealing with pathological meticulousness. Their initial advice is to assess the seriousness of the perfectionism. You can do this by checking for the main areas where the problem arises. From preceding chapters you will have guessed that the most practical way to do this is to keep a diary, which you can label your perfectionist journal. You can then more easily assess these areas that provoke this behaviour and look at triggers such as situations, people, or activities. You will see how high you set the bar, how this interferes with your life, and especially how it interferes with your relationships.

According to Antony and Swinson (2009) the diary will help you set realistic goals. Being a perfectionist, you may be tempted to set the bar too high, so keep your goals simple and specific. In doing this choose a few specific areas where you wish to tackle perfectionism. This might refer to your work where you spend too much time over planning or over preparing and, therefore, fall behind in your work. It might be about preparing an assignment where you spend innumerable hours writing, changing and checking, bringing on anxiety, or it might concern how you tend to be critical of others. The diary will also help you to recognise thinking that promote perfectionism. You will find that there are irrational beliefs behind the perfectionistic thinking that inevitably provoke anxiety. If you suffer from Ellis's *'musturbation'* you are probably perfectionistic. One of my clients, whose basic belief was that he must always please his boss, suffering severe anxiety as a result. He was perfectionistic and weighed down with shame as he struggled under an unreasonable workload, which made it impossible to satisfy his perfectionistic tendencies. It was a matter of changing the irrational thought to 'I will try to please my boss if that is feasible'. It is essential and relatively easy for a perfectionist to make such a radical change. Look back at cognitive restructuring in the chapter on anger for further information on how to change your thoughts.

Obviously, since perfectionism is bred from an insecure attachment it will be accompanied by other issues outlined in Appendix 1. Some of the issues that can accompany perfectionism are depression, anxiety, anger and eating disorders including body image problems. There are others, but it is easy to see how perfectionism can lead to those listed; for example, the treadmill of continuous striving and failure can lead to a low mood and confirms your feeling of not being good enough. This in turn can stoke anger and resentment. The concretisation of not feeling good enough in body image problems leads to eating disorders in a futile striving to be physically perfect.

Another book you might like to read to help heal your perfectionistic tendencies is *The Green Platform.* This was written by Declan Coyle, who was fortunate enough to have the Holocaust survivor and internationally famous psychiatrist, Viktor Frankl, as his visiting professor during his post graduate studies in Ottawa. The green platform is a metaphor for positivity and one of the most positive outcomes is the demise of perfectionism, the acquisition of boundaries, the dissolution of negativity and a corresponding sense of being in control of your life. Being in control of your life is personal power and should not be confused with power and control over others. It is an internal state of calmness with a sense of direction and is a necessary ingredient for living. It is profoundly disrupted if your childhood has been negative. Even if you are outwardly successful, not being in control is like being chronically ungrounded and uncertain. In the nineteen fifties Julian B. Rotter, a prominent psychologist, explored the concept of control and came up with a theory, which he labelled locus (location) of control. He differentiated between an internal and an external locus of control. If you have an internal locus you believe that you are in control and in charge of your life. You are unfailingly positive. If, however, you have an external locus you believe that your life is controlled by external factors and you are by and large powerless to properly dictate the course of your life. In one you give yourself credit for success and in the other you complain about external obstacles, normally obstacles you feel you cannot overcome. These are the obstacles you often erect yourself and are the by-products of perfectionism.

The word locus seems to be liked by psychologists. Carl Rogers uses the term an external locus of self-evaluation, which means that your self-esteem is based on external factors such as your work, wealth or some other factor that you value. Without question, those who have an external locus of control also evaluate themselves externally and lack confidence and the ability to dictate their lives. I cannot think of a greater recipe for unhappiness or fear of failure. I remember a client telling me that his self-esteem lay in being good at his job. When I asked how he would be if he became ill and could no longer do his work, his answer was 'I would feel empty. I would feel nothing.' When your self-esteem lies outside of yourself you are constantly on the treadmill of shame. You should realise that you are more than your job or whatever external reality you rely on for your self-esteem. It must lie within yourself.

But, first you have to eradicate that false self who carries your wounds and it is helpful to realise that the false self contains a saboteur, who continuously whispers negative messages about yourself in your ear. Creating an image of the saboteur is one good way of concretising the negative thinking that binds you and nurtures your fear of failure. Imagine that little black saboteur sitting on your shoulder, whispering into your ear telling you that you are not good enough, that you will fail, that you are not intelligent enough, that you will fail an interview, that you will not be able to do the job advertised and there is no use in applying for it, that you will never have a relationship, and so on. To make that little saboteur more realistic paint it, and make it as hideous as possible. Then feel your power over your creation as you tear it up or burn it.

When you have booted the saboteur out of your life, write down the different traits that you would like to have. If you have difficulty doing this, look at people you envy, who seem to have all the desirable qualities that you lack. You will find that despite your fear and feelings of inadequacy, you have many desirable traits. You may, for example, be helpful, persistent, diligent, honest, be good at sport, music and so on. It is worthwhile considering the concept of multiple intelligences (nine types) outlined in the writings of the American developmental psychologist, Howard Gardner, and you will discover that you may have a richer persona than you thought. Emotional intelligence is far more desirable that IQ. Spatial intelligence is also very advantageous. You also have an innate creativity. If you mistakenly label yourself as unintelligent, remember that creativity is your greatest gift. Those who succeed are invariably creative and studies show that child prodigies with high IQs frequently lapse into ordinary, uninteresting adults. All of us have an inner creative child. All you have to do is awaken her.

Part of your creativity is using your gut feeling. Your gut is your best adviser. You will find it a rich source of inspiration, when you become acquainted with it by constantly practising gut communication. This can take some time and effort. It may be true, as some writers claim, that those with fear of failure make poor choices in terms of careers, but they also make poor choices in most areas of their lives because of this debilitating underlying condition. One of the best ways to look at your precise goals, your judgement, and your proposed behaviour is to use your gut. Many people instinctively close it off, probably because they are not used to referring to it or because subconsciously they fear what it will tell them. I have studied the gut from my own experiences and made some important decisions on its response. I will give you an example. I once considered becoming a counselling supervisor. It would not have been difficult and I made enquiries from supervisor trainers. My head said yes. Statistics in my county showed that there were hundreds of counsellors and only a small number of supervisors. My head rightly said that I would make more money than the small amount I make from counselling. I asked my gut, confidently expecting its approval and was surprised when it strongly rejected my plan. The gut usually responds in about five seconds and using it will save you many headaches and prevent poor decisions. I try not to go against my gut, and whenever I do, I create problems. I do not immediately accept the gut's simple response of yes or no. I like to know the reason for its answer and your gut will tell you, because it knows everything about you. The reasons it gave me was that my job was to sit with people rather than telling counsellors what to do. It also hinted that my health would be under too much strain and that I had sufficient money. The gut is always right, because it knows you. It cannot, however, predict how others will react, but that is not your problem.

Using your gut helps you to avoid mistakes in what direction you should take in different circumstances, but it does not give you an insight into the extent of your fear of failure. One of the best ways to get an overall view of this is to keep a fear and avoidance diary. This should be as comprehensive as necessary, recording your **thoughts**, **feelings**, and **behaviours**. Let us take a brief example of how this might look in the context of the lecturing job I once avoided.

Thoughts

That would be a very attractive job. It is highly paid and I need the money badly now, with a large family and a big mortgage. I like history and lecturing does not carry a big workload. I'm also well qualified and am a good writer. I could easily write plenty of articles and a few books, perhaps. But, I would have to give up my profession which I really love. I would have to say good bye to that. I would have to move and sell the nice house I built. I like where I'm living. I like the countryside. I like the voluntary work I am doing. Worse still, I would have to leave all my friends. What would I do if I made a mess of this? After all some of these third-level students will be more intelligent than me. I might be a laughing stock.

Feelings

I feel a bit uneasy about this. I can feel this in the pit of my stomach. I feel worried that something will go wrong and I can feel some element of shame in my body. I am afraid, because I think this is too much. I feel angry that I am so stuck, because this would be a good opportunity for me career-wise. I feel angry that I am like this. What makes me like this? I feel like a child.

Behaviours

I can't let this opportunity go. I'll apply for the job, but I'll outline the difficulties in my way. I'll tell them that I want the job but I want to remain on here for another year to finish out my Leaving Certificate class.

I would clearly have seen from this diary how I sabotaged my future in the lecturing field. My initial thinking was positive, but then I buried it beneath a morass of negative and irrational thinking. The feelings coming from this thinking are clear – fear, anger and shame. The behaviour is one of subconscious avoidance, one of the most prominent saboteurs attached to fear. I would not have seen this at the time. Fear clouds clear thinking. Writing it down makes for clarity and good judgement.

Yet despite my fears, I found fulfilment in my life as a teacher, a principal and a counsellor. I believe that this was my destiny. In my training as a counsellor I had to undertake fifty hours of personal counselling. This changed my life in the most positive way possible. I regret how my fear prevented me from speaking at the Oireachtas and perhaps arousing the anger of others, but I have let that go. I have accepted that I once had a deep fear. Letting go of regret is important, because those with core fear live in a world of regret, a futile world, a negative place that they wallow in, where the words 'if only' predominates. I believe that all of us has a destiny, and it is up to you to find it and banish fear from your world.

Chapter 5

Social Fear

ONCE KNOWN AS THE 'NEGLECTED DISORDER,' social fear is now seen as one of the most disabling conditions to beset human beings. There are widely varying statistics about how prevalent it is, but research shows that it affects up to twenty percent of people, making it one of the most common anxiety disorders. At some stage or another we all experience normal social fear. We are apprehensive when we have to make a speech, give a presentation, ask someone out for a date, sing a song or perform in some way in public. It is only when it becomes so distressing that it inhibits us from living happily and interferes with our life that it can be termed pathological and requires treatment.

Social fear is more formally known as social anxiety or social phobia, and is seen as an anxiety disorder that affects both men and women. Psychologists rightly distinguish between fear and anxiety. While they are distinct, they may overlap and the differences are well explained by the Swiss biochemist, Thierry Steimer, in his article 'The Biology of fear-and anxiety-related behaviors.' If you are interested in brain function this is an excellent article. Anxiety is a body sensation and has a large number of physical symptoms that arise at a possible or imagined threat. It is, therefore, a generalised response to an unknown danger. Fear is a primitive emotion in the face of real or immediate danger, or what is seen as a danger. Without fear, however, there would be no anxiety, although some psychologists argue that anxiety can be converted into fear. I think the opposite would be closer to the truth. I have never met anyone who had anxiety that was not accompanied by a silent and hidden fear.

John R. Marshall, Clinical Professor of Obstetrics and Gynecology at UCLA School of Medicine, is one of the pioneers in using medication to deal with social fear. In his book, *Social Phobia. From Shyness to Stage Fright*, he divides it into two categories, specific and generalised. Some people fear situations that may involve any type of criticism, including small everyday activities in the presence of others such as shopping, posting a letter, or dining in a café. I have met people who find going for a walk in an urban area a torture, because they feel conspicuous and exposed. They are acutely conscious that people are staring at them and commenting on them and they feel terrified and paralyzed as they walk with head bowed. Even shopping is torturous. They stand dumbly at the counter and are unable to make eye contact with the shop attendant and at the same time are intensely conscious of other shoppers. This hell is generalized social fear, since it pervades most areas of your life, where you strive to be more than human, where you are in the grip of perfectionism to avoid shame, where your boundaries are very defective as you strive to please everyone. You take in the feelings of other people very easily, and fear that the simplest of actions such as asking the price of some item will arouse their hostility and they will judge you as awkward. This generalized social fear is more crippling than the fear of specific circumstances.

Jason's main issue was social fear coming from fear of abandonment and an insecure attachment to his father. It was his main presenting issue. His narrative shows how utterly disabling it can be, how it encourages avoidance, interferes with normal functioning and interferes with self-care.

> By the time I had reached college, fear had, unknown to me, taken over my life. I did adequately in my Leaving Cert without ever reaching my full potential. The subject I was good at was English, as I had a teacher who took a keen interest in me and really pushed me. I did well in this subject, so it seemed logical to study this further in college. I accepted my place in University College Dublin, with just one other person from school doing the same degree. This was where my problems started. As my brother had gone to college before me, I decided, like him, that it would be a good idea

to live with strangers and make new friends. My brother had made a great new group of friends, but unfortunately I only realise now, what was good for my brother might not make me happy. It was, without doubt, the loneliest time of my life. I made one new friend, Darren, out of 200 students following the course. I relied on him heavily and if he wasn't going to lectures, there was no way I was. I just couldn't handle the house.

There were three girls and two lads living in the house. They were all nice people and in particular the lads, who had many of the same interests as me. I just couldn't put myself out there to spend time with them or to socialise with them. I would spend hours locked in my room. I couldn't even muster the courage to urinate and would often do it in my sink. I was paralysed by the fear of meeting them and I suppose being judged. I never ate or cooked in the house and only very rarely watched tele-vision in the sitting room. I would usually only do this when there was nobody around. If I left early in the morning to go to college, I would slip out the door and hope nobody spotted me. I then would often spend hours wandering through the college, putting down time until it was dark and time to go to bed. This could often be as early as 6 o' clock. I would lock myself in my room and read. Reading would keep my mind from thinking and I grew so dependent on it that I wouldn't be able sleep without reading. Not even my love of rugby could help me. I was too afraid to try out playing even though I know I was better than some of the players on the team. These were lads with similar interests but I just couldn't push myself to go to the trials. My only solace was my school friends. I would call down to my school friend, Jimmy, a lot, but as he was studying a different course, he was rarely around. I had friends across city in another college. This was my escape. I would throw some clothes into a bag and head for their place. I could spend days over there, missing huge amounts of college work. I felt comfortable with the lads I knew. We would head out drinking a few nights a week and this was my escape from my college worries. I was getting a bit of a reputation as the guy who loved going out, especially among the older lads from back home. I loved playing up this reputation and when they rang I couldn't say no. I loved been seen as one of the boys and a 'right lad,' but deep down I was really struggling.

Jason was mistaken if he thought that his fear would depart when he began working. It intensified and destroyed any attempt at happiness.

I would do my work to a high standard but I would lunch by myself, in a place away from work where my colleagues wouldn't see me. I was on a very busy team so people didn't go to lunch together. I asked one of the lads one day to go to lunch, but he told me he didn't have time. Instead of taking this as the truth, I thought it was my fault and he just didn't want to have lunch with me. I questioned myself and the rejection made me put up my guard. I wouldn't be asking again. There was another group of lads on another work team. They were friendly and sporty and liked the banter. This is the kind of group I would have got on well with. But I wasn't brave enough to ask if I could join them. The fear of being judged, 'the look at this loner' thoughts that was going round in my head, meant I never made the effort with them. College was happening all over again. I'd have a few scenarios were I'd have a laugh with them, but I wouldn't be able join them the next day for lunch or stop for a chat. If circumstances had been different I could have been on this team. They would have invited the newbie to lunch and I could have made some really good friends. Instead, I was left to go to lunch on my own in a restaurant up the road that I was familiar with from my college days. I was nearly 2 years working in the office before I could venture into the canteen. I had the feeling that all eyes from the office would be on me as I queued for my food. The thoughts of being in a queue having to make conversation with one of my work colleagues, especially those in higher positions, made me blush and sweat. This irrational fear meant I never went to the canteen. Work was really intense and some days I didn't have time to go to the restaurant across the way, so instead of grabbing something quick in the canteen, I would eat nothing. On bad days, I could arrive home from work around 8 in the evening and not have eaten since 7 that morning. At the time I didn't notice anything crazy about my behaviour. As I write this, I can't really believe how irrational my fears had made me. I thought this was all to do with college and I couldn't see the signs that my fears had taken me over.

Essentially, therefore, social fear is about oversensitivity of being judged, criticized or rejected by others; being acutely self-conscious and feeling embarrassed or humiliated. Barbara Markway, a psychologist in Jefferson City and an expert on social fear, makes the interesting point that people with social fear not only dread disapproval, *but exaggerate the threat of criticism.* Negative thinking, therefore, always tends towards exaggeration and the expectation of blame. It is allied to catastrophization (catastrophic thinking), a term coined by Aaron Beck, one of the founders of cognitive therapy.

This mindset means that even before you meet a group of strangers or attend a social occasion you are already internally embarrassed and crippled by your own negative self-appraisal. You sabotage yourself and are defeated before you set out. Social fear is all about yourself with an intense and paralysing internal focus and hypersensitivity to anticipated scrutiny by others. You imagine that they can see the false self with all its imperfections of shame, anger, low self-esteem and, above all, being boring. Almost every person I have met with social fear felt they were boring and uninteresting in the company of other people. The focus also shifts to physical manifestations of fear and anxiety, sometimes including sweating, blushing and stammering. Thinking about them is a trigger that will bring them on. All those defects that were planted in you during your childhood stand starkly in your mind, and this brainwashing paralyses you in many aspects of your life, and especially when interacting with others. It is about not being comfortable in your skin, ruminating about letting yourself down in front of others and being oversensitive about yourself.

While it is a silent and invisible saboteur, albeit with obvious anxiety symptoms, the negative thinking that drives it is very often translated into obsession with body image. You are conscious about how you look, blame yourself for these so-called imperfections, and become distracted, while others are oblivious to such supposed defects. A negative view of body image can affect how you interact with others, especially members of the opposite sex. Even if you have a defect, you exaggerate it out of all proportion and focus relentlessly on it. Jason, for example, was constantly aware of his hair, and felt distressed that he would go bald. This increased his pre-existing fear of forming intimate relationships.

Randy and Lori Sansone in their article, *Body Image*, have come up with an enlightened explanation of body image issues. They suspect that negativity tends to be concretized on a body level in shamed children. In other words psychological negativity is converted into a physical one. Generally they are unaware of body image as children, but become conscious of it in teenage years and bring this shame and negativity into adulthood, where the so called physical defects rivet their attention and fits perfectly with their low self-worth. The magnifying glass sees every defective speck in their bodily make up, and the mirror becomes the gauge of their self-esteem. For some individuals body image is pathological and is known as dysmorphophobia i.e. a fear that one's body is repulsive. This affects up to 2.4 percent of the population and is classed as a psychiatric complaint. I have met some handsome people who feel this way about their imagined ugliness. In many cases some of these turn to the plastic surgeon. Unfortunately, because body image has a psychological dimension, they continue to return for surgery in what is a distressing grindstone.

The body image dimension of social fear is strongly affected by culture. Because of the fear, you are vulnerable to how some modern magazines portray the ideal in terms of physical beauty. Such magazines are a powerful trigger to make you conscious of physical defects. The so-called beauty industry is colossal, and an increasing number of people, male and female, are being seduced by it. If you have good self-esteem you will not be swayed by the proclaimed ideal of physical beauty. You will be comfortable in your skin, even if it is wrinkled with age! If you define yourself in terms of physical beauty, you will ultimately be haunted by a sense of failure. This may sound ludicrous, but do not underestimate the power of cultural aspirations, which can make you feel flawed. Cultural views on physical beauty is just another way of being shamed, as you compare yourself to beautiful females and handsome males adorning the pages of these magazines. You may have thoughts like 'I am ugly, my hair is falling out and she will think I'm unattractive, my ears are too big, my nose is too long, or I'm not good looking enough for her, I'm too fat, I'm too thin, 'I'm too small, I'm too tall' and a whole myriad of other supposed imperfections. The lesson is to deal with the underlying cause of not feeling good enough.

Social fear is essentially detrimental because the human has evolved as a social creature. Some early civilizations were organized on a tribal basis, designed for survival. Social fear, therefore, can be seen as an evolutionary reaction in the face of danger. This provokes the fight or flight response. That was all very useful when danger surrounded us at every turn, but the underlying impact of an insecure attachment pathologizes social fear to the extent that it becomes debilitating, and instead of being a beneficial protective mechanism it renders you powerless and fearful of ordinary situations. Occasionally, this debilitating condition can begin in children as young as eight, but the average age of onset is mid-adolescence and it is rarely generated after the age of twenty-five. Children with social fear find it difficult to mix with others, are unfriendly and withdrawn, do badly at school and occasionally have depression. School is the place where these symptoms normally appear. Their anxious response to social situations with their peers can include weeping, freezing, tantrums, as well as some behaviours shown by socially anxious adults. These behaviours are often accompanied by physical symptoms such as stomach aches or headaches. Being in class can be extremely painful for teenagers suffering from social phobia. Being asked questions by the teacher fills them with fear, and for a small number of students can degenerate into selective mutism, which is discussed later. In extreme cases mixing with other pupils is a no-go area. Such children often arrive in school late when classes have begun and isolate themselves at break times. This tendency to isolate increases as they move through adulthood, causing significant interference in living. Sometimes the fear is so great that sufferers choose jobs that leave them solitary rather than take on more suitable jobs, where they would interact with others. There are cases of people who find it impossible to work during the day, and find employment where they work only at night and in a solitary capacity. I should say, however, that many teenagers who suffer extreme anxiety find healing in therapy and live a fear free adulthood.

Psychologists have categorised social fear as an abnormal personality trait, an avoidant personality disorder or a phobia. Psychological distinctions are not crucial to this book, but we need to know why so many people harbour this particular fear. It is strange that researchers still argue about the origins of social fear. Some, for example attribute it to biological or genetic vulnerabilities. Professor Martin Antony, for example, makes the case that genetics may play a part in social anxiety. Further studies now highlight some of the actual genes that contribute to social anxiety. Professor Gillian Butler and Dr Edmund Bourne outline some sources such as biological factors, temperament, environmental factors (parenting, traumatic experiences, life stage problems, and other stresses). Ray Crozier and Lynn Alden and their colleagues explore the biological factors in some detail in their book, *Social Anxiety for Clinicians*, but also discuss the importance of attachment as a factor in social fear. Overall, it may arise from a combination of genetic, biological and environmental, suggesting that a combination of counselling and drug therapy may be the best route to take. The drugs will deal with the genetic and the counselling with the effects of an insecure attachment. The appropriate drugs can only be created when we know the exact neural chemicals that are deficient.

We should be aware that people often mistakenly use genetic or hereditary terms without realizing that these more often than not are about our environment i.e. our parenting. For example, you frequently hear people making statements such as 'like father like son', which insinuates that there is a genetic factor involved. Anytime I have explored the generational and genetic themes it has become apparent that childhood abuse and neglect were rife in such families, going back for generations. The generational factor was not necessarily (but could be) genetic, but rather neglect that carried on throughout the decades. A genogram is an effective way to explore this. This is like a family tree and can be framed to look at relationship problems, medical issues, addictions and so on. You can download examples of genograms and instruction on how to use them from the internet. The further back you can go the better, but generally grandparents are as far as we can go. In examining the completed genogram you may be shocked to see the psychological pathologies in your ancestry associated with attachment problems.

Seeing a pattern of pathological issues in the ancestry and wider family is not at all about blaming them or blaming parents, most of whom do the best they can. Nevertheless, we must be realistic, and it can be safely argued that particular types of parenting can unintentionally sow the seeds of social fear. It can be learned from parents who show excessive worry or anxiety about social occasions, or can be created if a parent is overprotective, distrustful or critical of others. Parents can sometimes inadvertently give the impression to their children that the world is not a safe place. This arises from their love and concern for their children. *Repeated* warnings to young children about trivial behaviours, such as being careful on the road, or mixing with other 'undesirable' children, can create such an incapacitating belief in the child. Over protective parents can also make the child feel that he is not competent to meet the social challenges that life throws up. They can give the impression that others have certain standards and expectations, and the child can become self-conscious and made to feel that the opinions and evaluations of others are absolutely necessary. Without realising it, parental attitudes and beliefs help the child to develop an unhealthy mental representation of himself as supposedly seen by others. In short, he imagines that others see him as he does – inadequate and defective. This negative outlook is seamlessly transferred into all areas of your life including the arena of social fear. In short, your default setting is negativity.

The negative self-view is also reflected in a number of assumptions that fearful people have about themselves and about social behaviour. In his article, *A Cognitive Perspective on Social Phobia*, David Clark sees three divisions in such assumptions – unreasonably high standards for social performance, conditional beliefs about the consequences of acting in a certain way and negative beliefs about the self. The totality of such thinking is crippling and includes such thoughts as

'I must always appear strong',' I must always sound intelligent', 'I must disagree with others or they will think I am stupid', 'if I make conversation people will think I am boring', 'I'm unlikeable and different', to name but a few. This negative inner self-world was formed when you were very young and developed over the years with an accumulation of social experiences. It will be helpful if you check the existence of some or all of these assumptions in your case, because you may not even be aware of this negative and irrational thinking as it works away in your subconscious undermining you all the time, reinforcing negative self-beliefs and false assumptions. Your fleeting thought may be a belief that you are worthless and your assumption is that you must show that you are a worthwhile human being or else people will not like you and you will end up living a lonely life.

Gillian Butler, therefore, correctly sums up the components of social fear as thinking and behaviour, with physical and emotional symptoms. Thinking symptoms include consciousness of other people's opinion of you, lack of concentration, focusing on yourself and worrying about what might go wrong. Behavioural symptoms might be avoiding social occasions, mumbling, looking away from a person while speaking to them, and trying to avoid attention. The problem with these symptoms is that they more than likely will be misinterpreted by others as unfriendliness and people do not respond warmly to an unfriendly person. This then reinforces your belief that you are disliked, or worse still not worth liking, and a vicious circle is created, whereby you withdraw more and more. But, as mentioned elsewhere you can change your behaviours. You have control over them. Physiological symptoms have already been outlined and some of the emotional symptoms include apprehension, anger, sadness, helplessness and depression. These are seen, also, in Jason's narrative. All of these make up an unpleasant assortment in the recipe for fear.

Social anxiety is often part of a bigger problem. I have found that depression, lack of assertiveness, aggressiveness, worry, addiction and many of the issues listed in Appendix 1, are sometimes comorbid with social fear. In their book, *The Essential Handbook of Social Anxiety for Clinicians*, Rick Ingram and his colleagues discuss the relationship between social fear and depression in adults, and show that between twenty to thirty percent of people with social fear also have depression. Social fear normally kicks in before depression and for people afflicted with both, the lethal combination is painfully shackling. This chronic condition is frequently powered by rumination, one of the causes of depression. Ruminating means asking yourself questions that have no concrete answers. This keeps you on a treadmill of anxiety and keeps your head in a continuous spin. Here are a few of the questions you might pose that keep you in hyper vigilance –

What does this person think of me?
Is he staring at me?
Does he look unfriendly?

Does she recognise that I am incredibly boring?

Does she see that I have very little knowledge?

Can he see that I am beginning to blush?

Does he know that I have no self-esteem? That I am useless?

Can he see the perspiration on my forehead?

Does she know what I am really like?

Can he see what I am thinking?

He is a very educated person and I left school early. Will he see me as stupid and ignorant?

Will she will compare me to her friends, who are all better than me?

In the case of social fear the depression and anxiety are often accompanied by toxic shame, which is very often the basis of this condition. Some researchers, however, also theorize that social fear is a social issue rather than a personal one. That is true insofar as people with social fear often feel embarrassed or shamed because they feel they do not fit in. They feel on the margin, but the shame makes it personal. Shame often brings anger, and many people with social fear carry toxic anger and negative fantasizing. They are not paranoid in the psychological sense, but in a minority of cases indulge in violent fantasies about hurting or insulting others, a condition that also occurs in OCD. If they feel judged they in turn judge others and many are conflicted or confused. Their internal conflict with others is often accompanied by external meekness, although they feel cold, detached and suspicious.

There are ways to assess how serious your social fear is and to examine its particular underlying causes. The following list of questions will help to clarify this –

> Has the fear fettered you and limited your capacity to make friends? Can you list the reality and the details of this? Find good examples and speculate how you might have handled the situation better. Do you ever remember being like this at a younger age? What prevented you making friends when you were young?

> Has the fear changed the course of your life (as fear of failure did mine)? Are you happy with the life you are living or do you feel thwarted and unhappy? Have you ideas about how you would have liked your life to have gone? If so, what type of life would you like to have and is it possible to achieve it? If there is a vacuum in your life how can you fill it? Were you unhappy as a child? What was your life as a child like?

> Has the fear prevented you from having the type of job you would have liked to have? If so what type of job would you like to have? Is it possible to change your job? Check training opportunities.

> Has the fear interfered with your ability to work in your current job? If so, how? Are you

constantly watchful and fearful of authority? Do you spend a lot of time thinking about your job? Are you constantly checking your work? Do you compare yourself unfavourably with your colleagues?

Has the social fear prevented you from going to work? Check your thoughts to see how they undermine you. Did you miss many days at school as a child? Did you drop out of school early?

Has the fear stopped you from getting a job? Write down the avoidance mechanisms that fetter you and prevent you from applying for available work. How did you deal with college? Did you finish the course you were doing?

Has the fear prevented you from entering into intimate or romantic relationships? How many romantic relationships have you had? Were you able to make dates? Were you conscious of your so called defects when you tried to make dates?

Has the fear damaged an intimate relationship you have? If so, how? Explore the dynamics of the relationship and your thinking, feelings and behaviours. What could you have done to prevent the damage caused? What can you do now?

Has the fear affected your ability to relate to family and friends? If so, how? Are you isolated from family and friends? How serious is the isolation? Is it entirely your fault? What can you do to change your situation?

Has the fear stifled your creativity? How have you curtailed your creative inner child? How can you release her and allow her to be free and spontaneous? Do you feel yourself to be dull and restricted in that spontaneity?

There are many more questions you could pose to assess the impact of social fear on your progress in every part of your life and to help you cast off this fear.

Martin Antony and Richard Swinson in their book, *The Shyness & Social Anxiety Workbook*, suggest a simple technique for self-assessing the seriousness of your social anxiety, where you can measure on a scale from 0 to 100 the level of your fear and the extent of your avoidance for various situations that cause you anxiety. This will enable you to deal with the fear using situations which are easy to deal with and those which require the greatest effort. So if you rate yourself as 80 on the fear scale you are extremely fearful and if you put yourself at 90 on the avoidance scale for the same issue you often avoid. In this way you can produce a hierarchy of situations based on this way of measuring fear and avoidance, and you can then take appropriate measures to counteract this.

Jason, for example, had severe social fear registering at least 90, and would have a similar score on the avoidance scale. It remained with him for the entirety of his college years, and it gradually resulted in his isolation from his friends and the loss of their previous respect for him.

> For 3rd year, we all moved in together. As I didn't know the new guys well, I was feeling very uncomfortable about the move. In the first week there, all the old feelings came back from my first year in college. People called to the house every day and were always in in my sitting room when I came home. There was a party one night and I didn't know anyone there. I couldn't hide in my room as before, because I knew Simon and Darren too well. They would see this as weird and I didn't want to be judged like that. I panicked and decided to move out. I slept on the couch of a friend from back home. The lads were ringing me wondering what the story was, and after a few days I told them that I was moving out. They couldn't understand it, so friendships were lost. I ended up avoiding them altogether and became a loner again. It was a very difficult time and I felt very isolated and avoided college as a result. As there was still group projects to be done, I was in a group with Simon and Darren. The day before the project was due, we were to meet. Another friend asked

me to go to the races down the country. I went, met some friends from home and did not return to help with the project. They handed it in and reported me to the lecturer for not contributing. This was well and truly the end of the friendship. I felt very aggrieved that they would hang me out especially as the project wasn't far from completion and in a previous project, I had done most of the work. I told the lecturer what happened and she was understanding and docked me only a few small marks. As we were on work experience for second semester, there was no contact between us again for months. I felt really bad that I lost Darren as a friend, because we got on great and we had met the first day of college.

Jason lost these friends due to his fear and avoidance, but resolved to move in with friends from home. He found new excuses to avoid facing the fact that this was now a deep rooted coping mechanism with detrimental results.

As I knew nobody in college now, I decided the best plan would be to move across city and live with the lads from home. I promised myself that I would get the bus over every day and stay all day. It would work out better, I was convincing myself. I moved in with Rob and Dave. Week one came and went. My routine was going out on Sunday night, when we'd come down home, hungover for Monday, back out drinking on Tuesday night, hungover for Wednesday, Thursday was too late in the week to go to college while Friday was going home time. Each week would roll out the same. I thought of every excuse to avoid college. If I stayed in on Sunday I'd be too tired Monday and then it was going out Tuesday. I fell into a rut and while the lads were attending their college in the mornings, I'd stay in bed until one and get up when they would come home. College became a place I just couldn't go. A fear would keep me from going. Fear of sitting on my own at the back, fear of being judged by people as a loner. To cope with the fear I avoided people and situations. This would be my means of defence against everything. I even went one day and got as far as the college and went home. For the first semester I went to the college once, to register. I decided I'd give one of the exams a bash and I ended up passing. As I didn't have notes for the rest, I skipped them. I even hit a new low. The realisation that the good grade I had from the first 3 years would slip away prompted me to go and talk to the college year head. I lied about being badly depressed. I asked them to postpone my exams until the summer. They said they would consider this if I went to counselling sessions. I said I would, but by semester two

I had given up on the year and had decided I would repeat it. I tried not to think about what I had done, three years of an English degree wasted. All my parents' money down the drain. The guilt and the shame was eating me up, so again I ended up going out or doing anything to get my mind off it. I watched as my friends graduated, while I knew people were talking about me failing the year. My mother at this stage was extremely worried that I'd go out for 3 days and not come home. She didn't push me on it. I think she hoped this was a phase and I would come through it. My father and me would just not talk, full stop.

Going to lectures is only one of hundreds of specific situations that provoke fear and avoidance, so it might be helpful to further mention a few of the more common ones. One of the most widespread is fear of giving speeches or presentations. This is labelled per-formance fear, which is not so much fear of making a mistake as of others seeing your fear.

Most people suffer mild stage fright, but when it becomes debilitating it is pathological. Such extreme fear is expressed in the body is several distressing ways – increased heartbeat, palpitations, raised blood pressure, feeling dizzy or weak, dry throat, weak voice, nausea, perspiring, stomach knotted, and intense anxiety, which John R. Marshall calls anticipatory anxiety. I have met people for whom the very thought of standing in front of an audience and making a brief thank you speech caused days of worrying, lack of sleep and extreme anxiety. It is very difficult for those who do not suffer social fear to understand such an extreme reaction to what seems a minor issue.

Barbara Markway and her colleagues give valuable advice on preparing for a presentation and David Leisner, the famous classical guitarist and composer, compiled six golden rules to counteract performance fear, which can be used in any areas where you are facing an audience. The first and most important rule is to remind yourself that you have practised to the best of your ability. When I was a school Principal I had to make numerous speeches, and I found the best place to practise was in the car as I drove to and from work. In that way I repeated my speech many times. There was always some difference with each rehearsal, so I knew that the speech I ultimately gave would be slightly different to the ones I rehearsed, but I also knew that I could go on autopilot and keep the same theme.

Having prepared well, your second golden rule is not to become over-conscious of how you are performing. This will distract you and destroy the natural flow of your speech. You will find yourself concentrating on the form or style of your speech rather than upon the content.

The third golden rule is to avoid being sucked into the audience by trying to second-guess their reaction to how your speech is going. If you yield to the temptation of looking at the faces of some of those present, you will be even more distracted from your presentation as you vainly try to imagine what they are thinking. So if you see one person looking out the window you will be sidetracked by the thought that you are boring, and this negative feeling will be reinforced if you see someone with her eyes closed, apparently asleep. If you see someone yawning it may simply be that they are tired. You cannot tell what a person in an audience is thinking, so look over their heads as you speak. You cannot focus on your presentation if you are focusing on the audience.

The fourth and fifth golden rules can be combined and remind you to remember that your task is to clearly communicate a particular theme to the audience, a theme that you have practised until it flows easily and naturally.

Finally say what you mean and believe in what you are saying. In that way you can enjoy making your speech, which is about informing and sharing with others what you have learned. Even if you are simply making a thank you speech, let it be sincere, enjoy praising others for whatever contribution they made to the occasion.

Another common but less well known form of social fear is that of urinating in the presence of others. This is known as parauresis or shy bladder syndrome and generally starts in childhood, but can also begin in adulthood. It is a particularly distressing type of social fear and can be extreme, affecting not only males using urinals at sports fixtures, but in some cases people are unable to urinate if another person is in the same building.

Dating is another specific situation, where social fear can be crippling and is an almost impenetrable boundary to forming a relationship. I know many people, who have no fear of giving speeches or meeting people, but are unable to ask for a date. Research shows that those with social fear are less likely to get married, or do so later in life. Consequently, one of the most prominent feelings they experience on a daily basis is loneliness. My client, Jason, struggled with this since he was in his early teens, and used an unhealthy defense mechanism to cope. He found Dutch courage, appropriately known as liquid courage, through alcohol, but was still unable to make a date. For years he was on this treadmill of drinking to find courage to make a date, followed by depression and lack of motivation for several days, which left him vulnerable to addiction, but fortunately he escaped that tragic consequence. He never made a date and never had a girlfriend, because his negative thinking paralysed him. He clarified these as

I'm not good enough for her. She's so attractive, and look at me. She's bound to say no. what could she see in me? If she says yes, I won't know what to say. She'll think I'm boring and what if I get tongue-tied. I have no experience of dating and I'll make a mess of this; I'm just not good enough for her. She'll see me blushing and think I have no confidence.

You can see the contradiction in this thinking. Jason has a fear of being rejected or accepted. Both, however, are based on a feeling of inadequacy. He fears the shame of rejection, which would confirm his supposed defectiveness, yet if accepted he fears that she will see the false self and leave him. He is still working on this issue using EMDR therapy. If his fear still persists following EMDR then a technique called EMDR Flashforward can be used. This is explained clearly in an article by Robin Logie and Ad De Jongh. I am struck by the stranglehold this particular problem has on Jason, and have only come across one other case so resistant to therapy. It is something of a challenge for me!

For many men social fear also includes an anxiety about sexual performance, which can contribute to erectile dysfunction, reinforcing your belief in your sexual inadequacy. You can create some manageable boundaries to deal with this. Many men leap ahead and imagine that they will be expected to have intercourse early in the relationship. They are convinced that this will be the expectation of the possible partner. There are many stages in entering a relationship, and for many people having sex is the last one. Setting boundaries at the beginning of a relationship creates respect both for yourself and the other person. You can choose to move slowly, beginning with meeting for a coffee, going for a walk, or something that seems very achievable. Barbara Markway and her colleagues hold that you must have a plan to deal with social phobia, and creating a relationship is ideal territory for this. Nevertheless, my clinical experience shows that for some people, even such simple boundaries create fear. They see having a coffee with the intention of ultimately asking for a date, as an intimate situation and the sexual agenda is generally present in their awareness.

Nonetheless, I found that continuous challenge in a counselling setting sometimes worked and reluctant clients were able to make the first manageable steps, leading to long term relationships. I found that systematic desensitization (explained later), relaxation techniques and social skills training provide an effective way of dealing with fear of dating and relationships. Social skills can be learned from an expert, who will teach you techniques that will make you comfortable in social exchanges. You will receive the opportunity to practise new skills and receive constructive criticism in simulated conditions. If you search the internet you will come across many institutions and individuals who teach social skills. As regards desensitization, one of the best ways to prepare for dating is to meet the other person in social situations, at work, at workshops or in college. Getting used to interacting with them and their friends may ease the fear of going a step further and asking for a date, but it may also cause you severe embarrassment. If this is the case your social fear may be complicated by shyness.

For many years there has been confusion about the differences between shyness and social fear. Now it is generally recognised that they are different, although they share some similarities. As a personality trait, many people who have social fear are not necessarily shy, and many shy people do not necessarily have social fear. Shyness can be defined as a combination of anxiety, inhibition, reticence in social and interpersonal situations and nervousness about being judged by others. The context is generally the same as for social fear. It lies dormant and only surfaces when the shy person finds himself in situations that cause him unease and embarrassment. Normal shyness is often seen as an attractive quality, and in some cultures shyness and reticence are seen as desirable characteristics. They do not over-pathologize it and there is some evidence that those with normal shyness keep their friends for a longer period of time, and can be more highly regarded by their friends.

Pathological shyness, however, is a different matter and is not to be dismissed too lightly. It becomes toxic when it prevents you functioning properly, such as having an inability to make a date or mix with ease. It can begin in childhood and longitudinal studies show that shy children, who are wary and anxious in new situations, are most likely to be shy adults and have social fear. Studies on shyness and anxiety in children indicate a very complicated picture. Ironically, at the other end of the life span, the elderly may be more affected by it than people in the other life stages. Research shows that older shy people experience greater sensitivity to the problems of that stage of life than the non-shy elderly. They are more emotionally affected by loneliness, isolation, vulnerability to crime, having social networks, widowhood, retirement and reduction of income. The lesson here is that it is important to deal with shyness in early life so that all stages, especially the final stage, offer appropriate fulfilment.

Morbid shyness may also be linked to some unpleasant psychological problem such as depression, anger, shame, loneliness and fear. Its physiological features include blushing, stomach turning, dryness in the mouth and a pounding heart that stimulate acute self-consciousness. These are accompanied by negative thinking and feelings of worthlessness that feed into social fear and reinforces the avoidance defence mechanism. Many people who are friendly and kind by nature are regarded by others as cold, withdrawn or snobbish because of shyness. This can have serious consequences in terms of relationships. Some morbidly shy people may be so self-conscious that they resort to social media as a way of concealing it and avoid human contact as much as possible. In that case shyness and social fear are very much related.

Professor Arnold H. Buss in his paper, *A Theory of Shyness*, describes two types of shyness, fearful and self-conscious, which helps to explain the different triggers that spark this distressing trait. Fearful shyness is more primitive and affects very young children who become distressed at novelty and change. Older humans are more likely to experience self-conscious shyness, which arises from a sense of being scrutinised, predominantly in formal situations. Buss attributes fearful shyness to adverse circumstances during childhood, particularly bullying or aggression, or being isolated from strangers. He argues that those with self-conscious shyness may have been over-conditioned by parents in areas like good behaviour, proper manners and so on. This makes them feel conspicuous and exposed. Professor Jonathan Cheek and his co-writers, when discussing adolescence shyness, make the point that fearful shyness may indicate somatic (physiological) anxiety and self-conscious shyness may point to psychic (cognitive) anxiety. I have no doubt that people with social fear have a mixture of both that cripples them in living healthily.

John R. Marshall in his client work discovered that some people compensate for shyness by assuming a role. Noreen, one of my clients long ago, was always the life and soul of the party. She was seen as extremely friendly and was never in bad humour. Her work colleagues were drawn to her because of her good humour and ever ready smile. It was only when I got to know her that I realised that she was a shy, serious woman and that her invented self was the ever-happy individual, who seemed to sail through life in a carefree mood. In reality she was anxious, depressed and under great stress. She accepted my challenge and changed. She lost some friends, but experienced a new sense of peace by being real.

Reticence has already been mentioned as part of shyness and more often than not is an element of social fear. It can be found in children as well as in adults, particularly where parents are over solicitous and controlling how the child behaves in social situations. Adults suffering from reticence lack skill at social speaking and have difficulty interacting with others and having romantic relationships. They find it stressful to take part in group activities, make small talk and experience problems in making and maintaining friendships. Some are acutely conscious of it and others unaware. It can range from silence to hesitancy about speaking. A basic belief by some sufferers is that it is best to stay silent and be thought a fool, than to speak and prove it. Yet reticence is a distressing condition bringing loneliness, isolation, boredom, anxiety and a sense of failure. The symptoms reticent people experience are similar to those with social fear.

The late Professor Gerald M. Phillips, an expert in speech communication and shyness, devised a programme called Rhetoritherapy as a way of dealing with shyness and reticence, which he explains in some detail in his article, *Rhetoritherapy. The Principles of Rhetoric in Training Shy People in Speech Effectiveness*. It is based on the premise that any skill or art can be improved through understanding, assisted performance and proper feedback. Antony and Swinson (2008) have a chapter on communication skills which include listening skills, interview skills and public speaking skills. On a practical level Toastmasters would be an ideal setting for you to deal with reticence. Not only would you acquire communication skills, but you would find members of the Toastmasters club to coach you and ease your fear.

Toastmasters, however, is not an effective platform to deal with a complaint called Selective Mutism, which is at the extreme end of the shyness spectrum. Dr Elisa Shipon-Blum, President and Director of the Selective Mutism Anxiety Research and Treatment Centre (SMART) in Pennsylvania, defines it as the inability to speak and communicate effectively in particular social settings such as school. In my long experience as a teacher I have only been aware of two cases in the classroom. Both were teenagers. Ninety per cent of sufferers also experience social phobia and loneliness. They are also more vulnerable to anxiety such as separation anxiety, moodiness, and sleep problems from infancy. Studies show that it is a genetic problem and there seems to be no evidence that Selective Mutism comes from childhood abuse, neglect or trauma. Of the two cases I have seen I am now aware that one had a happy childhood and the other suffered frequent emotional abuse.

Teenagers with this complaint find it difficult to form romantic relationships and suffer other symptoms such as bowel issues, dislike of bright lights, dislike of loud sounds, or being touched by others. They can be disobedient and are easily frustrated. Many of these children have sensory processing problems which cause them to shut down. This neurological condition results from the brain's inability to integrate and process information from the body's five basic sensory systems, enabling it to react appropriately to the world around them. Some of these difficulties are similar to autistic children, but Selective Mutism is not part of autism.

Other children suffering from this debilitating condition may not freeze in such an extreme way, but may be able to whisper or say a few words in the particular situation that causes them anxiety. It is essential that children suffering from Selective Mutism receive prompt treatment, otherwise a plethora of psychological issues will arise later in life. Parents should lessen any pressure on these children and educate themselves on Selective Mutism. In therapy, reducing anxiety is essential but more is needed such as teaching communication skills. A wide ranging series of investigations are required, such as speech and language evaluation, occupational therapy evaluation and a thorough physical examination, followed by treatment from a specialist in that area. The Spectrum Speech have clinics in Dublin and Kildare and will advise you if you have a child with Selective Mutism. The internet contains information for clinics in other countries. It is also important that teachers are aware of this and do not misinterpret the silence as insolence or indifference.

Shyness can also trigger fear of blushing (erythrophobia), an extremely distressing and exhausting condition, which is surprisingly difficult to treat. Pathological blushing is not about embarrassment, but can happen in the most ordinary situations, such as meeting an acquaintance. Blushing differs from flushing, which refers to redness of the body in general. The human is the only animal that blushes and that is because he possesses social awareness, and hence is vulnerable to embarrassment and fear of being judged. Some people who are prone to blushing may also perspire excessively, especially in the face or hands, thus adding to their discomfiture. It is estimated that about seven percent of people suffer from chronic or pathological blushing, which is frequently connected to shyness or to social fear. Some studies show that up to ninety percent of those presenting to counsellors for blushing have extreme social fear. Those with a fear of blushing often have an overactive sympathetic nervous system, and hence it can also have a genetic or physiological cause. The sympathetic nervous system is part of the autonomic nervous system and stimulates the fight or flight response. In the face of danger, or imagined danger, it expands the blood vessels to your face, which heats up, and makes you conscious of blushing. Other factors, apart from social fear, that bring about blushing include alcohol, especially red wine, hot drinks, a hot atmosphere, being near a fire, fever and spicy foods.

In the context of social fear, blushing becomes abnormal or pathological when the acute distress it causes makes you avoid social situations or interferes with your capacity to function properly in areas of your life. It can also send the wrong signals to others that you are lacking confidence, telling lies or hiding some-thing. When you are acutely aware of such messages, blushing adds to the distress of social fear. Pathological blushing can also affect your promotion prospects at work, because you will avoid exposure to such situations as job interviews.

The most upsetting aspects of blushing is that it is an automatic reaction, is difficult to control and assumes exaggerated importance in your thinking. The more conscious you are the more likely it is to happen. One of the best ways of dealing with blushing is to understand that it is part of a much bigger picture of core fear and shame, and of other themes addressed in this book. If you deal with these core issues, the blushing (if it is not genetic or caused by a medical condition) will become less of a problem. Understanding the physiology of blushing will also help you minimise it. Debilitating blushing originates in your mind and should be dealt with there. Part of minimising it is also to get a proper perspective on it. It is only getting a red face. It is not a catastrophe. While some individuals may notice it and draw the wrong conclusions, do you honestly think that most people have nothing better to do than ruminate about your red face?

Some people heal their blushing by using their imagination, for example visualising themselves by the sea experiencing a cool breeze blowing across their faces. Try and create appropriate visualisations for yourself.

As you can see by now social fear is a complex condition with several distressing components, based upon the simple premise of not being good enough. It may not begin as a phobia, but can develop into one if not treated. Social phobia is a more extreme and consistent fear. It is chronic, because it is the anticipation of the fear that will arise on being observed, judged and possibly rejected by others. A phobia is always excessive and irrational and the DSM (Diagnostic and Statistical Manual, the bible of psychiatrists) defines it as a persistent fear of situations where the sufferer feels she is being judged by others and expects that her behaviour will lead to humiliation and embarrassment. Phobias can reach extreme panic levels and have a combination of severe physical and emotional symptoms such as your heart pounding, experiencing a choking feeling, becoming dizzy, feeling your stomach churn, feeling detached or unnerved and being overwhelmingly anxious. This is a panic attack, which, ironically, is panic about getting a panic attack. It is fear about fear, and a fleeting subconscious thought can trigger it. You may not even notice the thought because it comes and goes in the blink of an eye. It is almost subconscious. Basically, if you are afraid of fear you empower it. Fortunately, you can effectively deal with panic attacks that can suddenly ambush you even in sleep. There are several ways you can proceed. Firstly it is essential to understand what a panic attack is and this will lessen the fear. As with anger, analysing what is happening slows and defeats the fear. In the first place, understand that intense and constant fear over a long period puts your body under stress and ultimately it reacts in a very strong fashion. You will find that your heart begins to pump adrenalin around your body. This is a primitive reaction to prepare you for danger creating the fight or flight response, and would have been a normal physiological response in ancient times, when the human was faced with the many dangers that existed in the wild. In many, but not all cases, the individual begins to hyperventilate i.e. take in more air through their mouth to concentrate oxygen. Again this prepares for flight or fight. Panic attacks can occur at any time, even in your sleep. They bring feelings of helplessness and terror and sometimes resemble heart attacks. The important point to remember is that they are not heart attacks and will not cause you harm, however, unpleasant they are. By understanding them you will minimise them. When the panic attack occurs rather than catastrophising, have an internal conversation with your body. When you are addressing it say something like the following –

> *My heart is beginning to pound and it is sending adrenalin throughout my body to prepare for danger. I am hyperventilating to get more oxygen to meet the danger. My body is reacting and telling me to prepare to run or fight. This is a primitive response, but there is no danger now and this will pass. My body is my friend. My body is intelligent. It is telling me that I am filled with anxiety and that it is time to do something about it.*

You can extend this simple technique by using interoceptive exposure, which is experiencing all the unpleasant physical symptoms that accompany panic attacks. You dwell on the dizziness, the trembling, the pounding of the heart and the sweating. It is important to remember that this is only an extension and should not be used until you have practised the simple technique for dealing with fear and panic. It is also important to use abdominal breathing. You can devise your own formula for dealing with panic attacks, and my experience is that this works and takes the fear, but not the unpleasantness, out of these unwelcome guests. You can use the same cognitive technique for dealing with the less severe symptoms of social fear i.e. they are unpleasant but essentially will do you no harm.

In the overall context, EMDR, exposure therapy and systematic desensitization are the most effective ways to control social fear and social phobia. I have already mentioned exposure therapy in the context of jealousy as exposing yourself to the person, place or situations that cause the fear. It is interesting and hopefully helpful to see how exposure works on the brain. Research in Tufts University School of Medicine in 2013, for example, shows that exposure therapy deactivates to a significant extent a group of neurons that are triggered in a fear causing situation. It activates and increases the perisomatic synapses that inhibit the fear neurons. This experiment, however, was conducted on mice and there is now evidence that the storage of fear in our brain differs is significant ways from animals, but this does not take away from the validity of exposure therapy.

Exposure is difficult and even distressing but vital in healing social fear. Systematic desensitization is a type of exposure therapy that involves exposing yourself on a very gradual basis to the stressor, thus desensitising or soothing yourself, so that the fear arousal is lessened. There are several aspects to this technique. It includes thinking about the anxiety-rousing situation, when you are in a relaxed state. Because fear provokes anxiety, the first step is to learn relaxation techniques, which are mentioned throughout this book. These include meditation, progressive relaxation, abdominal breathing and progressive muscle relaxation.

When you have mastered these techniques, you then begin the actual exposure to the stressor, where you expose yourself gradually to the situation and withdraw when the anxiety begins to reach an unbearable level. You will feel an element of control because you can choose when to withdraw and when to return to the feared situation. It is best to have a plan, rather than a haphazard system of exposure. In other words, you practise on your good days and on your bad ones according to your plan. Do not try to achieve too much too quickly, but it is important to be tenacious and not give up. It is also necessary to practise on a daily or even more frequent basis. Be comfortable with each stage of the exposure before you move on to the next one. You may sometimes fail. In fact, you will fail, possibly on many occasions. This is a reality. Understand that it is normal, and try not to blame yourself, but use the coping skills outlined in this book. Do not be surprised if all kinds of suppressed feelings arise as you go through the desensitisation process.

Allow these feelings. Be aware, too, that it may take up to a year or more to banish your phobias or panicky feelings. The more you succeed the greater will be your confidence. EMDR is also about desensitization, but is a much faster process.

Flooding is a more radical type of exposure therapy than systematic desensitisation and for many too extreme. It simply means full exposure to the stressful event, place or situation without any escape or means of avoidance on at least a daily basis. Generally there is no preceding relaxation techniques, but the advantages are that it works quickly. Generally nowadays counsellors use a less severe form of exposure called graduated exposure. It is similar to systematic desensitization, but it exposes the person to other less fearful stressors, progressively graduating to more severe ones. Initially the person will outline a list these dreaded situations, and the counsellor will discuss them at length.

If actual exposure is a step too far for you, imaginal exposure is a useful technique, but it is not as effective as systematic desensitization, graduated exposure or flooding. This involves imagining yourself taking the steps in the actual exposure exercises. Create a detailed picture of the situation, using as many of your senses as you can to make the experience as real as possible. Look around at the scene you have created, see what is happening, and pay attention to your feelings and your thoughts. Be aware of your body sensations, look at your behaviour, listen to sounds and check for particular odours. Remember that the fear comes from experiences blocked in your brain containing images, sounds, thoughts, feelings and body sensations. The more accurate the picture you create the greater will be the fear you experience. You will, however, know that you are safe, that you are minimising the fear – inducing experience. When you have practised this for some weeks or perhaps months, move on to the actual gradual exposure knowing that you have already familiarised yourself with the situation in your imagination.

If your fear stems from meeting other people in groups where you feel inadequate and judged, consider the dynamics of conversation. Do people really prefer a knowledgeable person? Do they prefer someone who takes over the conversation, or do they like someone who listens to them and shows and interest in them? If you are plagued with social fear it is easy to forget that people prefer listeners to talkers. Train yourself to listen better. The biggest compliment you can pay another person is to show interest, and this is evident if you train yourself to listen. It will also remove your own self-focus, bring you out of your head and make you attractive to the talker. When you listen carefully, you can ask the right questions, make the right comments and become a better conversationalist. You must be careful, however, not to use listening as an avoidance behaviour or confuse it with reticence.

You can also condition yourself for meeting people by becoming more aware of them as they go about everyday life. This will not involve contact but observation of them and of how you feel about them. As you walk down the street become aware of how you are as people approach and pass you by. Notice if you feel interest, apathy, hostility or fear. Notice if you feel open or closed. This will increase your self-awareness and perhaps increase your empathy for others. It is a type of indirect desensitisation.

Antony and Swinson (2008) suggest that one of the most effective ways of dealing with social fear is to set general aims and then lay out specific goals to achieve these. I have seen this work wonderfully well. You are taking control, deciding what you need to enrich your life and then exposing yourself to the fear of the specific areas you wish to become involved. One of my clients, William, suffered from serious social fear and decided that he would like to learn dancing, swimming, and debating. These are three difficult areas for people suffering from social fear. His specific goals were to join a dancing class in the local town, talk to the swimming instructor in the local gym and join Toastmasters. We explored the possibility of doing one of these to begin with rather than risk being overwhelmed by taking on too much. He successfully joined a dancing class.

Put a section in your fear diary on social fear. If you have difficulty in expressing yourself, writing it can be very therapeutic. It also brings safety, because there is no danger of retaliation or humiliation in a public place. When you write something down in a planned way it can give you a better insight into what is happening to you. Some headings in your diary should include the date, the situation, the triggers, other feelings accompanying the fear, the negative thought patterns that arose, the beliefs that gave rise to the thoughts and how you behaved as a result of these. When you become aware of your beliefs, you can test how rational they are by checking on your past behaviour based on those beliefs. You will quickly see that many of the anticipations of disaster you had never came true, because your beliefs were not based on reality. They were suppositions and irrational. As mentioned, Antony and Swinson (2008) have different examples of diaries and journals that you might find helpful.

One of the important factors of journaling is the perspective it gives you. You can see if you are making progress and this gives you confidence to continue with this technique. On the other hand if you see that you are not progressing you can analyse what is happening and focus on that. Such regression can be helpful, because it makes you pause and focus on some aspect that is holding you in the fear. It also helps you to look at your behaviours, especially how you practise avoidance, what you avoid, and how bereft your life is and how enjoyable it could be. The human is a social being and it is distressing to detach from other humans. We need company sometimes, even if we have an introvert personality. Introversion is not linked to social fear. It is a personality type, and it is neither better nor worse than extroversion.

You can also use your journal for another effective technique for changing from negative to positive thinking. Divide a blank page in two. On one side write down the negative thoughts from your diary and on the other put in positive and contradictory comments; for example on the left hand side 'I am not interesting. I don't fit in' and on the right hand side write 'I am an interesting person, I am kind, I am loved by my family.' The positive and opposing thought must be relevant to your life and must be true. Pema Chödrön introduces us to the useful idea of positive slogans and how relevant they are to change. If you work with them and practise them they will become part of you. This takes time, patience and perseverance. You can buy posters with positive slogans on the internet, a method Jason used with some success. When he awoke each morning he was confronted by these positive posters staring at him from the walls of his bedroom.

Much has been written about the positive impact of pets on stress and anxiety. Andrea Beetz and her colleagues examined sixty nine original studies on the beneficial effects of owning a pet. There is proof that interacting with a pet has many beneficial results not least on fear and anxiety. Caressing a dog, for example, provides comfort, calmness and a sense of well-being as well as other physiological benefits such as the lowering of blood pressure. There is also a sense of being loved. Equine-assisted therapy has also found to be useful in dealing with many psychological issues. There are equine assisted therapy centres in Europe, including Ireland.

I would like to close this chapter with the reminder that acceptance is one of the best ways to deal with distress. There is a poem by the medieval Afghan poet, Jalalludin Rumi, called *The Guesthouse,* which offers a difficult but worthwhile philosophy to help you, as you explore your distress in counselling. The poem is about greeting all the unwelcome visitors (listed in Appendix 1) that come to you every day.

This being human is a guesthouse.
Every morning a new arrival.
A joy, a depression, a meanness,
Some momentary awareness comes
As an unexpected visitor.
Welcome and entertain them all!
Even if they're a crowd of sorrows,
Who violently sweep your house
Empty of its furniture.
Still, treat each guest honourably.
He may be clearing you out
For some new delight.
The dark thought, the shame, the malice,
Meet them at the door laughing
And invite them in.
Be grateful for whoever comes,
Because each has been sent
As a guide from beyond.

Chapter 6

Fear of Death and of Dying

DEATH HAS EXERCISED THE HUMAN MIND since ancient times. Images of death abound, some originated in ancient civilizations, but that of the skeletal figure with a hooded cloak and scythe goes back to the fifteenth century. This chilling presence was named the grim reaper in the nineteenth century and is the representation most associated with death today. Many philosophies about death have poured from the pens of inspirational thinkers, be they believers, atheists or agnostics. Death is the ultimate existential crisis and is probably the most written about reality of all. Much of what is written is profound, much cynical and intolerant of religious belief and much is common sense. Death is so mysterious and so moving that it has inspired some of the best poetry ever composed.

While fear and depression are widespread, death applies to all from the beginning of human existence. Professor Thomas Langner in his book, *Choices for*

Living. Coping with Fear of Dying, maintains that children as young as three may fear death, although they generally do not have a conscious fear until nine or ten. Childhood neglect and its accompanying sense of danger to survival may bring on a fear of death in children. Other writers also hold that children think about death as well as adults. Based on research about prenatal life, fear of death, i.e. of not surviving, may sometimes be present in the womb. But, the emotional nurturing of the child alleviates fear and helps it to attach securely to a reliable and trustworthy source of protection. Overall, I believe that fear of death is alien to most young people and for those focussed on it, their fear is morbid and pathological. Being young is being vibrant and looking long into the future with optimism. There may be exceptions, but in general children and teenagers are not unduly concerned about death, but have an occasional hazy discomfort about it.

Both birth and death are times of separation, and both can bring fear. Birth, however, soon brings familiarity, but death is possibly a journey into nothingness. It is lonely time when we are separated from our family, our friends and from the world itself. Loneliness is probably the universal feeling experienced by most people irrespective of religion, who pause to think of their demise. It is an existential loneliness, where you realize that no one can travel the path with you, or share your experience. It is probably most pronounced for those lying on their deathbed surrounded by their family. Irvin Yalom, in his beautifully written philosophical discussions on death, argues that loneliness increases the anguish of dying. That loneliness comes from the human as a social being, ending the accustomed connection with other human beings.

Many researchers hold that everyone at some stage has a fear of death, or at least push it into their subconscious. Fear of death is innate, although culture is also an important mediator. Professor Sheldon Solomon and his colleagues are right when they claim that people do not consciously think about death and are oblivious to it, but that it has a pervasive impact on our lives insofar as we are surrounded by it, with stories of war and death in the media. Our immediate world is a place where living and dying are ever present realities. These authors also show that fear of death can be present in various psychological disorders which, unlike death, are partly controllable. They illustrate phobias, OCD, social fear, anorexia and severe depression as examples.

Despite such arguments, it is difficult to accept Amy Wallace's point that death is always in our awareness. She is strongly influenced by the writings of Irvin Yalom, which explore that theme of the ever present fear of death. Even with the benefit of research, writers are influenced by their own experiences, internal and external, conscious and subconscious. The very honest and very open Yalom is aware of that as he draws on his vast experience in dealing with seriously ill people. But, if fear of death is as present in all of us as

Yalom and others claim, why is it that so few present to counselling with it? The conclusion is that they can shelve it and not allow it to interfere with their lives. Amy Wallace makes the interesting point that even therapists are afraid to talk of death. But, when I ask clients about the fear death only a small minority admit to this fear. Yet, there is ongoing research into how to prolong life through genetic means. It is a certainty that someday a way will be found to stop cells from dying.

This type of research and experimentation do not necessarily imply that people wish to live longer because they fear dying. For most it may mean the possibility of enjoying life's benefits for longer. That would be relevant for wealthy people, but for many it would be a never ending life of mediocrity and for others an eternal nightmare of poverty. I was a school Principal for twelve years. The thought of being one for a hundred years would fill me with alarm, to say the least. Death is part of the natural order and living for hundreds of years would disrupt that order with serious repercussions. We would certainly have to migrate from earth to find living space, and the possibility of having children would be severely curtailed. For an interesting view on life extension in the context of immortality you might like to read the very interesting book, *The Worm at the Core. On the Role of Death in Life,* by Professor Sheldon Solomon and his colleagues.

Some Negative Realities Relating to the Fear of Death

WHAT I HAVE FOUND FROM QUESTIONING clients is not a fear of death *per se*. Most people are able to blot this out, but they have other fears which adulterate it, so that dying is a unique experience for each individual and makes fear of death in some form or other relevant to all people. Consequently, you have to check beneath the phrase 'I am afraid of death' for the reason that generates the fear. There are, nevertheless, certainties that we must acknowledge. We must admit that we will get old, get ill, die and leave our earthly goods, families and friends. The young mother may fear leaving a young family, the process of dying inspires fear, facing the unknown can make you fearful, losing control affects others, leaving friends can be an issue, leaving worldly goods is not easy. Being forgotten can obsess some people and this can be seen by elaborate headstones in graveyards. The fear of getting cancer or Alzheimer's are prominent fears in relation to death. Retiring and declining and losing meaning are also part of fear of death, while losing a spouse, a child or parents inspire fear in others.

Of all these related fears, the *process of dying* is a prospect that few care to consider. Yet, in exploring it you can become desensitized to its impact. Any nurse working in a nursing home sees this process on a frequent basis and becomes desensitized to it. Barbara Karnes small pamphlet, *Gone from my Sight. The Dying*

Experience, has a concise account of the dying process. She is the clinical supervisor at the Hospice Care of Mid America in Kansas City and has long experience of witnessing people dying.

While you might be fearful about exploring the process, it is helpful to realise that the dying person frequently get consolation from it. They are very much internally involved and they feel some level of control. Changes begin in the dying person up to three month prior to passing away and the dying process usually begins a few weeks before death. From one to three months prior to death they begin to withdraw from the world and even from family and loved ones, and they prefer touch to conversation. This is the final separation and is accompanied by an inner world of reflection and self-examination. Sleep increases, but the internal processing is active and may include all the fears surrounding death discussed in this chapter. Following this reflection and as they enter the final process two weeks before death, it seems they get a comprehensive understanding of their own mortality. With that comes a decrease in eating, symboliz-ing the withdrawal from life and the move towards death. Sleeping then increases further and some dying people seem to become confused and restless. Their blood pressure lowers, the pulse rate fluctuates and the body temperature varies. They may perspire and their skin colour changes, where it becomes flushed from the fever, blue from the cold, and yellow as death approaches. Breathing fluctuates from very high to very low and congestion occurs, producing a rattling noise in the lungs and throat. Sometimes the dying person gets a surge of energy and is lucid and normal as death gets closer, usually a day or two before passing on, but in the final two weeks the symptoms mentioned above become more intense. The dying person's eyes become glassy and hands and feet turn purple. As death approaches they become non-responsive and slowly slip away.

While many fear the dying process, for a significant number of people the most feared aspect is the possibility of going to Hell. Fear of Hell (Hadephobia) is a real issue for some religious people, especially the elderly. The concept of Hell (and the question of an eternity there) differs in various world religions, but it is never pleasant. Even the different sections of Christianity have refined the concept of Hell and for Muslims one of the names given is Jaheem (blazing fire). Catholic children of my generation (1950s) learned the Butler Catechism by heart, and Hell was defined as *a place or state of punishment in the next life, where the wicked undergo everlasting suffering with the Devil and his angels.* In this dreadful place they were *deprived of the vision of God and suffer dreadful torments, especially that of fire, for all eternity.*

Catechism teaching found its way into folklore with chilling stories about the Devil roaming the land at night, or his cloven hoof under the table as he played cards with rural dwellers. This reinforced the idea of hell and its torments, which inculcated a false sense of sin, guilt and fear among people. Those of my generation had an ambivalent attitude to death, where the darkness of malevolence tainted the brightness of goodness. Many will remember the words of Christ that they learned by rote from the Catechism about His condemnation of the 'wicked' on the last day – *Depart from me, you cursed into everlasting fire, which was prepared for the devil and his angels.*

If you are a believer, the type of God you worship has a profound effect on your fear of death. If you believe in a harsh, condemnatory, unloving judge then your fear of death will be exacerbated and you will incur psychological distress. That was my type of God, and one of the side effects on me was scrupulosity, a tormenting condition, which the historian Joanna Bourke calls a fear of having sinned or offended God in some way. I was tortured by scruples when I was a novice in the Jesuit order. I remember going to confession three times a week confessing the most ridiculous 'sins'. I remember the distress, the stomach churning, and the heaviness in my head when I was tormented by an irrational guilt.

Hell and the idea of a judgemental God are not the only images that strike fear of death into us. Many people standing at the edge of a freshly dug grave are briefly reminded of their own mortality. Cremation does not seem a more acceptable alternative. Being buried or roasted offer no softening of fear of death, although cremation might allay fear of being buried alive! Joanna Bourke in her book, *Fear. A Cultural*

History, traces the history of fear throughout the ages. She reminds us that horrifying images of burial, such as the skull and crossbones, were replaced by more palatable images when graveyards were sculpted into neat lawns with gravel or tarmacked paths. Ancient headstones sometimes contained timely reminders of mortality. Once, when passing through a neglected ancient graveyard near Kilcooley Abbey in County Tipperary, I saw a poem on a faded headstone reminding me, a child of eleven, that someday I would lie in the clay just like the long forgotten occupant of that grave. I am not sure why at such a young age I learned the verse and have never forgotten it.

> *Remember, man, as you pass by,*
> *As you are now, so once was I,*
> *As I am now, so will you be,*
> *So remember, man, eternity.*

Sometimes a death in the family or a serious illness brings us face to face with our mortality and inspire fear. This is seen in the case of Cath Filby as she battled with cancer and underwent frequent checks after her cancer operation. Her husband was profoundly affected by her struggle. You might like to read her book *Breast Cancer. A journey from fear to empowerment.* Some authors believe that suffering such a trauma, or losing someone close to us, can bring on a fear about our own death. The American writer, Erica Brown, writes about the fear of death her grandparents carried long after their liberation from Auschwitz. Forty members of her family died during the Holocaust, and Erica became petrified with fear of death. Her grandparents never spoke about their experience.

While understandable, that is not the experience of everybody. When our child died, the faith of some family members waned, but it returned slowly and became stronger. We believe we will meet him again. While we confronted our own mortality through this loss, none of us experienced fear of death as a result, but our apparent lack of fear and our belief did not shelter us from the pain of loss, which went on for a long time. What I felt was utter terror that my child was snatched away and I could do nothing about it. Rather than a fear of dying, some of us briefly lost our desire to live. Our fear, too, was more about something happening to our other children and having to go through the same unbearable mourning again.

I believe that an insecure childhood attachment impacts on how we think about and deal with death. It makes it more difficult for us to properly deal with the challenges the different stages of our lives, and this includes the final stage. The basic premise is that if we fail to negotiate any stage this causes problems in later stages. Fear of death then becomes toxic. The case of an old woman, Kathleen, clearly illustrates this. I knew Kathleen for many years before her death. She frequently maintained that her faith was important to her. She attended weekly Mass and was involved in parish activities. But, despite her protestations, she seemed to struggle with her religious belief and tried too hard to convince herself of an everlasting life. Fear was always in her eyes as she discussed sickness and death. From the many conversations I had with her down through the years, I knew that her childhood had not been good. Her father was withdrawn, and she described her mother as cold and punitive. In such a home her dependency needs were neglected and she brought some of the issues in Appendix 1 into old age. The most evident of these were fear, anger, a negative outlook, anxiety and an extremely strong controlling impulse. The older she got the less comfortable she was in her skin. When she was in her early eighties I could see that even then she never emotionally envisaged dying, maintaining that she would live well into her nineties. That was enough to momentarily allay the reality and dread of death. She was using what Professor Sheldon Solomon call distal defences, which allay terror by putting death into the distance and relying upon her shaky faith. Unfortunately, Kathleen got incurable cancer in her mid-eighties and knew she did not have long to live. She felt terrorised because of the toxicity injected by her core fear of abandonment. As she lay on the hospital bed, she resisted the dying process, and was unable to deal with the unfinished business that is part of that process.

I felt compelled to write the following poem and capture a moment when I went to visit her in hospital shortly before her death. I was shocked by the sharp stare of her eyes and the terror etched on her face.

I stepped into the ward, gently and softly.
She was half turned from me,
Staring out the window.
A blanket of terror lay across her face,
Her angry eyes were wide with fear.
She turned and stared at me
And at the eternity that called to her,
And she could not go.
Her anger held her in its mute clasp.
I sat by her and bowed my head,
Sadness seeping through my being
At my helplessness and her terror.
Then I took her by the hand and said
'He is waiting for you.'
I meant her husband long departed.
She closed her eyes and I sensed her letting go.
It took her less than an hour to leave.

Kathleen knew that she was mortal and that ultimately she would die. When I saw how she convinced
herself that she would live on, I wondered if the human
has a deep psychological desire for immortality. Pema
Chödrön writes about impermanence, and how change
is part of life. According to her if you seek permanence,
you will always be sad as you witness change at every
turn. Nature dies in winter and comes to life in spring.
Millions of creatures from tiny insects to large animals
die each day. At this time, over fifty million people die
every day. Our youth dies every moment and finally
our old age perishes and we leave. Our world is a living

dying entity and we are part of that eternal process. Death daily stalks the land in some survival societies in Africa, in Middle-Eastern conflicts, and decades ago in Ireland when cruelty, war and disease swept many away. As recent as the 1930s and 40s Tuberculosis was rampant in Ireland and touched many families, including my own when my grandmother and 18 year old aunt perished. Kathleen would have remembered this era and perhaps been affected by it. She was an old woman and it is also likely that the ravages of the Great Famine was in the memory of her family through her grandparents, and subconsciously impacted upon her fear of death.

Younger people, however, also experience fear of death. Peter, one of my friends, is open about his fear of death and his uncertainty about an afterlife. He is happily married and emotionally stable, but experienced an intense fear of death from teenage years onwards. I was startled when he outlined the struggle that can beset younger people with a fear of death. It is a very instructive passage, because it also contains many of the reasons people fear death.

> Blackness. Nothingness. The very very end. No hope. Non-existence. The deepest sense of panic. Dread. Aloneness.

> The above are some of the words I could use to describe how I feel when I wake in the middle of the night with a deep sense of panic about the

end of my existence. I am a healthy middle aged man. I consider myself to have a great life with a wonderful wife with two fantastic children. We are all healthy and financially sound. I lead a busy life, one that I thoroughly enjoy. I am lucky to have a lot of interests and am surrounded by many friends from my school days, to college days, to work, to my local community, etc. There is never a dull moment, in fact my challenge mostly is fitting everything and everyone in – this, I consider to be a good complaint. I travel a lot both with work and with my family. I consider myself well educated, street-wise and a person of the world. Then why do I have this massive fear of dying??????

I don't fear much in life except for the usual things like the safety of my children – the normal things that a parent may fear. But, I don't get engrossed in such a fear. I take a positive approach to life and don't allow myself to live in fear of what might be. I consider dwelling on the negative to be a waste of time. Unfortunately for me there is one big exception to this – the fear of my own death haunts me at times. I cannot say how often I think about my own death as I try to banish these fearful thoughts from my head as quickly as they enter. But I will say that this feeling is the most awful panic I have ever felt. I usually get these feelings at night, either as I am dozing off to sleep or sometimes in the middle of a deep sleep, or what feels like a deep sleep. A sudden sense of darkness comes over me, a sense of what I describe to myself as "nothingness". It is the most terrible feeling of non-existence. I suddenly start to think about what my death would be like – not the act of me dying but what of my existence after my death. I sometimes break out in a panicked sweat thinking about the fact that after my death there may be nothing. What if there is no God? What if there is no heaven? What if the human being does not have a soul after all? What will I do if I simply don't exist? What is the point of it all? Will I ever see my loved ones after I die? I can sense all of these thoughts running through my mind. I sometimes wake myself up saying the words "no, no, no"..... In the moment I wake up, panicked and scared, I immediately try to banish these thoughts from my mind. I immediately tell myself that this could not be the case. There must be an after-life, there must be a God, there must be a heaven! I have learned over the years to move on fairly quickly and get back to sleep. But I have never learned how to banish these thoughts from my mind or my dreams for good.

When I dwell on my fear of death I sometimes wonder if my biggest fear is not have a meaning or a purpose in life. In my life today I have a purpose. I try to be a good husband to my wonderful wife. I try to be a great parent and do everything I can for my children. I continue to learn about parenthood every day (mostly from my wife) and provide my children with a happy and fulfilled life. I think about everything I can do to ensure a safe passage for them into adulthood. I take the time to continue to a big part in the lives of my family of origin. I try to take the time to engage positively with my parents, my sisters and my nieces and nephews. I work very hard in whatever job I do. I take a caring leader approach to my role as a manager and devote a lot of time to people's wellbeing and professional development. I genuinely care about the people who work for and with me. I deliver top quality results and make a difference in whatever role I am in from a work point of view. I carve out a significant amount of time to working in the community. I feel like I mean something to those people in my life and I truly value this. I guess the question is do I fear dying or do I fear losing my meaning/purpose in life?

I have never really spoken to anyone about this fear. I do not think that this fear has a negative effect on my life or on the lives of those around me. I often think about when these thoughts, this fear started but I cannot say when they started. I have had this fear for many years but do not know if it started when I was very young, a teenager, after I was married or after my wife and I had children. I cannot think of anything that has triggered it. Now that I write about it I cannot even say the last time I had a "fear of death panic attack". It feels like I experience this deep fear about once every month or two – but I cannot say for sure. I am guessing the reason for all this lack of clarity is the fact that I do my very best not to pause on these thoughts and in fact to banish them from my thoughts as quickly as I can. Maybe this fear is something I should "deal with"? Maybe I should think about seeing a professional who could help me deal with it? Or maybe this fear will go away or fade away over time as I get older? Maybe I will be able to find safety in a deeper faith and belief in God? Maybe there is a wonderful after-life when I will live on after my death and continue to mean something in the new world I will live in............................I do wish I could find a way to dispel this anxiety from my life."

So, despite his emotional stability, Peter is afflicted by a pathological fear of death, whose roots are not clear. But his train of thought is clear. The words he uses at the beginning are significant – *Blackness. Nothingness. The very very end. No hope. Non-existence. Dread. Aloneness.* The fear of annihilation is a very real one for most people who think of death, but the issue with Peter is his obsession with it. That makes his fear morbid.

Margaret, one of my younger clients, however, had a clear perception of why she had such a strong fear of dying, and probably mirrors the thinking of other younger people. I was surprised when, tears welling in her eyes, she expressed the depth of her fear. She had everything to live for, a kind husband, plenty of money and three lovely children. When I helped her explore her fear, I discovered that she had a strong fear of dying because her children would be left without a mother. She told me that she did not fear death itself or of going into the unknown, but of her children being left without a mother. Margaret's fear is about losing the love and connection she had with them, but this is true about all connection ceasing. We are born to love but that too must be relinquished. The 23 year old poet, John Keats, in his 1818 sonnet, *When I have fears that I may cease to be*, while recognising the swift passing of time, laments the prospect of losing the world of love and romance, which ultimately becomes insignificant in the shadow of death. He died three years later. There is much to learn from the sadness and reality of his poem –

> And when I feel, fair creature of an hour!
> That I shall never look upon thee more,
> Never have relish in the fairy power
> Of unreflecting love – then on the shore

Of the wide world I stand alone, and
   think
Till Love and Fame to nothingness do
   sink.

The prevailing and more mundane image I get with the passing of time is that of my house. I built it in 1972 and it represented stability, family and putting roots down. It was **my** house. I made many alterations to it throughout the years, but it was always my house. Now as I enter my seventies, I am beginning to see that it is my house for a time only. I always knew that, but it is now a more frequent thought. I want to hang onto it for as long as I can! That is a sad thought and it reflects the reality that we own nothing, that we will leave all our possessions and wealth. There is nothing wrong with being rich. Wealth can enhance our lives, but we cannot base our happiness on it. If we do, the thought of death may be much sharper and more painful for us. Death is a cold reminder that possessions are temporary. They are symbols of effort, achievement, happiness and sadness. They are emblems of living and we should enjoy them and then let them go.

As we get older we have more reminders of the passing of time. I had two fiftieth anniversaries in 2013. One was for the Leaving Cert Class of 1963 and the other for my entry to the Jesuit Novitiate in Emo that same year. In both cases, most of us had survived the fifty years and we all seemed to be in good health. My memory, particularly of the novices, none of whom I had met in fifty years, was of lively teenagers all with full heads of hair of different hues. Now before me I saw a large group of elderly men, some with thick white hair and some, alas, with shiny bald domes. It was a shock and I wondered when the scythe would cut a swathe among us. That thought lingered for a while before finally drifting away. I found it interesting to suddenly see aging in the context of those fifty years, a 'sudden' transformation from teenagers to elderly people. I began to understand Milton's preoccupation with the passage of time, that 'subtle thief of youth,' when he was only twenty three.

Sadly, there are many twenty three years olds who have a greater fear of living than of death. Many young people for various reasons opt out of living by taking their own lives. It is difficult to comprehend the agony and distress this causes to families and friends. This thought prevents many people from committing suicide, but for others the pain is so great that they cannot bear to live.

When I was a child in the 1940s and 1950s suicide was practically unheard of in Ireland, although that does not mean that it did not happen. But, certain factors probably kept the suicide rate down. In those days, for example, there was a severe stigma attached to it. It was also illegal and was termed *felo de se* (felon of himself) and in England continued to be a crime until 1961. It was a crime in Ireland until 1993. This criminalisation goes back to the Middle Ages, when those who attempted suicide were cruelly punished.

From the Fourth Century onwards the Christian church considered suicide a serious sin and the Council of Braga in 563 ordered that suicide victims be denied funeral rites. Ultimately suicides were forbidden burial in consecrated ground. That has ceased, although like most Christian churches, the Catholic Church opposes the act of suicide. The 1997 Catechism of the Catholic Church maintains that *everyone is responsible for his life before God who has given it to him. It is God who remains the sovereign Master of life. We are obliged to accept life gratefully and preserve it for his honour and the salvation of our souls. We are stewards, not owners, of the life God has entrusted to us. It is not ours to dispose of.* This is similar to Plato's teaching that life is a gift from God.

Ironically, in the first part of the twentieth century the factors mentioned above probably prevented many suicides, but at the same time caused suicide to be a source of shame to families, and prevented reporting. It was a failure to understand the suffering of the suicide victim and to grasp the reality of divine love. It was an outrage and a contradiction of the love shown by Jesus in the gospels. Thankfully, at parish level in recent years those who commit suicide are treated with compassion like all other deceased people. The stigma seems to have largely gone also. It is also true from current research that church goers are less likely to commit suicide than others.

Whether there is a relationship between this and the increase in the rate of suicide in some countries is debatable. It is now generally agreed by researchers that there is an under-reporting of suicide in all countries where the classification of death is falsified and suicide is coded as something else. What is clear is that it is universal and is one of the leading causes of death today. Currently there are 800,000 suicides on a global level, with one in a hundred fatalities caused by suicide in the UK and the US. On average there are 117 reported suicides per day in the US, while at least half a million people self-harm. The Samaritans reported 6,188 suicides in the UK and 451 for Ireland for 2015 . More women than men attempt suicide, but about five times as many males as females commit suicide, although it is suspected that there may be greater under-reporting of female suicide due to the methods they use. The trend is reversed in China where more women than men commit suicide. Suicides range from adolescence to old age. The greatest number of suicides in most countries, however, is middle age, although in Ireland the number of young men committing suicide is alarming. George Howe Colt in his well-researched book, *The Enigma of Suicide*, refers to studies maintaining that many teenagers think about suicide quite frequently.

According to Adele Ryan McDowell in her excellent book, *Making Peace with Suicide. A Book of Hope, Understanding, and Comfort*, there are three common factors in all suicides – pain, disconnection and disenfranchisement. The pain is not only physical, but also psychological, emotional and spiritual. Disconnection is a survival mechanism to protect us from the awful pain of loneliness, but it only adds to our feeling of isolation. As you have learned at the beginning of this book, children who have an insecure attachment to parents generally disconnect and they bring that disconnection into adult life. Disenfranchisement is a feeling of total alienation, a complete lack of connection with others and feelings of powerlessness and helplessness.

Yet despite being disconnected or emotionally chaotic about a quarter of suicides leave notes. Some are clear and some are confused, reflecting the state of the suicide victim's mind. The notes with most clarity ask for forgiveness, express love, give advice and accept full responsibility. This may play a small role in helping the survivors of suicidal loss to manage their grief.

As you will see there are many reasons why people commit suicide, but there is one certainty that fear of living is greater than fear of dying. As he stood on the edge of a cliff, Matt Haig uses the symbol of the balance, with fear of death finely balanced against fear of living. He writes that an ounce more terror and the scales would have tipped and he would have jumped to his death. Fortunately, the scales tipped the other way and Matt lived to write his book *Reasons to Stay Alive*, which is one of the best books on depression.

The suicidal impulse is a symptom of some other problem that people have. Research shows that 90% of suicides come from three sources – mental illness, substance abuse, or a combination of both. I am concerned about the term mental illness. What is the definition of mental illness? Psychiatrists label depression as mental illness, although it is frequently no more than a reaction to negative circumstance. It is the experience of having a low mood. When my child was killed I suffered from depression. I was not mentally ill. It is difficult enough for those left behind to deal with suicide, but to be told that the person who committed suicide was mentally ill is intolerable. It is, however, true that depression is closely linked to suicide and there is some evidence that depression may have a genetic component. About 13% of those suffering from Schizophrenia, a mental illness, also commit suicide.

Apart from depression, people find living intolerable for other reasons such as broken relationships, the breakdown of a marriage, or having major financial problems. Others commit suicide because of severe anger, out of defiance, serious illness, alcohol abuse, the imposition of austerity during economic downturn, loneliness, severe loss, isolation, bullying, feeling worthless, hopelessness, confusion and childhood abuse. Studies show that parental suicide makes other members of a family vulnerable to taking their own lives. An absence of meaning is probably one of the greatest causes of suicide. Generally, it is a combination of factors that drive people to suicide. But, many people endure these problems and do not commit suicide, which suggests that behind all of these lie other underlying reasons. If you wish to examine the many reasons behind suicide you might like to read *Suicide. A Modern Obsession* by Derek Beattie and Patrick Devitt, which also contains a detailed list of suicides per country on a global level, showing an extremely uneven pattern.

Suicide can also have a cultural aspect and some ancient societies such as the Celts, the Goths, the Vikings and many more, encouraged suicide as a way of entering Paradise. George Howe Colt has many examples of cultural suicide in his book.

When fear of living, for one reason or another, becomes stronger than fear of dying many people wish for death, although most do not commit suicide. This has always been the way. In nursing homes very old people frequently express to care nurses their wish to die, and their frustration at living. Many people would like help to die, and assisted suicide has become a major issue in recent years. Assisted suicide is where the physician provides the patient with a lethal dose that is administered by the patient at a time of his choosing, whereas euthanasia is where the physician administers the lethal dose.

There are different organisations advocating assisted suicide, mostly operating in US, although the movement is spreading throughout the world now. John Wyatt's book *Right to Die. Euthanasia, assisted suicide and end-of-life care*, lists various writings, legislation and organisations on the right to die from 1870 to 2015. One of the earliest and most prominent was the Euthanasia Society of America founded in 1938, whose work was affected by the Nazi policy of euthanasic atrocities in the 1940s. In the 1960s and 1970s the right to die movement recovered its dynamism and the president of the ESA founded the Euthanasia Educational Council established in 1967. This was followed by the Hemlock society founded in US in 1980 by Derek Humphrey, who helped his wife to die when she had terminal cancer. This was later changed to Compassion and Choices. Currently, the World Federation of Right to Die Societies encompasses thirty eight right to die organizations in twenty-three countries.

Such organisations were always beset by controversy not least encapsulated in the campaign by Dr Jack Kevorkian, who was eventually sentenced to imprisonment. You can read about this in Michael DeCesare's book *Death on Demand. Jack Kevorkian and the Right-to-Die Movement*. Kevorkian served eight years in jail for assisting death in 130 cases. He invented an apparatus that the person who wished to commit suicide could operate.

Since most world religions condemn suicide, it can be expected that they vigorously oppose euthanasia and assisted suicide, although a few individual senior clerics are beginning to change their minds. Their theology is clear, but Governments are in more of a dilemma. Legislation has been passed in some countries such as Belgium, the Netherlands, parts of Canada, Germany, Switzerland (the Dignitas Clinic), and some states in the US, which allow assisted suicide. The laws in these countries are carefully crafted and unique to each country in dealing with a sensitive and complex subject that arouses high levels of controversy. In most countries after decades of debate, a majority of the populations support assisted suicide, and, therefore, it is likely that governments will eventually pass laws allowing it. You can get a good insight into the current public debate on what is a moving target in John Wyatt's book. He also looks at the pros and cons of taking one's own life, and makes some strong philosophical and religious arguments against the practice.

Wyatt points out that the debate among people has changed from the issue of escaping from pain to one of choice, control and independence. The diseases in question have also changed from physical pain to neurological diseases such as motor neuron disease, stroke, MS, and Locked in Syndrome. Physical pain can be greatly eased by hospice staff who address the physical, psychological, spiritual and relational dimensions of the patient's distress. This means using the best medicines, providing a suitable psychological environment of human contact, counselling, and emotional support, encouraging family visits, and placing prayer and worship (if appropriate to the patients beliefs) at the centre of the process. That is the essence of palliative care.

Positive Mediators of fear of Death

LEAVING ASIDE ALL THE ABOVE MENTIONED negative factors relating to the dark side of death, we have to ask why some people can prepare so calmly for it, if, as some writers claim, fear of death affects most people? I have known many Catholics with fatal illnesses, who write detailed plans for their funeral ceremony, with specific prayers and personal items for the Offertory. My friend and counselling colleague, Catherine, got terminal cancer in her late forties, and laid out particulars of her funeral Mass in great detail. She invited me for tea shortly before her death and greeted me with a smile of dark humour, inviting me to partake of the 'last supper.' Perhaps, instinctively, she was using humour to diminish death, which, as she knew, was then very near. Thomas Langner writes that humour is one of the bulwarks against the threat of death and devotes a chapter of his book to it. It could also be that Catherine was subconsciously trying to get some control over the crisis that could have been overwhelming. Control in that respect is empowering and comforting. While dying from cancer is slow and distressing, Catherine went through the dying process peacefully. She was surrounded by love and care. The hospice nurse provided solace and practical assistance that prepared her for her journey.

Catherine was not a particularly religious person, but she had an innate spirituality. Research shows that for many people a strong religious faith is a significant comfort when facing death, providing that a deep conviction lies behind that belief, and an equally strong conviction of the loving goodness of God. Catholic children who grew up in the aftermath of the Second Vatican Council (held from 1962 until 1965) saw the

Devil and the flames of Hell relegated and that element of fear of death no longer exists for the younger generation, who experience a more gentle theology based on forgiveness and love. Yet, formal religion is generally more important to older people, and is a positive mediator of the fear of death. I was puzzled that my father seemed to wish for death, and as he lay dying for six weeks, until he lapsed into silence, he quietly spoke to me of his desire to meet his parents and siblings, who had predeceased him. The paternal side of my family had one common characteristic. They had a deep religious faith and a strong conviction that there was an afterlife. People who lived from the early to the mid part of the Twentieth Century would have been imbued with a strong religious faith, handed down for centuries and passed on to people of my generation. Most studies show that fear of death decreases with advancing years and many of the people I met who approached death with equanimity were elderly. This is somewhat puzzling, considering how they were brainwashed with fear of hell, but they strive to live a good life and that supplements the positive impact of their religious belief.

Apart from formal religious belief, the concept of reincarnation also lessens fear of death. Reincarnation is an ancient spiritual or philosophical concept also termed metempsychosis, meaning the transmigration of the soul. It literally means 'entering the flesh again' and is similar to the Buddhist concept of rebirth, which in effect, means never dying, but living in different ages, in various bodies that may be human, animal or spiritual. These include winged creatures, underwater creatures and even existence on different planets such as Mars. Some tribal civilizations also believe in reincarnation and up to one third of Christians believe in it, although it is opposed by the Christian, Islamic or Orthodox Judaic religions. The Christian churches see it as conflicting with the doctrine of Heaven and the salvation of man through the sufferings of Christ. But, for many it is a comforting concept and in that context you might like to read the accounts given by Richard Bullivant in his book, *True Real Life Stories of Reincarnation*. Bullivant holds that several famous scientists believe in incarnation. He refers to hypnosis as a method of discovering previous existence, but does not challenge the concept of false memories in relation to that particular discipline.

While there is evidence that religious faith and reincarnation are positive mediators of fear of death, atheists and agnostics have written inspirational material about death and many have no greater fear than believers. Interestingly, some writers believe that there is no such thing as atheism, but that there is an evolutionary reality that is deeply wired in the human that makes all people believe in a higher power. These writers claim that atheism is psychologically impossible. What is certain is that all humans are intrinsically creative and spiritual and have the ability to connect, and this is also seen in some works written by atheists and agnostics. We can discard those that criticise or scoff at religion, but there are many that teach us how to live and, therefore, how to die. In his book, *Love's Executioner*, Irvin Yalom, a confessed atheist, makes the valid point that fear of death is always more severe in those who have not lived their lives fully. The agnostic writer Julian Barnes admits to fearing death and his humorous writing may be a conscious effort to moderate it. He does not believe in God, he writes, but he misses Him and he dislikes atheists!

The question arises as to how nonbelievers get the emotional comfort believers get from their faith when facing death? Atheists rely on their own individual philosophies. They may see death as the final farewell of a long series of goodbyes throughout life, and experience sadness at that ultimate ending. For others, the present life is merely part of the timelessness of eternity. They will return to that timelessness where they 'existed' prior to conception. For them it is lights out and then nothing, and many do not fear that. They see death as a unique experience in life's journey, although others fear its finality. There are atheists who seem to find strength and comfort in becoming part of the earth, which gives new life. Some agnostics tend to rationalise about their ambivalent belief. They see the possibility of life after death as at least interesting. If there is another life, all the better. They will experience it gladly. If there is not, they will be without awareness in their nothingness. Some, however, admit to being uncomfortable with the doubt and the uncertainty.

Believers and non-believers find comfort that they live on through their offspring. Many years ago I brought a small headstone for my grandfather's grave. He was a school teacher and is buried in another family's grave, because there was not a vacant grave in the parish's ancient graveyard. I worry about that little headstone and hope that my children and grand-children will maintain it to keep his memory alive. I am his eldest grandchild, but was only a baby when he died. So, while I have no fear of dying, I would like to think that I will not be forgotten. I do not see a contradiction in this. It is a recognition that death is part of life and life is part of death.

Apart from personal or religious beliefs and philosophies, many people have been exposed to cir-cumstances, which lessened or obliterated their fear of death. Near-death experiences are a widespread phenomenon and have been written about for decades. No doubt, they have existed for as long as the human has been on earth. The American Orthodox monk, Seraphim Rose, details many examples in his book, *The Soul After Death,* and if you are interested, he has an appropriate bibliography. The psychiatrist, Thomas S. Langner, also mentions some best sellers about this interesting phenomenon.

There are different theories about near-death expe-rience, such as neurological, scientific, psychological and supernatural. Some researchers argue that these experiences do not come from the brain, because it cannot create images during unconsciousness, and the source of consciousness cannot even be located. They maintain that during cardiac arrest the brain ceases to function and cannot produce clear, well ordered, thought processes and images. Other neurological theories, however, suggest hallucinations caused by electric stimuli or lack of oxygen. The supernatural theory points to another world beyond ours in which we are connected to a cosmic consciousness. Dr Maureen Venselaar, a Dutch researcher, who has studied many near death experiences, proposes an interesting astro-physical theory that as life ends a process releases exotic energy (light energy or photons) that allow us to travel through space and time. As the body dies more and more photons are released and a new body of light is created. The interesting American lawyer, Nanci Danison, has written three thought-provoking books about her unusual near death experience. She claims that she was immersed in new knowledge and understanding, undergoing a process of spiritual awakening. She outlines this process in great detail, which involved merging with the Source and acquiring new knowledge of creation and the evolution of mankind. She calls each insightful journey a documentary and her unusual narrative has drawn the attention of skeptics and would probably be disowned by the churches.

Of the thousands of stories that have been told, most show the near-death experience in a favourable light with a minority describing it as terrifying. The vast majority of people, however, felt comfort and peace, and subsequently acquired a deep belief in another existence. As research deepens, the scepticism of scientists about near-death experiences as evidence of another existence seems to be changing. One important factor is the similarity of the experience across cultures. In most of the positive ones, the clinically dead person frequently has an out of body experience and sees a white light increasing in brightness and containing a mysterious and welcoming being. The common understanding is that this being has come to guide them. Generally there is mind communication from the being challenging the 'dead' persons to reflect on their lives.

Many of these clinically dead find themselves in the presence of deceased members of the family, who form a protective presence around them. Some also hover above those who are trying to revive them and show an interest in what is happening, but feel a deep loneliness because they cannot communicate with them. What makes these stories credible are accounts of how they can describe not only what is happening in the immediate room, but even in adjoining rooms or at a distance. Others relate that they found themselves in places of great beauty and serenity in rural settings or in cities of light, which they understood to be Heaven. People of all religions and no religion have reported similar experiences and few wished to return to their mortal state. Significantly, their fear of death vanished from then on and they looked forward to it as a comforting and even enjoyable experience.

There are other positive mediators of fear of death that you can employ that will help you to emotionally accept the reality of death. They provide a comfort zone that lessens its impact. The most crucial one is to appreciate life and feel that you have lived it well. The title of Amy Wallace's book gives the most appropriate message – *Fear of death. It's about life actually*. Try and reshape your thoughts about life and death. Remember that human life is much more than survival and dying, but about being in the moment, about living and experiencing as much as possible in the short time that you are here. About relating to others. No matter how long you live, it is only a short stay and you should try to make the best of its joys and sorrows. There is an adage in the story *An Beo* by Liam Ó Flaithearta that sums up the brevity of our lives – *'is gairid é an t-aistear is faide ón mbroinn go dtí and fód* (short is the longest journey from the womb to the grave). The Gaelic speaking people on the islands were close knit and their saying *ar scáth a chéile a mhairimid* (we live in each other's shadow), had an underlying message of sharing and interacting in times of hardship and of happiness. The autobiography of Peig Sayers, *Peig*, is inspiring, although the sanitised version was probably boring for the thousands of school children, who had to study it for their Leaving Certificate. Peig lived on the Great Blasket for many years, where she suffered enormous distress through poverty, illness and the death of her husband and five of her eleven children. Yet, she managed to remain cheerful and patient. Despite her suffering, she combined kindness with a jovial and mischievous sense of humour and a philosophical acceptance of death.

Peig had a deep sense of empathy for others, and this is something we should strive to have. Empathy empowers us more than any other feeling and takes away our fear. It is a formidable cushion against fear of death. It is almost a way of being and applies not only to those with whom we interact, but is an emotional understanding of all people. It is about neighbourliness. Whether you are a believer or not, the Butler catechism has an all-encompassing definition of being a neighbour. The brief question *who is my neighbour?* has a remarkable answer – *My neighbour is all mankind, even those who injure me, or differ from me in religion.*

Focusing upon living rather than upon death, means being conscious of the goodness within you and what you have achieved in your dealings with other human beings, so that when death beckons you can sit in the consolation of having done your best in your mortal existence. It is also about appreciating life and what it has to offer and about having or creating meaning. If you were told that you only had a few months to live, you would experience a profound change not only in how you would deal with others, but in how you would view the world around you. Urban and rural life have their own beauties. If you live in a rural area slow down and remind yourself to look at the countryside – the green fields, the blue or cloudy sky, the hills in the distance, the birds flying across the land, the trees swaying in the wind, and the animals living quietly in the fields. Being aware of the eternal beat of existence is part of your intrinsic spirituality, and makes dying easier. It gives you a sense of gratitude, which enriches your life no matter what obstacles you meet. Gratitude is the greatest of gifts you can give yourself and opens the door to joyfulness. So, appreciate nature in its many guises from the harshness of winter to the warm beauty of the summer. Patrick Kavanagh's poem, *Advent*, is a good source for learning to appreciate nature. Let us look at a few lines from it.

And the newness that was in every stale thing When we looked at it as children: the spirit-shocking Wonder in a black slanting Ulster hill Or the prophetic astonishment in the tedious talking Of an old fool will awake for us and bring You and me to the yard gate to watch the whins And the bog-holes, cart-tracks, old stables where Time begins.

From this you can see that the child finds meaning in ordinary life. The banal is as important to him as some exotic wonder. Meaning not only enriches your life, but it is life giving and it is absolutely essential to gain happiness and to dispel fear. If you underestimate the importance of meaning in relation to fear, take time to read the little book by Viktor Frankl, *Man's search for meaning*, which proposes that no matter how bad the circumstances you can find meaning. Frankl came to this conclusion when he was in Auschwitz and Kaufering (part of Dachau) concentration camps and when all his immediate relatives (apart from his sister, Stella, who was in Australia) perished under the Nazi regime. Meaning comes not only from achievements but from a positive inner life, which enables you to look outside of yourself and to make a connection with a higher power. That connection applies to believers and non-believers and fashions our spirituality, our cushion against fear of death.

Meaning is relevant to all stages of our lives, but it is vital for people who have retired and are entering the final stage of the life span. Work gives meaning and when you retire you can find a vacuum in your life. There is conflicting evidence about the impact of early retirement upon mortality, but the vast majority of studies in Europe and the U.S. show that those who retire early have an increased risk of premature death, especially among the male population. The reasons given are smoking, drinking, poor diet, lack of exercise and reduced income, all of which can lead to anxiety and fatal heart complaints. According to a study in France, delaying retirement can also reduce the risk of dementia. A survey in the U.S. involving 60,000 retired women show that many suffer depression, sadness and anger. These studies do not mention meaning, but there is an obvious case to be made that lack of meaning may underlie these behaviours and emotional symptoms.

You can also find meaning in death itself. When I was a school Principal, one of my teenage students, Linda, died suddenly from a heart attack during school hours. She was taken to hospital and most of the school community were unaware of the tragedy. I locked the office door to prevent news of her death leaking out and causing distress and panic among the students. When I told the staff after school the silence in the staffroom was palpable, and a darkness lay over the school for several weeks.

I drove home with a sorrowing heart that day and spent a long time that night thinking about what I would say to the school community. The word meaning kept coming up in my mind and I realised that it is as important to dying as it is to living. I tried to explain it to the school community at an assembly next morning. To really understand meaning in death I considered the death of an infant, either pre or post birth. I explained to the students that death itself has profound meaning, because it has such an impact on those who are left. If, for example, an infant dies, it leaves the family devastated, sensitive to the brittleness of existence, sensitive to the lives of others, ultimately appreciative of life and changed forever. In dying we can have a greater influence on others than in living. As adults, meaning gives us some degree of control, for an infant it is in being and in dying. If we never had meaning in our lives, the death of our own child drove us to look for it. Julian Barnes jokingly dismisses the death of us poor humans as being of no relevance to the world in general. Yet, although we are individually unknown, our meaning comes from the impact we have in our own very small circle, where we dispense what Wordsworth calls 'little, nameless, unremembered acts of kindness and of love'.

The question now is how would you feel if you were told that you would have to live your entire life again, exactly as you have already lived it? Would you feel happy and joyful or would you feel sad and fearful? If it is the latter, take stock of how you live, how you appreciate the world around you, how you treat others, how you treat your family, how you create meaning, and see what changes you might make in the years left to you. That would be a powerful way to meet the challenge of mortality and the fear of death. You can change your legacy to humanity for the better. That is your choice. Only you can make it.

If you find that there are behaviours you regret, or if you feel that you have not lived a fulfilled life, or have a dearth of meaning, the best way is to look at the life stages, as outlined in the next chapter. Developmental psychology is particularly relevant when it comes to the final stage of our lives, when death is on the horizon. As I mentioned at the opening of this chapter, there is much to be said for the argument that we find it difficult to deal with death, if we are stuck in an earlier stage. So it is imperative that we emotionally explore these earlier stages to enable us to clear the final hurdle. The emotional or soul wounds of early childhood that silently hurt us must be exposed and healed. It is not easy at an advanced age to do this. Elderly people feel that it is disloyal to parents long dead to rake up times of hardship and lack of love. They have to be reminded that they are not criticising their parents, but rather their parenting.

Not appreciating life and not having meaning also prevent how we take care of ourselves, another essential way of dealing with fear of death or its attendant fears. Self-care, both physical, emotional and mental should be a vital element of our lives and will be looked at in more detail in the final chapter of this book. The case of James, one of my clients, is instructive.

> I worked really hard all my life. I never had time for myself or my family. It was all work, work, work. I was driven and had done well in life. I did not smoke or drink, but eventually the hard work, stress and constant rushing affected my health and my heart was affected. I also got vertigo, tinnitus and anxiety. I became exhausted and retired from my job, but eventually found other work. This made me feel good, but my poor self-care dogged me. It was a lifetime habit not to look after myself and it did not change, when I found other work. In autumn of 2015 I had a bad fall in Galway when my head struck a large rock. Unknown to me my brain began to bleed the following week. I was on a blood thinner and that made the problem worse. An initial scan a few days after the fall did not show the bleed and I felt happy, but after eight weeks I was still getting headaches, and my voice began to slur. My handwriting deteriorated and

another scan at my request showed a substantial bleed. The doctor took me off the blood thinner and then the fear began. Many years previously I suffered two mini strokes (TIAs) and now I felt unprotected. The fear grew that I would get another TIA or a stroke. If that happened what would I have in my life? I would no longer be able to go about my normal activities. I would be dependent, unable to physically function. There was a chance that my brain would be flooded and I would die. My fear accompanied me day and night and my mind became negative and began to race. My anxiety and fear built up and became an obsession. I could not sleep and I felt depressed. Eventually my GP calmed me and the fear of getting a stroke receded to some extent. Eventually the bleed stopped and I was able to resume the blood thinner. Looking back I realise that my fear of being disabled outweighed my fear of death.

It might be difficult to see the connection between a large deficit of self-care and the inability to deal with that dangerous crisis. But, the reality is that previous neglect undermined James's capacity to deal with it. How can a work addict suffering constant stress and failing to practise self-care cope with the prospect of getting a stroke and becoming incapacitated or even dying? How can he deal with the loss of meaning that would come if he got a stroke? You can see how the fear increased and he had no techniques to deal with it. James, however, learned from this experience and began to look after himself. He began to walk several times a day and following strong challenges in counselling, practised some of the self-care suggestions in the final chapter.

If you are a non-believer, recall that fear of death is somewhat akin to fear of abandonment, because they are about a threat to survival. Death is the ultimate loss of survival, and people fear annihilation, non-existence, disintegration and ultimately being forgotten. For some the survival threat exists in the early stages of life, and certainly for all at the end of life. Fear of annihilation is a psychic trauma at any stage from beginning to end of life. If you do not believe in an afterlife and you fear annihilation, remember that nothingness holds no memories, all is left, so it is the thought not the reality that frightens. The reality is an abyss, where there is no sorrow, no happiness, no regrets, no anything, and so no need to worry or to regret. You will return to where you were before you, a potential person, were given life and your final mortality will become absorbed in the universe, an insignificant crumb in an infinite cosmos.

Whatever you believe, it is essential to cultivate an attitude of acceptance, which as I have mentioned is the key to healing. Begin with small things such as minor illnesses so that a philosophy of acceptance becomes part of your psyche. This is easier said than done. It is a frame of mind or a personal philosophy built up throughout life. The more you resist the greater the distress you will suffer, the more you accept the more ease you will get, even in the midst of a fatal illness. You saw the impact on Kathleen, who never cultivated an attitude of acceptance in any aspect of her life. Acceptance works. Accept your mortality and your ultimate death. Accept that you will sometimes get ill and will not always feel well. Accept that you might get a serious or fatal illness. Acceptance is about the here and now. Pema Chödrön rightly states that resistance causes suffering. We can say the same about fear. Resisting fear gives it greater power over you. Accepting it loosens its grip.

Acceptance will help you to shun the undesirable defence mechanism of avoidance, which has been mentioned in different contexts here. Most people avoid talking about death, because it causes too much discomfort. In extreme cases some avoid funerals, funeral homes or burials. Desensitisation is as important in fear of death as it is in social fear. More often than not, however, people avoid going to graveyards because of the distress caused at the death of a loved one. The more they avoid, however, the less likely they are to grieve the loss of a loved one. But, the prospect of death, either through old age or serious illness, can also bring grief and grieving is essential to our mental well-being. The grief that accompanies fear of death is known as anticipatory grief, where you experience a milder version of the feelings that come with actual grief. It is important to be open to the feelings of anticipatory grief, knowing, ironically, that you will never experience actual grief! The feelings are the same – shock (being told that you have incurable cancer), anger (that God could allow this to happen), disappointment (that you will be leaving a familiar life), bargaining (that this can somehow be avoided for the time being), and loneliness (at the prospect of leaving family and friends). You can prepare for all of this by accepting the reality of death. If you are a believer or perhaps an agnostic, you could put all of this in a letter to God. If you are an atheist you could write to your higher power. This might seem to be a somewhat bizarre suggestion, but I have seen some good results from it. When our child died, my eldest daughter wrote to God in her despair and the healing power she got was deep and lasting.

As you have seen, the process of dying is one of the most feared aspects of death. Yet most people seem to negotiate that phase and arrive at a calm acceptance of death. At any rate, that is my experience in dealing with dying people. If you have fear of the process of dying I recommend that you read Dr T Sky's book, *The Joy in Dying. Restoring Love and Peace to the Dying Process so Living can Begin.* She helped her brother Neil, through the process and learned about how we can find joy in dying. Neil was a difficult patient for the hospice nurses. He was always an alienated and bitter man and now he angrily fought the process of dying, partly because he had a fear of hell and partly because he feared the process. Because of the type of dissolute life he lived he was unable to access the mental capacity to explore it. In a gentle and loving way T helped him explore his fear, which evaporated when a hospice nurse explained the process in detail to him. T helped him examine his life and the question of self-forgiveness. Her assistance helped Neil to embark on the process of withdrawal and self-examination. What she learned is that unconditional love, forgiveness and acceptance without judgement that death is near, are the key ingredients to the joy of dying.

I will finish this chapter and this book with a poem by Henry Scott-Holland, who was canon in St. Paul's Cathedral of London and a Professor of Divinity at Oxford University. This poem came from one of his sermons in May 1910. Whether you are a believer or not I hope you will find something consoling in it.

Death is nothing at all.
It does not count.
I have only slipped away into the next
    room.
Nothing has happened.

Everything remains exactly as it was.
I am I, and you are you,
and the old life that we lived so fondly
    together is untouched, unchanged.
Whatever we were to each other, that we
    are still.

Call me by the old familiar name.
Speak of me in the easy way which you
    always used.

Put no difference into your tone.
Wear no forced air of solemnity or sorrow.

Laugh as we always laughed at the little
    jokes that we enjoyed together.
Play, smile, think of me, pray for me.
Let my name be ever the household word
    that it always was.
Let it be spoken without an effort,
    without the ghost of a shadow upon it.

Life means all that it ever meant.
It is the same as it ever was.
There is absolute and unbroken continuity.
What is this death but a negligible
    accident?

Why should I be out of mind because I
    am out of sight?
I am but waiting for you, for an interval,
somewhere very near,
just round the corner.

All is well.
Nothing is hurt; nothing is lost.
One brief moment and all will be as it
    was before.
How we shall laugh at the trouble of
    parting when we meet again!

Chapter 7

How to heal the wounds that come from an insecure attachment.

THIS BOOK ILLUSTRATES THE MANY WOUNDS that come from an insecure attachment. Thankfully most people who had an insecure attachment do not suffer all of them, but my experience as a therapist shows that many people suffer some of these wounds. This includes myself. I know that they can be healed to a greater or lesser degree because that is what happened on my own painful journey. I have already looked at some of the ways to deal with specific issues, and I would like to end the book by outlining an overall strategy for dealing with the problems shown in Appendix 1. The impact of these acts like a domino effect, whereby in dealing with one, the others become more tolerable.

I have laid the strategy out under headings, and you can treat them like a menu, choosing ones that appeal to you or that you might feel will help you.

Relationship with Yourself

LIFE IS ALL ABOUT RELATIONSHIPS, RELATIONSHIPS with lovers, parents, children, others and above all with yourself. Relationship with yourself is the most fundamental one, and if that is negative it is very difficult to have a good relationship with others. People with an insecure attachment never have a good relationship with themselves because their basic belief is one of being flawed, which sometimes leads to a degree of self-loathing. The result of this belief is one of self-blame, being hard on yourself, burying your feelings, overworking and abusing yourself in other ways. So learning how to heal it involves the long road of forging a good relationship with yourself that becomes core, irrespective of the circumstances you find yourself in. This is not always difficult, but it is slow because you are dealing with something that has been installed on your brain from an early age. It has become part of you and you know nothing else. I remember long ago, when someone rather crossly turned on me and said '*You had better get a good relationship with yourself*' I felt shock and distress, and was puzzled, because I did not know what he meant. That is how far I was removed from myself! Clearly education or status does not mean self-awareness.

Awareness

AWARENESS IS THE FIRST STEP TO healing the wounds of childhood, and then having the courage to expose and explore the false self. This is about being vulnerable. We often misinterpret what vulnerability really is. If you consult the word vulnerable in a dictionary you will find words like 'weak,' 'susceptible,' 'defenceless,' 'helpless' and 'exposed.' These interpretations are correct in some circumstances, but in the context of healing it means having the strength to reach out, to admit that you need help. Being 'strong' means that you will never ask for help, but carry your burden until it crushes you. And crush you it will, because many of the symptoms in Appendix 1 get worse as you grow older. It might help you to read an informative book on vulnerability by Brené Brown, *Daring Greatly. How the Courage to Be Vulnerable Transforms the Way We Live, Love, Parent and Lead.* It makes the most relevant point that to feel is to be vulnerable. Vulnerability means honesty where there is no hiding, no cover up.

Self-Care

IT IS ESSENTIAL TO BEGIN THE process of healing with the concept and practise of self-care. The whole tenor of this book is about self-care. The idea of looking after themselves is alien to many of those who have an insecure childhood attachment. They are unwittingly harsh on themselves because of their subconscious belief that they are not worth it. They are more inclined to neglect themselves and, for example, may become addicted to work and be driven. In a sense they mirror how they were treated in childhood. If you do not practise self-care you are simply carrying on what was done to you in a childhood in terms of emotional neglect. Self-care, therefore, is about putting value on yourself as a worthwhile human being. It is a holistic concept and involves physical, emotional psychological and spiritual self-care.

Looking after your physical needs is more important than you may realise. If you exercise every day, have regular medical check-ups, and get sufficient sleep and rest you will begin to feel better about yourself. The ancient proverb of the Roman poet, Juvenal, *mens sana in corpore sano* (a healthy mind in a healthy body) is forever true. A healthy diet is also an essential part of self-care. This is well illustrated in Edmund Bourne's workbook, *The Anxiety & Phobia Workbook,* which discusses the type of food that can either increase or decrease anxiety. There are many books on diet, but I would particularly recommend Bernadette Bohan's *Eat Yourself Well* for an interesting exploration of how you can change your diet and achieve better physical and mental health. Cath Filby's story also illustrates the importance of self-care, particularly in the area of diet. Cath was only 53 when she got breast cancer and went through a complicated process of occasional panic attacks, fear, loneliness, physical pain, self-consciousness, chemotherapy, nausea, resentment at losing her hair, and a determination to live. Her instinct was to gain control while struggling with uncertainty and fear on an almost daily basis.

She also practised yoga, specialised visualisation (meditation) and deep breathing and managed to slow down and get a better perspective on life. Sometimes being still is what you need. Listening to water flowing or to gentle music is a soothing and healing exercise. Such gentle behaviour will engender a feeling of peace and well-being in you, and will also make you more inclined to meet your emotional needs. Meeting emotional needs is about self-empathy. If you have not experienced emotional warmth as a child it will not be easy for you to have self-empathy (or, perhaps, empathy for other people). It can take a long time, but if you have the right friends, who affirm you, and if you open yourself to your emotions you will succeed in recognising your emotional needs and ultimately meet them.

Psychological self-care is about self-awareness of how you came to be as you are with the destruction of the true self and the creation of the false self. This involves looking at your thoughts, core beliefs and values. Ultimately it is about healing.

Spiritual self-care is about connectedness to yourself, to others, to nature, to a higher power, to God, to the universe through intuition and positive thinking, cherishing a love for others, trying to see the good in them, and learning to have an optimistic view of human nature. Connecting includes developing a spirit of curiosity. Healing the inner critic is essential to meeting your spiritual needs.

Below is a brief list of practical and simple ways to practise self-care. Choose a few that appeal to you and remember that great benefits can come from a small change of behaviour. There are several internet sites offering numerous suggestions that might suit you, for example Gateways-To–Inner-Peace.com. Other calming techniques are included throughout the book.

Stress reducers

- Get up 15 minutes earlier in the morning, having prepared for the morning the evening before (prepare lunches etc.).
- Use a notebook for reminders of what you have to do.
- Keep all kitchen and outside equipment maintained on a regular basis.
- Carry a book in your car so that you can read if your partner is shopping (or you might like to join him or her!).
- Plan ahead and always have a plan B.
- Allow a quarter of an hour extra to get to appointments or meetings.
- Don't put the bar too high. Keep your expectations and standards at a normal level.
- Count your blessings rather than dwell on the negatives.
- Do things slowly. Begin by tying your laces slowly.
- Turn off your phone when you are relaxing and try to mix with non-worriers if possible.
- Try and walk around for short periods if you have a sedentary job, and even if you take

exercise once a day. **It is now known that sitting all day will undermine the benefits of exercise.**

- Go to bed early and make sure your bedroom is for sleeping/sex.
- Try and be neat. Know where everything is.
- Have a nice environment to live in. Get comfortable chairs and decorate your house nicely (you deserve it).
- Live one day at a time and do stuff you enjoy.
- Be thankful for your health.
- Realise that you have a lot of control over your life and you can choose many behaviours.
- Have a pet.
- Try to look and dress well. This shows that you value yourself.
- Don't cram your day with too much work.
- Be positive in how you think and eliminate destructive and negative self-talk.
- Take proper breaks during the day.

Self-nurturing activities.

- Take a warm bath/bubble bath or have a sauna. Go for a massage, or have a manicure/pedicure.
- Walk on a scenic path in a picturesque park, where you can stop and smell some flowers. Go to the beach, or take a scenic drive. Visit a zoo or fun park.

- Wake up and watch the sunrise, or watch the sunset in the evening or the stars on a clear night. Watching the stars will give you a sense of wonder at the universe.
- Relax with a good book, or play soothing music, or watch a funny video
- Browse in a book or record store or in a clothes shop in a leisurely way. Otherwise do some window shopping.
- Buy yourself a cuddly stuffed animal and play with it.
- Go see a good film or show, or read a book that inspires you. Perhaps visit a museum or another interesting place.

Boundaries

BOUNDARIES ARE SEVERELY COMPROMISED BECAUSE OF childhood insecure attachment. When enmeshment occurs, a parent is unwilling to allow the child to separate and possessive (enmeshing) bonds are preserved, inflicting a long-lasting emotional wound. What happens is that the process of building boundaries is destabilised and when adulthood is reached the individual has poor defences. Boundaries are the key to happiness and it is vitally important to understand what they are. A boundary is a psychological barrier to protect us. There are four main boundaries types – spongy, rigid, gapped, and elastic. Those with a childhood insecure attachment usually have spongy boundaries and are more likely to be people pleasers because they tend to take on the feelings of other people and to fear confrontation. Like a sponge they absorb the feelings of others. Rigid boundaries indicate fear of commitment and make intimate relationships difficult. These, too, are often the result of an insecure attachment, where the child automatically and subconsciously protects himself from the pain and distress of neglect. Rigid boundaries are necessary to protect the child, but are more often than not counterproductive in adulthood. Gapped boundaries mean that there are times when the boundaries are effective and other times when they vanish. They are most likely the result of an ambivalent insecure attachment. Elastic boundaries are the ideal, because they enable you to protect yourself when necessary by pushing away someone who harms you or shrinking to allow others get close. If parenting is healthy you learn boundaries automatically as a child. Parents who emotionally neglect their children, or who are controlling, lack proper boundaries and are unable to demonstrate them to their children. They are most likely to show poor boundaries and frequently infringe upon their children's boundaries.

If you have not learned boundaries as a child, it is encouraging to know that they can be quickly learned as an adult. This can be done through awareness of your behaviour, which is explored with the help of a professional. Listening to your story on a weekly or fortnightly basis, a counsellor will educate you on where you have failed to maintain boundaries. Gradually you will become aware of boundary issues in your interactions with others and erect them accordingly. I have seen this happen on many occasions.

Negative Thoughts Based on Irrational Core Beliefs.

Irrational core beliefs, generating negative thinking, are the hallmarks of emotional childhood neglect. They often stem from frequent direct or indirect criticism in your childhood that generate shame and anger. It is essential that you challenge your beliefs and change your thoughts as part of the healing process. Part of this is changing the negative belief/thought to a positive one. Michelle Skeen, a psychologist practising in San Francisco, has a detailed section in her book *Love Me Don't Leave Me* on core beliefs and a series of questionnaires that would help you to identify them as you try to make sense of yourself. The list below consists of negative and positive cognitions compiled by Robbie Dunton and used in EMDR, which will hopefully will be of help to you in changing from the negative to the positive. This will demand constant practice, but it will empower you. When you substitute a positive for a negative belief the impact can only be beneficial, even if initially you do not fully believe the positive one. If you wish for a more rapid and powerful acquisition of positive thinking you can avail of EMDR, where the installation of positive thinking is one of the eight phases of this therapy. Researchers were astounded at brain activity during this installation.

NEGATIVE	POSITIVE
I don't deserve love	I deserve love
I am a bad person	I am a loving person
I am terrible	I am fine as I am
I am worthless/ useless	I am worthy/ worthwhile
I am shameful	I am honourable
I am unlovable	I am lovable
I am not good enough	I am fine/deserving
I deserve only bad things	I deserve good things
I am permanently damaged	I am/can be healthy

I am ugly	I am attractive
I am stupid	I am intelligent
I am insignificant/ unimportant	I am significant/ important
I am a disappointment	I am ok just the way I am
I deserve to be miserable	I deserve to be happy
I am different	I am ok as I am
I am inadequate	I am adequate
I cannot trust anyone	I can choose whom to trust
I cannot protect myself	I can take care of myself
I cannot be alone/I'll be abandoned	I can be on my own
I am powerless	I have choices

I cannot stand up for myself	I can make my needs known
I cannot be trusted	I can be trusted
I cannot trust myself	I can learn to trust myself
I cannot trust my judgement	I can trust my judgement
I am a failure	I can succeed
I have to be perfect	I can be myself/ make mistakes
I need to be taken care of.	I am independent.
I am to blame.	It is not my fault
I cannot heal my fear.	I can take steps to heal my fear
I have no one to support me	I will make friends
I am unlovable	I am lovable

Remember my client, Nancy from chapter 1! You can see from her situation that she is bound by negative thoughts. She did not feel good enough and that negative feeling coloured her entire outlook. Nancy did not have a good childhood because her dependency needs were not met. Although I have no doubt from her overall story that her parents loved her, she did not *feel* loved, and if you do not feel loved you feel negatively about yourself. If you feel negatively about yourself all your thoughts are contaminated with negativity and you quickly enter into a negative world. It is immensely sad that some people live in a pessimistic bubble all their lives.

The beliefs Nancy learned from such neglect warped her outlook. Beliefs underlie your thoughts, values and behaviour. Beliefs are concepts that you hold to be true and the assumptions you make about yourself. Values are ideas and characteristics that you hold to be important, about how you think things ought to be. Do you think that you are *not good enough,* that you are *worthless, unlovable* and a *disappointment?* If so, you are suffering from childhood insecure attachment, because these four most poisonous beliefs are how you define yourself. Such a definition is crippling and depressing, and of these four maladaptive beliefs that of not feeling good enough is the most pernicious. It intensifies many of our pathological issues. Think of it! Jealousy is certainly based on the belief of not being good enough. If you harbour fear of failure you are convinced that you are not good enough, and similarly social fear, focusing upon being negatively judged by others, is based on your own judgement of yourself as being inadequate. You can even connect the existential fear of death to this belief. For those who believe in an afterlife this negative self-judgement will sharpen a sense of sin, and hence of being judged by God. This irrational fear can also be linked to anger. The more negative your self-belief about yourself is the angrier you are towards yourself and towards the world.

Your Pessimism may be Bred by an Insecure Attachment, but Neural Wiring can be Changed.

BUT, IF NEGATIVE THINKING IS **BRED** in us from emotional neglect as children, we can also **learn** to be pessimistic from the domestic atmosphere, where a negative outlook and critical thinking are the norm. Emotional growth is stunted in a home where parents are in conflict on a continuous basis. Conflict can be physical, verbal or psychological, where weeks of silence prevail following a row. It stands to reason that such children as adults will always expect the worst possible outcomes. But, it is a basic premise that what is learned can be unlearned. It used be thought that the adult brain was inflexible, and that negativity following childhood neglect was hardwired and lifelong. Now we know that our brain (i.e. the neocortex) is pliable and can be rewired because of its capacity to grow new neurons and to create new synaptic connections between neurons. (A synapse is a junction allowing communication between nerve cells). The brain has 100 trillion cells. It is only in the last twenty years that we have learned that it is possible to rewire the brain and this has enormous implications for human development. Looking at it another way, the brain is like an enormous computer with a vast data base of all our experiences and feelings. As mentioned earlier the brain is wired by experiences and relationships as well as genetic factors, and if something happens to you very early in life, the same feelings aroused in those early years will also be triggered later in life, if a similar incident happens. Technically, the Amygdala is alerted. As already mentioned it is one of the important processors of memory, decision making and *emotional reactions*. Astonishingly it only only takes the amygdala 200 milliseconds to trigger the fight or flight reaction. When a childhood trauma occurs it is stored in a neural network that is activated by any subsequent similar negative experiences. The network is thus triggered with its central thought of feeling flawed being stimulated. Positive experiences are not stored in that particular network and only negative ones link to the original trauma. Fortunately, that can be changed to a greater or lesser degree.

How you can Step Back into the Shoes of the Child

A LESS COMPLICATED WAY OF LOOKING at this process is that in certain circumstances you step back into the shoes of the child. Occasionally, I became an eight year old Principal whenever I met a particular 'strong' female trustee of the school, who had authority over me in my role, and who reminded me of my mother. My anger, shame and fear immediately surfaced when she (unfairly) blamed me. All the negative feelings I had in my childhood were immediately resurrected and poked their unpleasant heads into my consciousness. This is a common experience of those who had an insecure attachment to a parent.

Stepping back into the shoes of the child can be explained in various ways. Understanding the triggers involved is helpful. For example, in the above case there were several factors that triggered old memories that were trapped unprocessed in my brain – a resemblance to my mother, the attempt by this woman to shame me, her forceful personality and the fact that she had authority over me. When I reflected on this I made the connection and it made sense to me. I was then able to repave my negative neural emotional pathways with positives. This takes patience and perseverance using many of the techniques discussed throughout this book, particularly substituting the positive for the negative. As you do this, listen for the ancient voices that criticised you so often and hand back the negative messages to them. You are handing back the shame that a parent, a caregiver or perhaps a teacher has poured on you. Susan Jeffers makes the point that actually saying out loud positive statements make them more powerful, so when you have handed back the shame go back to the list and say out loud the positive statements you have written. Speaking the positives should then be practised frequently. The frequency adds to the power of the spoken word and creates a program in your brain that eventually will largely overlay the negatives stored there. I practise this when I arise in the morning and the positive statements become rooted.

Concentrating on your strengths in a concrete way is very helpful in reinforcing positive thinking. I did a long course with the Dublin Rape Crisis Centre and the facilitator showed the group a technique for bolstering confidence following a trauma. It takes about two hours and consists of highlighting your strengths in writing. You will need a helper for this who will write each strength that you mention on a card and lay them around you. You may be surprised at the number of cards surrounding you. Strengths might be simple realities such as having a job, a car, house, good education, kind partner and good friends.

Forgiveness

WHEN YOU HAVE PROCESSED AND HEALED your childhood wounds, you may arrive at a stage of forgiveness, which will give you power and enable you to stand in adult shoes and dissolve your fear. Forgiveness, however, is a complex issue. It is not about condoning the narcissistic parenting, which caused you distress in your adult life. Neither is it about the reaction of the person that you forgive, but about you. As I was writing this book one of our priests spoke about forgiveness in his Sunday sermon. "Forgiveness is about healing your own heart", he said. This puts the focus on you and makes it easier to forgive, and allows you to forgive even if a parent denies or fails to own up to his or her behaviour. This so rarely happens that we would seldom forgive if we felt only repentant parents deserve forgiveness. Marcia Cannon offers a three faceted explanation of forgiveness, which involves accepting the reality of what happened, accepting that you have grown and become more self-aware and where you wish healing and growth for those, who caused you such pain. This does not mean that you condone the emotional or physical neglect that you suffered, but understand that the person who tries to hurt you has their own issues and their own hurts. Forgiveness and compassion open the gateway to freedom.

Forgiveness is a feeling not a thought. For me, at any rate, cognitive forgiveness is not healing. You can tell yourself as many times as you wish that you forgive somebody, but unless you feel it you will not find healing. It can come suddenly, but it may only come following a long period of emotionally processing your childhood. We cannot force forgiveness and it may never arrive. But if it does, embrace it and its healing effects. I was fortunate to experience this feeling of forgiveness, but only after years of processing my own pain and healing my emotional wound. I believe that forgiveness, like grief, is a very personal process and comes to each one of us differently. It arrived suddenly and unexpectedly for me, and it is difficult to describe the sense of calmness and of peace I experienced as the forgiveness flooded my spirit.

Forgiveness can also come from recognizing not only the pain of your parents, but the problems besetting your wider family. Using a genogram can help get an insight into distresses within the wider family. Thich Nhat Hanh reminds us that we carry the wisdom, happiness and sorrow of generations before us. The therapist, Fr Jim Cogley, does helpful workshops on ancestry, and you might like to read his series of creative books, *Wood You Believe*.

Grieving

FORGIVENESS CAN OCCASIONALLY BE PART OF grieving, and grieving is one of the most important ways of healing the loss of a childhood from an insecure attachment. Grief is ultimately about acceptance and letting go. This will bring peace, but letting go is a process not a thought. If the process is not completed letting go will be superficial and the loss will continue to torment you. Effectively, it is not only about letting go of grudges, but rather about letting go of hurt. A lost childhood and almost a loss of self (identity) is a major trauma. In order to grieve properly you first of all have to make sense of your story so that you have a coherent narrative and then you feel the pain. In a sense this coherent narrative is part of the cognitive part of grieving. You cannot heal from the trauma of insecure attachment until you understand what happened to you.

Grieving is one of the painful paths you will automatically tread as a way of dealing with so profound a loss. It is also one of the most important ways to heal. Grief comes from the Latin *gravis*, meaning heavy, and reflects the heaviness that falls upon us when we are bereaved. Bereavement comes from the word 'reave' which is to snatch away or to plunder. The robbery of our childhood is a long drawn out affair and equally it can take some time to come to terms with it. The traditional way of dealing with grief was laid down by Elizabeth Kubler Ross, a Swiss-American psychiatrist, and involved a five stage cycle of denial, anger, bargaining, depression, and acceptance.

If grief refers to the personal experience of loss, mourning refers to the process that occurs following the loss. The word mourning is related to the Old Norse *Morna*, meaning to pine away. Grieving is about thinking, feeling, and behaving. Feelings are the door to healing and sadness is the key to that door. Everybody grieves differently, but there is a recognised range of feelings, and we must remember that it takes great courage to open up to these grief feelings of loneliness, anger, regret, longing, sadness, depression, guilt, disbelief and anger. But, because of the shell that the child constructed in the face of abandonment and which now envelops the adult, it can be very difficult moving from a cognitive exploration of your loss to emotionally re-experiencing it. It is tempting to turn away from the pain of loss when exploring childhood.

One of the most important grief feelings is anger and it is dangerous to bury it. I am not even sure if it is possible to do so, although some people assure me that they do not feel angry at childhood injustices. Anger in grieving childhood is justified and can be very strong. When you become aware of the distress from childhood you will then direct your anger at the appropriate person, although it can also be projected at an innocent caregiver until it is properly explored. If being angry was not acceptable in your home when you were a child, it can be very uncomfortable. Perhaps you might feel that it is wrong or at least disloyal to feel angry with a parent, who has done her best for you. If so, try to remember that anger is only a feeling, distinguish it from angry behaviour, and realise that your anger is not at the person you tried to love but at her behaviour. The trauma of anger must be healed or you will suffer physically and mentally.

J. William Worden, Professor of Psychology at Rosemead Graduate School of Professional Psychology, California, created another construct for grieving, which I find useful when facilitating the grieving of losing a childhood. He outlines the **tasks** of grieving which is empowering because it means you have some say in how you heal. The first is to accept the reality of this loss, which is one of the biggest losses the human can endure. I am convinced that the loss of childhood has to be fully explored, if possible on an emotional level, to understand its enormity. It is a decision we make, and not everyone is able to do so. The second task is to work through the pain of grief, which means experiencing the wide range of feelings that accompanies loss and mentioned above. Loneliness is one of the most poignant feelings you experience if you suffer the loss of a childhood. I have never yet met a person whose dependencies needs were not met, who did not have an internal and unique loneliness. This type of loneliness is a lack of connection by the inner child with the primary caregivers, so it does not matter whether you are with people or alone, that ancient loneliness lives in you. It is a type of existential loneliness. When you have the courage to open yourself to the distress of these feelings then you can move on with life, the other task of mourning.

Because the loss of childhood is so complex, it helps if you know what you are mourning. When you grieve the loss of childhood you mourn many things –

- The loss of feeling loved.
- The loss of warmth and affection.
- The loss of being attended to where your parents were interested in you as a developing child.
- The loss of a parent who would have nourished you emotionally.
- The loss of a parent with particular character-istics which you value.

- The loss of a parent who values you and includes you in his or her emotional life.
- The loss of connectedness.
- The loss of self-esteem
- The loss of inner peace.
- The loss of a close confidante.
- The loss of confidence.
- The loss of inner calm.
- The loss of being directed and learning how to do things.
- The loss of identity and knowing who you are.

Check for other losses that you experienced in the context of a lost childhood and if you grieve the loss of childhood successfully, you will gradually emerge from confusion and claim your identity. The severity of these losses will determine the intensity of your grieving. Such losses can range from mild to severe. I remember long ago sitting in the lobby of a hotel in Galway reading Carl Rogers book *On Becoming a Person*. I had little self-awareness at that time, but when I saw the words 'the real self' I suddenly realised that I did not know who I was, a psychological condition that John Bradshaw rightly describes as the 'greatest tragedy of all.' Despite being in a public place I was unable to stop the tears of loss running down my face. That was the moment when my rehabilitation began, and I travelled a long road after that to find peace. My grieving has long since stopped, but I am still travelling.

Knowledge of Defence Mechanisms

WHEN OUR CHILDHOOD IS UNDERMINED, IT is very common to develop what are known as defence mechanisms, which we may find momentarily useful, but ultimately they are counterproductive in trying to deal with childhood issues, so understanding the most common ones will help you to deal more effectively with them. A defence mechanism is a (generally) unconscious mental process to avoid distress or distressing situations and the following are ones that you should be particularly aware of when dealing with attachment issues.

Avoidance. This can be conscious or unconscious. If it is conscious it is more a coping strategy, and unless it is to avoid harm it is an unhealthy behaviour. It is most often used in the context of social fear, and may become habitual and stifling. Ultimately the consequence of avoidance can be isolation.

Denial. This is an inability or even a refusal to accept reality. Because the reality of a neglectful childhood is 'normal' to the victim, it can take a long time for a person to even see the link between childhood and adult problems. When cases like this arise there can be no emotional experiencing of childhood when there is not even a cognitive connection.

Regression. This is a reversion to an earlier stage of development. You may recall my own regression as a

Principal in the presence of one of the trustees of the school, who reminded me of my mother.

Acting out. This is a physical expression, when you are incapable of expressing how you are feeling or thinking. Aggressive behaviour is a form of acting out, and can be seen in the context of domestic violence. Essentially it is an unhealthy way of releasing internal tension and shows inability to self-regulate and practise self-control.

Dissociation. This is one of the worst results of an insecure attachment. It is vaguely related to avoidance, and happens when we escape to a fantasy world devoid of the pain and distress we have suffered in our childhood. It is disengaging from the unpleasant reality of such childhood neglect. People who dissociate carry a painful and serious emotional or soul wound.

Projection. This means attributing an unpleasant trait of your own onto another person, for example, if you are controlling, accusing another non-abusive person of being controlling. This defence mechanism helps a person avoid the pain of looking at an unpleasant personal characteristic.

Introjection. The opposite of projection, it involves subconsciously taking in another's traits, including attitudes, prejudices and other negative as well as positive traits.

Rationalisation. This is about blaming another person for your own failures. It is a way of explaining away your own negative traits or behaviour. It is often used by controlling people, who generally are far removed from their feelings.

Reaction Formation. People who are unable to express negative emotions and substitute them with positive ones are using reaction formation. Those whose dependency needs of approval are not met often have this and, in their search for approval, constantly try to please, even if they feel hostile and angry towards a person. It means behaving in a completely opposite way to how you feel.

Repression. This is an unconscious blocking and burying of negative thoughts, feelings or memories. The purpose of counselling is to bring these into the conscious, and care must be taken because the repressed memories may be false, or may be traumatic.

Suppression. This is the same as repression except that it is conscious, in which case it is more like a coping strategy.

Displacement. This is when we redirect our anger and frustration onto an innocent person. We may be angry at person B and redirect it at the innocent person C (our partner!).

Intellectualisation. This is when we avoid our feelings by concentrating on our thinking. It is a fatal defence mechanism if, for example, we use it to avoid the feelings of grief at the loss of our childhood. We discuss situations but cannot make emotional contact with them. Sometimes intellectualisation is necessary because it can protect you from being overwhelmed.

Developmental Life Stages

UNDERSTANDING LIFE STAGES IS AN EXCELLENT way to understand how we may have been wounded in childhood, insofar as we can look at the original wound, realise what caused it and see how it affects us as we move through life. Developmental psychologists argue that our life span is divided into stages and we must meet the challenges or crises of each stage to safely negotiate the challenges of the next one. Understanding these challenges and needs helps to heal attachment issues, if only by giving you an excellent format for exploration. It can also increase your awareness of good parenting. As already mentioned, one of the principal challenges we have in life is to separate properly from our parents and if we fail to do so in the early years it creates problems in every life stage, including the final one of very old age. The pain of arrested childhood development is shown in adulthood, where the inner child's anger and shame infects the adult's ability to love, parent and emotionally survive to a greater or lesser extent. The type of dysfunctional family dynamics where the child is prevented from separating is one of the prime causes of adult distress. The parents create the reality of life for the child. That is the only reality the child knows

There are three dimensions to the life stages – biological, cognitive and psychosocial (psychological development in a social environment). From the emotional and psychological standpoint psychosocial development is relevant to this book. Very broadly this development involves separation and identity formation. The latter is called individualisation and is crucial in our development. Failure to form our identity results in confusion and instability. Sigmund Freud and Erik Erikson were pioneers of life stage psychology. Erikson had nine stages (originally this was eight, but his wife Joan provided material which outlined a ninth stage – very old age). I propose to use an 11 stage model compiled from the writings of different theorists, which might be useful as a practical way to help you deal with the crises you experience in each stage as you move through life. Each stage impacts on the other like psychological dominos. If you wish to gain a deeper insight into how the human develops at the different stages you might like to consult the writings of Erikson, John Tracy and John Travers, and Helen Bee and Denise Boyd.

We cannot be prescriptive as regards exact ages in these stages and different theorists slightly vary in the ages involved. Each stage naturally flows from the other as the child develops and separates moving towards autonomy, independence and the final separation – death. It is worthwhile recalling the significant importance of meeting the dependency needs in the early stages of the child's development. We can recall that if these needs are not met, the emotional bond between the parents and child will lie dormant. Neither will there be a bond between the siblings. This bond radiates from a parent and envelops all the siblings. That is the difference between a happy, warm adult family and a disparate group of individuals, who criticize and are even hostile to each other as they struggle with the issues that arise in the adult developmental stages. I see this in my counselling.

Stage 1 – Prenatal life.

I have already discussed the extraordinary life of the foetus in the womb, its sensitivity to external stimuli and how it can be born traumatised. I do not think this can be dealt with satisfactorily in counselling, but you need to be aware of how you can be affected before you are born. Trauma from the first trimester can affect the human, even if the second and third trimester are positive and the birth is without complications. If you are suffering from fear, anxiety, depression or mental distress, it is advantageous to find out about your parents' relationship circumstances, emotional and otherwise, during your prenatal life. If you are adopted and feel anxious or depressed without any visible evidence of causes, knowledge of your prenatal life would be important.

Stage 2 – Birth to two years old.

This is a vital stage in the person's development, where the child is totally dependent on parents for everything to sustain physical and emotional life. The child must trust that the parents will respond to give that security, which is necessary for emotional and physical survival. This sense of security lays the foundations for psychological well-being in adult life. Stage 2 depends on stage 1 in that respect, because a baby who has experienced trauma in the womb may be mistrustful in those early months following birth. This mistrust may be mistaken for well-being and independence, for example, by the child's refusal to allow efforts to comfort and console her. The really unfortunate consequence is that a secure attachment is hindered and pathologies enter the core. In those early months and years the child is wary of strangers, and even four year olds will baulk at staying overnight at grandparents. Only the parents or caregivers are the objects of attachment and we recall how the nature of the attachment has a profound effect upon later adult life. In other words this early stage lays the foundation of future mental health. During this stage the child needs encouragement and praise around the areas of feeding, toilet training and dressing. At the end of the stage the child begins to become more independent and to interact with other children. Most people do not remember much, if anything, from this stage, although I have met some who instinctively know if they were valued during this time of their lives. Alan Schore argues that this is the time to intervene to prevent adulthood psychological problems and ensure mental health.

Stage 3 – Three to six years old.

This is an important stage, where the child tries to gain some type of control over her environment. This reaching for autonomy and separation can be misinterpreted by parents, who may see it as rebelliousness and naughtiness. How the parents impose boundaries and discipline in the face of this behaviour may have lifelong effects on the child, instilling either a negative outlook or a sense of purpose. The parents' relationship with each other also comes into play here and impacts positively or negatively on the child. During this stage the boys begin to incline towards their fathers, and failure by fathers to respond will be detrimental to the child's emotional development. The female children lean towards the mother, and paternal failure will not have as big an effect on them, although the importance of fathers should not be underestimated. Maternal failings have a detrimental lifelong impact on girls. This is also the time when children begin school and signs of the type of attachment they have soon begin to appear. The child with an insecure fearful attachment will usually be upset, cry and want to remain at home. The child with a secure attachment will present as content and comfortable in his new environment. The child with a dismissive attachment will cope in the way that this attachment operates – matter of fact! Professor Manford Sonstegard's booklet *Creating Harmony in the Family* contains some practical information for dealing in a kind way with the child's so-called rebelliousness. Similarly, if you wish to improve your parenting the booklet *A Parent's Guide to Understanding and Motivating Children* by Amy Lew and Betty Lou Bettner is very helpful.

Stage 4 – Seven to nine years old.

The child now identifies with certain qualities and attitudes of others. Learning how to befriend other children and to socialise in a more sophisticated way is an important part of development. The child also becomes aware of the family's status in the locality. In particular he becomes conscious of family economic circumstances. A sense of achievement and competence is engendered (or not) during this stage, and any shame that may have lain hidden comes more to consciousness. The child becomes aware of the importance of peer groups as he further separates and peer pressure is generally an issue.

Stage 5 – Ten to twelve years old.

The child now begins to struggle with identity, based on his experiences in the other stages. The subconscious question 'who am I?' emerges, and separation from the family accelerates. The child also becomes sexually aware and this can create further identity problems. Sibling rivalry may also be an issue in this stage and moral awareness increases.

Stage 6 – Thirteen to fifteen years old.

This is an important stage where significant changes occur in the brain. It is the beginning of possibly the most turbulent period of your life – adolescence. At the beginning of adolescence the process of neural wiring records previous experiences, positive and negative in its circuitry. This is where the seeds of good or bad self-esteem will begin to germinate and pre-adolescent experiences, now wired in the brain, impacts on the teenager's behaviour. The child now becomes (perhaps vaguely) aware of his sexual orientation and issues of identity strengthen. Parent-child conflict are more likely as the child increasingly seeks to separate and become more independent. These young adolescents seek more intimate friendships and peer pressure increases. They now enters second level schools and in some cases of extreme childhood neglect, depression or anxiety may begin to appear.

Stage 7 – Sixteen to nineteen years old.

Mid to late adolescence can be a time of serious disturbance for a minority of youths and it is also a period of significant brain development. Due to these brain changes, and possibly because of aberrant synaptic pruning, the result of a negative childhood shows as a lack of concentration, as psychic energy is diverted to take care of the emotional wound inflicted in earlier years. Teachers will experience this type of student either as disruptive, absent (daydreaming), constantly doodling, or all three. Any counsellor who asks a client what his concentration level was at sixteen and gets the reply 'forty out of a hundred' can immediately conclude that his childhood was problematic. My clinical experience is that most clients who score thirty will have dropped out of school, not because they were unintelligent, but because they did not have the level of concentration necessary to survive. Those who remain are exceptionally intelligent and live off the scraps they can focus upon. I find that it is a relief to clients to realise that they were not good at school not because they were unintelligent, but because they could not concentrate. Further, if they have school reports for that stage I always rewrite the comment ('not paying attention, not working, disrupting the class') with the words 'nursing an emotional wound'. It makes perfect sense to them.

As well as coping with a loss of concentration at this time of life, young people also have to cope with developing their identity on the cusp of the adult world. Dating and having intimate relationships is part of the process. They also struggle to find their place in the world with behaviours that may bring them into conflict with parents and other authority figures. During this stage they become more precisely aware of their sexual orientation, and the difficulties associated with being gay, lesbian or bisexual. Peer pressure can also be an important factor at this time. Young people have to cope with a world of high-risk behaviours such as binge drinking, eating disorders and drug taking. They may also begin to challenge the values and norms of their parents' world. Many of those in their late teens may reject attending religious services and cause confusion and anger in their parents, although most parents now accept the inevitable and understand that their teenage children are trying to create their own independent world. They still depend on their parents and this can create inner tension in them as they try to extend their boundaries and assert their independence.

Stage 8 – Twenty to forty years old.

This is a period of great variation. Childhood is slowly left behind as we find our feet in the adult world. Adolescence, however, can continue into this stage as many youths go to third level college and still live at home. Parents may find that they are surrounded by twenty-six year old adolescents! Significant development continues between the ages of twenty and forty, but this is the period when the seeds of an insecure attachment sprout into full bloom, and some of the issues in Appendix 1 come to fruition, making it more difficult to meet the adult challenges of the stage. By the age of thirty issues of intimacy and identity should peak, although late adolescence may delay this. During this phase the need for connection is filled by friends or by an intimate relationship and parental skills are learned and tested. Work is also extremely important to foster the need for achievement, and it is a truism to say that loving your job is a sign of success in life. In a sense you have three major roles at this time – being in an intimate relationship, succeeding at work and successful parenting. These are three extensive and complicated roles, but no matter how complicated, the core issue is whether you have the capacity to emotionally connect, and that brings you back to the earlier stages.

Stage 9 – Forty to sixty five.

Your intimate relationship and to a lesser extent your friendships continue to be central to your life during this time. You experience the somewhat sad reality of your children further separating as they move away and set up their own way of living. This can be somewhat of a crisis as you seek to redefine your relationship with your spouse. Up until that phase your attention has been focussed on your children and now your relationship comes more sharply into focus. If you have not prepared for this stage you may experience difficulties in your relationship. To do this you need to learn about the three spaces in a relationship – your space, your partner's space, and your mutual space. In other words both you and your partner have space to pursue your individual hobbies and social networks, while also making time to do things together. If you have neglected to do this in the previous stage, you may find that you are now thrown together with much work to do in relationship terms. On the other hand you may feel a new sense of intimacy with your partner and grandchildren may enter your life. You may also have to cope with a so-called mid-life crisis as your sense of identity is disrupted by the challenges you experience in this stage.

Stage 10 – Sixty five to eighty five.

Most people retire during this stage and face all the challenges that a possible loss of meaning can bring. Many cope well by having new hobbies and interests and feel a sense of well-being, while others find it difficult to separate from their working life, which is now redundant, and feel depressed and unwanted. I, and many like me, do not believe in retirement until I feel a need to retire. I have retired from being a Principal, retrained and become self-employed, which gives me the latitude to arrange my working conditions to suit my lifestyle. You can decide how you will spend this stage. You can train for a new profession or you can devote your time to leisure. Daily exercise must be built into your life irrespective of whether you are working or devoting your time to leisure. There is now good evidence, for example, that fresh air alone can have a beneficial impact on depression. This stage is a particularly difficult time for those whose partners have died. Stress may increase with a reduced income or more frequent medical problems. Stress is relieved by adult children and perhaps grandchildren, providing that your previous relationship with them has been positive.

Stage 11 – Very old age.

More and more people live to be very old. Decades ago when I was visiting my aged mother-in-law in a nursing home in Dublin I discovered that at least one hundred of the residents were over ninety years old. I have no doubt that this figure has increased substantially today. Very old age presents enormous challenges as in most cases infirmity increases, and the psychological foundations laid long ago are required to meet these challenges. A once meaningful role in life has diminished and vanished unless there is a satisfactory transition from one life stage to the other. Of course many of the same challenges also exist for those in the previous stage, especially as they enter their eighties. But these challenges are greatly increased in very old age. There is the certainty of death not being far off, and it cannot be assumed that the very old are emotionally prepared for it or that their faith in an afterlife is so immensely strong that that they have no fear of it. Remember Kathleen! Faith may be the only thing that gives a very old person meaning, but it is not easy to maintain that in the face of medical issues, frailty and decline. In many cases the enormous physical loss has a profound effect and brings a decrease in confidence that can border on despair. According to Joan Erikson, they may lose the trust in survival they had as children, although, despite their physical handicaps, they sometimes fiercely protect their autonomy. My experience is that they deeply fear being put into nursing homes even if that is sometimes inevitable. Nursing homes are symbols of dependence, loneliness, sometimes hopelessness and uselessness, where the loss of intimacy experienced in stage eight and the loss of involvement in so many areas in stage nine is mourned. Ultimately, it is part of life and we must learn to celebrate what we have achieved, not least having so many years on earth.

Inner Childwork

INNER CHILDWORK IS PARTICULARLY EFFECTIVE IN dealing with the loss of a childhood. It can be nicely combined with developmental work, because the inner child is alive and functioning in all the stages.

Inner childwork involves the inner parent. In a sense you re-parent yourself, and help your inner child meet the dependency needs, which did not happen in real life. You can have three inner parents – critical, loving and protective. The loving one recognises that the inner child was starved of love and now provides it. In my clinical experience I notice that those with a loving inner parent invariably feel a warmth across their stomachs, when they make contact with the inner child. On the other hand, the protective parent is very necessary for the inner fearful child. The critical inner parent, however, is created from the internalised blaming voice in the adult, entrenched from childhood. This inner parent can sometimes see the inner child, but cannot make proper emotional contact with her and blames her rather than empathises with her. The suffering and toxicity of childhood hurt can be passed from generation to generation for hundreds of years until it is broken by a parent, who either chooses to behave in a nurturing way, or who finds healing. I have known cases where the toxicity spreads its tentacles throughout the wider family resulting in much suffering and distress.

The hurt inner child will **never** respond, unless you have undergone significant healing and are able to emotionally connect. The child will turn away, because she does not need a parent who is maimed by distress, anxiety, depression, or coldness. She wants a parent who is grounded and capable of parenting, so initial work must be done on the adult. Following the work I did on myself, I can see my inner child immediately, no matter where I am. Sometimes he is playing, sometimes happy, sometimes flushed and sad, but he is always looking at me and I take care of him. When I have negative thoughts I know that my child is sad or angry or lonely, and I reassure him. That is where I would like you to be.

As an introduction to inner childwork, you should practise a simple 15 second meditation every day where you try to see your inner child, smile at her with compassion, which is looking at her with a soft heart and empathy. Empathy is vital for emotional healing and its importance is well illustrated by Maia Szalavitz and Bruce Perry. Thich Nhat Hanh suggests that we become aware of the wounded inner child and show friendliness and embrace her with tenderness. If you find, despite repeating the meditation for some time, that your inner child is turned away from you, you can take it that you are still disconnected from her. Nonetheless, the meditation is important in establishing some type of connection, until you are emotionally in the right place. Initially, you may not even see your inner child, but perhaps a shadow, the back of her head, or her face hidden by a fringe. If this is the case, you may need to use photographs as a way to get some contact with her. When you have made contact she will look in your direction. After some time you could begin to talk to her. John Bradshaw's book *Home Coming* is the best known book on inner childwork and has plenty of exercises that you can do to connect with your inner child. In her book, *Recovery of Your Inner Child*, Lucia Capacchione gives examples of written dialogue with the child and highlights the many different inner children we have. It is a surprisingly large family. You may see the lonely child, the spoiled child, the sulky one, the brat, the angry child, the mischievous one, the lost child, the hurt child, the rebel, the good child, the kind child and so on. All humans have a spiritual and creative child. Contact will also bring many emotions such as love, sadness, a desire to protect the child, or perhaps anger at how the child has been treated. Praise her, hold her, reassure her, and express your love for her. In other words, you become the loving parent to your wounded inner child and soothe her fears.

As the inner parent you could write a letter to the child telling her that you will always be there for her, that you love her and will take care of her. It is also very beneficial for the inner child to write to the inner parent. With this technique you use your non-dominant hand, which enables you to access the child's feelings and express her needs. Your letter will be written in a childish scrawl and will empower the fearful inner child that sometimes cowers inside you. Check the age of the child who wishes to have a voice after all those years. Allow her to open up and show the hurt, rage, fear, or other feelings that she has harboured throughout the years, when she has remained in hiding crying out to be heard. Allow her to ask for what she needs and respond with love to her request.

Inner childwork can be enhanced by using a technique called the empty chair, which was first introduced by the pioneering psychiatrist and psychotherapist, Fritz Perls, who was assisted by his wife, Laura. This is normally done with the aid of a therapist. Basically the counsellor will set up two empty chairs and you will shuttle between them. In one chair you will be yourself as a child and in the other you assume the personality of the parent, who wounded you. As you sit in the child's chair you try to imagine in as much detail as possible the parent who was so powerful in his behaviour towards you and filled you with fear. In this technique the parent is the Topdog and the child the Underdog. That particular technique is known as external dialogue, which allows you to voice your childhood trauma and enables you to challenge the person who neglected you, to express your anger and your grief, to demand an apology, and to express your determination not to allow childhood neglect to affect you anymore. It will help you to grow, to stand in the adult's shoes, and to reclaim your power. The person involved may be dead and this will give you the opportunity to deal with unfinished business and to say goodbye, if you wish. It is also useful in helping you to become more assertive not only against the person who caused you childhood fear, but in everyday relationships.

Another aspect of the empty chair technique is using internal dialogue. This is a good way to deal with irrational thoughts and the inner critical voice that you internalised as a child. As you shuttle between the chairs, you can be the critical voice in one and the challenger of the unjustified criticism and irrational thoughts in the other. The therapist can also use the image of the courtroom and advocate on behalf of the victimised child (much as a barrister might do) and refute the irrational and destructive thinking. You can also use the corrective dialogue, which is close enough to the internal dialogue. You begin by outlining your distorted thinking and flawed ideas about yourself and your relationship with others that took root in your childhood and caused you to have a negative self-view as you grew older. You move back and forth between the two chairs disentangling the illogical framework you have constructed throughout the years and putting in place a more realistic and positive one about yourself.

Recognising Your Adult Needs

AS A CHILD YOU HAD DEPENDENCY needs, and now as an adult you have adult needs. Unfortunately, those who suffer childhood neglect to any significant degree are normally unaware of their needs and are inclined to overwork, constantly blame themselves, drive themselves, and severely judge themselves. The inner critical voice reigns uninhibited, causing constant stress and misery. This abuse of the self is a way of being, a continuation of childhood neglect.

There are several theorists who enlighten us about human needs. Abraham Maslow, an American psychologist, was one of the pioneers in writing about them. His prescription for psychological health is called Maslow's hierarchy of needs and includes the need for love, respect, connection, safety, freedom from fear of poverty, from ill health and harm, freedom to be creative and much more. The American psychiatrist, William Glasser, also emphasised that meeting our needs was necessary for happiness and the creation of a quality world. He defined our needs as power, survival, love and belonging, fun and freedom. All these needs are interconnected. Power is an innate and a complex need that seems to apply to humans only. It ranges from the negative desire to control others, as a means of getting satisfaction, to establishing a positive and nourishing way of life. If you use power negatively, it will damage your need for love and belonging and will fracture your friendships. As a need with a positive foundation power is about feeling alive, having meaning, getting a buzz out of life. You need power, but not power over others. In a sense it is related to the freedom need. It allows you to be as you wish to be. It also allows you to help others and to deepen your interest in becoming involved with others without diminishing them.

Survival is obviously your most basic need. Take the infant as an example. No one wants to live more than an ill infant, who will fight with all its might to survive. Survival is a genetic instinct programmed into all living creatures. It drives us towards intimate relationships with the basic need of keeping the human race in existence. To do this you establish a way of living that ensures an intimate companion and all the means necessary for survival, such as having money, living healthily with a good diet and adequate exercise, having a suitable residence, and all the means to raise and educate a family. But, it is more than that. It is a way of living to ensure pleasure, happiness and companionship. It is about self-care and in a wider context, working to ensure a society that cares for all where peace reigns. On a global level you can see societies where war ravages comunities and prevents happiness and for many survival.

Love and belonging is related to survival. It not only drives you to establish nourishing relationships with others, but also to care for others. If you lack the need of love and belonging you feel lonely, abandoned and unhappy. It is a lifelong need and is achieved through your relationships with family and others. It demands a mindset of giving as well as receiving, of loyalty and fidelity where sex is used as a means of meeting a need, not as a way of controlling. Friendship is the essence of love and belonging. The ability to acquire friends begins in the earliest of the life stages. When you meet the need for love and belonging with an intimate circle, it enables you to reach out to others and to have your own individual interests and hobbies to enrich your life.

Fun is the need that is easiest to meet. Glasser describes fun as the genetic reward for learning. Your ancestors learned better ways to survive and be happy, creating space for fun, which became genetic. Glasser rightly asserts that when a marriage begins to fail, fun in the first casualty.

Freedom is a complex need. Glasser rightly sees it as a buffer against power, in this case power used as a control mechanism over others. Freedom is about being as you wish to be, not to do as you wish. It is also about having a voice and being heard.

This is a simple outline of your five needs and if you wish for a fuller explanation of them you can read Glasser's book, *Choice Theory. A New Psychology of Personal Freedom*. When you understand what they are, there are some pertinent questions that will help you explore further – do you feel loved and do you belong? If not what is thwarting this need? How can you address it? Do you have fun in your life? If not, why not? What is preventing this need from being met? Do you have freedom to be as you wish to be, or are you carrying a negative burden such as fear or anxiety, or perhaps you are in a controlling relationship where freedom is stifled? If you feel powerless, what are the circumstances involved. How can you change them? How can you change yourself and put yourself in a position where you feel your personal power? Are your survival needs compromised? What can you do? Is there a question of self –care involved, of poor diet, lack of exercise, lack of an intimate relationship.

You could also use an excellent technique of drawing your hand on a blank sheet of paper (as you did when you were a child in school), with each finger representing one of the five needs. You simply write on each finger how the needs are being met. This is a very personal way of checking where you stand. Sadly, I have met many people using this technique, who have not met a single need. The 'hand' remains empty and bare. Try this technique and it will indicate if you need to take steps to meet any need. Not only have you the capacity to meet all of them, but it is not an impossible task. It is a matter of choosing what steps you will take to have power, intimacy, a sense of belonging, fun and freedom.

Mindfulness and Meditation.

MANY PEOPLE ARE SOMEWHAT SCEPTICAL ABOUT mindfulness and see it as a passing gimmick, but it is one of the best ways to cope with the issues coming from an insecure attachment. It is an ancient meditation genre usually attributed to Buddhism, which is more a philosophy than a religion, but was also evident in Hindu meditations long before Buddhism. Thich Nhat Hanh argues that it heals the inner child. John Kabat-Zinn, Emeritus Professor of Medicine at the University of Massachusetts, is regarded as the guru of mindfulness as practised today, and his book *Full Catastrophe Living. How to cope with stress, pain and illness using mindfulness meditation*, is a best seller. He outlines the seven pillars of mindfulness practice which are worth knowing in themselves. They are the foundations of meditation practice and are as follows: –

Non-judging.

This is not easy to explain, but it means standing back from your experiences as if you are an external witness and not judging or labelling what is happening to you. Without realising it we usually spend all day categorising what happens to us and often keeping our minds in overdrive. So you suspend our judgement and see what is happening in your mind. As the American Buddhist nun, Pema Chödrön, teaches, it is about looking gently and honestly at yourself. Thich Nhat Hanh says that the first function of mindfulness is to recognise and not to fight, in other words to accept.

Patience.

This means allowing things to unfold in their own time. It involves slowing down your thinking, using, perhaps, abdominal breathing, which empties the mind. You accept the reality of your mind, of how you are. This will ground you and help you calm fear and arrive at good decisions.

Beginner's mind.

This is like seeing everything for the first time and putting aside what you know. You suspend your beliefs and your thinking. You open your mind to new possibilities and free yourself to look at things afresh. It reminds me a little of how poets look at life and the newness and essence of things. I think of Patrick Kavanagh, William Wordsworth and Seán Ó Ríordáin. Adopting the beginner's mind increases our empathy for others, as well as removing any attempt to put ourselves forward as somebody who knows everything.

Trust.

This is about developing a trust in yourself and your feelings. It is a matter of intuition. I often talk to people about this basic instinct, which always knows what is best for us. You have within you that instinct for your own welfare. It is about recognising your own uniqueness and not trying to be like others.

Non-striving.

This is self-explanatory. As Kabat-Zinn says 'meditation is a non-doing.'

Acceptance.

This is about accepting reality in your normal life and your normal way of being. As Kabat-Zinn is quick to point out this does not mean that you abandon your values or stop trying to change, it just means accepting how you are right now. If you can do that then you have a much better chance to heal, because you are not too preoccupied with your condition, and you can have patience in your journey of change. I have said elsewhere that acceptance is the key to healing, because it stops you struggling against yourself. It is a fundamental concept of humanistic counselling.

Letting go.

Kabat-Zinn sums this up as non-attachment. This reminds me of my few years in the Jesuits, where detachment might now be seen as part of mindfulness. Non-attachment was a major principle in our lives in those years. We let go of certain thoughts and feelings that we would like to hold onto. Letting go is very close to acceptance and it brings us refreshment just as we let go when we fall asleep. Think about what it is like when you cannot let go and lie awake, your head in overdrive, or spend years holding a grudge.

Bearing in mind the pillars of mindfulness, you can compile a gentle meditation as a calming way to soothe fear and some of its distressing companions. As the meditation progresses and the repetition of images occurs your sense of peace and being present will increase. The following is one you can use or adapt as you wish. Find a quiet place and sit in a comfortable chair, wearing loose clothes if possible.

- Close your eyes and become aware of any noise or movement outside the room. You may hear the noise of traffic in the distance, the wind blowing or the trees rustling in the breeze.
- Gently shift your focus to the inside of the room and enjoy the silence or perhaps the ticking of a clock.
- Begin to let go of your thoughts and notice

them floating away in a bubble into the distance.
- Become aware of the soft rhythm of your breathing.
- Be aware of your body being silently sustained by your breathing.
- Notice the coolness of your breath as you breathe in.
- Imagine the air being warmed inside your body.
- Notice your breath moving through your body and how warm it is as you exhale.
- Be aware of the feel of your body against the chair.
- Notice how the chair supports you.
- Feel the tension in the upper part of your body flowing through your arms and out through your fingers as you breathe out.
- Feel the tension in the lower part of your body flowing down your legs, into your feet and seeping through your toes into the ground.
- Breathe out your anger, your bitterness, your shame, regret, guilt and fear.
- Breathe in and experience your kindness, your gentleness, your love and empathy.
- Experience the love being carried through your body on your breath.
- Breathe out your sadness and your fear.
- Breathe in and notice your joy and your happiness.
- Breathe out your unease and any discomfort your body may be experiencing.

- Breathe in and experience your calmness and your serenity.
- Become aware of your mind as a deep, calm, pool without ripples.
- Feel the peace enter your mind.
- As you breathe become aware again of your environment.
- Listen for any movement.
- Shift your awareness back to your breathing and begin again.

You can keep repeating these until you feel fully present and relaxed. Usually four times is sufficient. You can also use your creativity and devise your own mindfulness meditation. You might also like to read Margaret Wehrenberg's book, *The 10 Best-Ever Anxiety Management Techniques*, which has an excellent array of meditations.

Pema Chödrön, has 108 brief sections in her book, *Comfortable with Uncertainty*, much of it on meditation and what she calls mindfulness – awareness. It is a soothing book, and for example looks at the simple process of using breathing to achieve loving-kindness, which she calls unconditional friendliness. She outlines four qualities that you acquire over time during meditation – steadfastness, clear seeing, experiencing your emotional distress and attention to the present moment. This type of meditation eventually brings about clarity, honesty about yourself, and being present; a recipe that combats emotional distress. The Zen teacher, Cheri Huber, feels that the most effective way to deal with fear and distress is to sit 'in compassionate awareness,' indicating that mindfulness works better when we are still. Stillness means slowing down and practising patience, one of its pillars. This will take time (and patience!) as you condition yourself to do things slowly and take time to think. One of my uncles, a most patient person, who was a tradesman, once said to me 'you always measure twice and cut once'. Begin with simple exercises and slowly expand them to include all your behaviour. Initially, I focused on my shoelaces, and conditioned myself so that now I automatically open them slowly with the word 'gentle' floating around my mind. The word 'shoelace' has become a trigger associated with patience. I also try to write slowly, because I used to write so fast that there were times when I could not read my own writing. That still sometimes happens, so I am constantly reminding myself to go slower, to write more slowly. I keep saying in my head 'slowly, gently' and I find that this works very well. It is also very soothing. I also like to keep my desk neat and tidy, an ongoing struggle!

You have to find your own way of slowing down, and you will notice that your new behaviour will have a psychological and calming benefit, as it lessens unease and anxiety. It is helpful, too, if you examine your perspective as to how important and urgent the task at hand is. Do you have to mow the lawn, do the weeding, trim the shrubs, clean out the sheds, sweep the yard and paint the gate on the same day? When you think of this you will see how you are driven by an unease, which prevents you from taking your time, having breaks and ultimately having a more easeful life. Ironically, working slowly will mean a quicker outcome.

On a practical level you can enrol in a mindfulness course. There are many courses on mindfulness which are highlighted on the internet and which you would find useful. Pádraig Ó Móráin, a therapist who writes for the health supplement of the *Irish Times,* gives excellent courses in mindfulness.

Redefine yourself

THE QUESTION 'WHAT AM I'? IS as important as 'who am I?' Redefining yourself is essential in healing attachment issues. Your definition of yourself as worthless will enslave you and keep you in a wounded state. Your definition must be based on your inner goodness, not on negative beliefs, not on outside factors such as wealth, achievement or success. The best way to define yourself is by your kindness and your genuineness and to put that into practice. I sense that love/kindness and genuineness are the principal attributes of the real self that become obliterated by a negative childhood experience. Pema Chödrön, teaches that being 'dearly loved' is the key to learning how to love and introduces the concept of loving – kindness in much of her writings.

Few people can love unless they have experienced it from someone during their childhood. Otherwise we have to learn how to love ourselves in our journey through self-awareness and to cultivate loving compassion towards ourselves. That is possible, and that is what I did in my years of being counselled, when I came to realise that I was not responsible for how I was.

Love is the great reward of change, and change is about having a new positive self-definition. Changing the self is not always easy, for some it is painful, not so for others, but this new definition will enhance your feelings about yourself. Regarding yourself as worthwhile will help you take better care of yourself, because you are worth it. You will find it easier to self-soothe and to reduce stress. People under a dark pathological cloud find it difficult to self-sooth and without exception are hard on themselves, but small changes in self-care can bring big benefits.

Counselling.

BECAUSE OF ITS INGRAINED NATURE, I do not think it is possible to effectively deal with moderate to severe attachment issues without some professional help. There are many types of counselling and they cannot be listed here, and there are many types of useful alternative therapies. Cognitive behavioural therapy is a good way to deal with some of the fallout from a negative childhood such as depression and anxiety, although researchers in the University of Amsterdam assert that it is only effective for a short time and that distress returns to most sufferers. Professor Mick Cooper in his book, *Essential Research Findings in Counselling and Psychotherapy. The Facts are Friendly*, also disputes the idea that it is the best therapy, and advocates that different people with different problems need different types of therapy. The important thing is that you feel comfortable with the counsellor and that you feel the benefits of the therapy offered. I feel that humanistic psychotherapy provides the warmth and supportive atmosphere in which you can emotionally re-experience the past and bring healing to the emotional or soul wound that is so hurtful to you. Humanistic counselling is effective in dealing with the trauma of a lost childhood. I agree with Dr Ivor Browne who recommends a holistic counselling to cater for the needs of those who carry the wounds of abandonment.

Research, however, shows that EMDR (Eye Movement Desensitization and Reprocessing), which has been mentioned previously, is probably the most effective way of dealing with trauma, including childhood trauma. It is particularly suitable if a client does not wish to dig too deeply into the past. EMDR has three prongs – past traumas, present triggers and future templates. All of these are key. This therapy is based upon REM (rapid eye movement) that occurs during deep sleep which allows the brain to process recent events. I saw how compatible inner childwork and EMDR were when I was doing my training with Dr Michael Paterson (EMDR Masterclass, Belfast), a leading expert in this therapy, who was trained by the creator of EMDR, Francine Shapiro. I have a handout on EMDR, *including copies of scans* showing how it activates the brain to process distressing events in the past or present, e.g. there is an increase in the hippocampus that explains why so many lost memories emerge during the therapy. The hippocampus is part of the limbic system and is the storage area of long term memory and includes past experiences and events. You can get more detail about EMDR and scans on the internet, but it is about accessing negative memory networks and shifting blocked traumatic events to adaptive memory networks, where they are properly processed. What often happens, especially with childhood trauma (not having the dependency needs met), is that the trauma (with its images, feelings, sensations, sounds and thoughts) gets blocked in the brain, and EMDR stimulates this blocked information and allows the brain to reprocess that unconscious material. If you decide to attend an EMDR therapist it is important to make sure that he or she is appropriately trained and has proper supervision.

Whatever type of therapy you opt for, the therapeutic relationship between you and the counsellor is vital, because the counsellor will be an attachment figure for you, and partly makes up for the bond that was never created in your early childhood. According to Babette Rothschild, there is evidence from brain studies that this is so. Consequently, an empathic counsellor is essential to allow you to play out the subconscious patterns of your preverbal life and reveal the false self that was created in those early years, which came to cause you such distress in your adult life. This will involve a great measure of trust on your part. Therefore it is important to choose a counsellor that suits you, and that at some stage you can feel an improvement from the treatment.

Counselling worked for me. As I trained for counselling and underwent a few years of personal counselling, I became aware of my shame, anger and fear. During that time I became interested in how I was parented and soon realised that my afflictions came from inadequate parenting, which I now recognise as giving rise to attachment issues, and when I became aware of attachment and, above all, the needs of the child, I discovered one of the sources. I would never blame my parents, they were good parents, they spoiled me somewhat, and they did their best, but somehow did not meet my dependency needs. My father was a soft loving man, and my mother loved as best she could, but was narcissistic, a woman you would not oppose. She carried a wounded inner child as do all parents who fail to nurture their children.

In my case, therefore, there was a combination of opposite parental personalities, which resulted in me having an ambivalent insecure attachment, which caused many emotional struggles in my life until I finally healed, although that process will go on for the rest of my life. Through my counselling I was able to understand what happened to me, by first of all learning about narcissistic people and how they must control others to gain momentary, illusionary peace. I soon learned to understand their angry, shamed and very vulnerable inner child and their inability to give their children unconditional love. If you wish to get an in-depth account of how a narcissistic parent impacts on us you might like to read Karyl McBride's *Will I Ever be Good Enough? Healing the Daughters of Narcissistic Mothers.* This explores the relationship between narcissistic mothers and their daughters. But, as I messaged Karyl, I have no doubt that narcissistic mothers inflict lifelong damage to their sons, especially if the father is quiet (and, more than likely, in a controlling relationship). I see this in my counselling. A narcissistic mother is the voice in the house and that voice can ring in your head all your life. Narcissistic parents are unable to meet a child's needs, and worse still they are prone to use the child to meet their needs, treating the child almost as an adult. Any child, who is forced to meet a parent's emotional and especially emotional-sexual needs, is destined for a bleak future, and will have a negative relationship with himself, with a deep rooted fear based on a shaky emotional foundation. This is a sad but, unfortunately, a widespread reality for many men and women.

Counselling also gives you other new insights to make sense of your life and bring healing. Early on in my counselling I learned about enmeshment. It was like a light bulb suddenly going on and filled me with sadness, as I now understood one of the main sources of my distress. It is very difficult to see an enmeshed childhood without the aid of a professional. If a parent loves you too much, you can be enmeshed or engulfed by meeting his or her needs. In a sense you become a surrogate caretaker, if not a surrogate spouse. Children in this unfortunate situation often feel suffocated, angry and a failure, because a child cannot meet the needs of an adult. It makes the child, and ultimately the adult-child, feel unloved, unlovable, angry, discarded and worthless. Enmeshment is now seen as a form of emotional sexual abuse because the child's sexual identity is compromised as he tries to meet the needs of a parent. It is an ongoing wounding process and has profound and long term sexual implications for a person's entire life, where the abused adult may more than likely view the opposite gender as sexual objects (sexual objectification). This is crucifying, unhealthy and breeds a fear of proper emotional relationships and indeed proper healthy internal communication.

It is now known through research that many people only go for counselling when their personal situation is desperate and their pain is unbearable. I would like to give Jason the last word, as he shares his experience of making contact with me, and a brief overview of how counselling worked for him. You might find his experience helpful, if you contemplate going down the counselling route. The context of this extract is his decision to leave his job and begin training for a different job, when fear of abandonment, social fear and fear of failure again began to haunt him. His courage and determination as he struggled against avoidance was impressive, and he eventually changed through his efforts in my counselling room. In this extract he is referring to the initial stages of his training.

The meet and greet day was getting close. I was a wreck from thinking about it. I could not sleep and every time I would think about it, I would do something else so I wouldn't have to think about it. The evening before we all met, I played a match. It didn't go well. I played poorly and was in a negative frame of mind coming home. It was a long trip home from the match and I was thinking about the college day. All of a sudden, I decided I was not going. I convinced myself that I would miss nothing and that I would go the next time. Immediately a weight lifted from me. I was happy with the decision I made and slept fine that night. I lied to my mother and told her the day had been changed. Once the college day was over, guilt, shame and a sick feeling consumed me. That night I couldn't sleep. This was my second chance and I was wasting it. I thought about it. I just couldn't go. I physically couldn't force myself to get into the car and go to college. I was consumed with fear and worry. I had a pain deep in my stomach and I broke out in a sweat just thinking about college. The thoughts of introducing myself to new people and talking in front of them crippled me. I just was unable to push past these feelings. I blamed myself. Why was I such a weak person that I couldn't go? Why couldn't I be normal like everyone else? Why was everyone so much better than me? I did what I always did and avoided the unknown. The fear of the unknown that day just wouldn't allow me to go. I thought about this over the coming weeks. The signs of my previous college experience were there and I knew it. I sent an email to the college apologising for not going and saying I was sick. This was exactly what I done when I was in college first – buy myself some time with lies until the inevitable happened and the house of cards came tumbling down. This was my second chance at college and it was meant to be different. I was finally going to realise my potential and see my efforts rewarded in good grades. I thought long and hard about where I was going. Deep down I knew this was not normal behaviour. Unfortunately I had started normalising it through the years. But now I knew that I needed help.

One of my friends confided to me that counselling had helped him greatly. It helped to know that a normal person, doing very well, was receiving counselling. I had always associated counselling with people who weren't well and had mental issues. To be honest, until recently it never occurred to me that I might need help from someone. I think I was at the right age to realise that my situation was not normal and that I didn't want to spend the rest of my life unhappy and in fear. I went home that evening and went on the internet, where I hoped I would find a good counsellor. I found an interesting website and my consciousness about confidentiality was eased by the information on the website. I was afraid to ring so I decided to send the counsellor an email. I just explained that I struggled with very low self-esteem and had little confidence to do simple everyday tasks. I was extremely nervous sending the mail but eventually I plucked up the courage to press send. I didn't check my mails for a few days. It was my way of avoiding the situation. Out of sight, out of mind was my philosophy. I would do this in college all the time, send a mail but I wouldn't have the courage to look at my emails for days. Eventually I would, but it would often be too late to do anything about them by then. A few days passed when I checked my mails again. The counsellor replied saying he could help me and to ring him on the number provided. This was half the answer I was looking for. I was happy that he would help me, but terrified about making the call. Around two weeks later, I rang. It took me that long to convince myself that I needed to do this. I look back on it now with pride that I was able to make the call that changed my life. So often before I'd have left it and struggled on. But there was something inside me telling me to call. My gut instinct was telling I needed help and make the call. I'm so glad I listened. For the call, I drove up to the local village and parked. I hung up before ringing once or twice before I went through with it. It was a simple conversation and we arranged to meet.

By the time I drove the few miles home, I was drenched in sweat. I had a date now to look to and I told myself that I had to go through with it. This was all that was on my mind for the coming week. As it got closer I thought about pulling the plug. Again something inside me told me to go ahead with it. It was a strength that I thought I never had. To ease my nerves I made the long journey the evening before. I just wanted to check out the directions I had been given and pass the place that I would be going to. This definitely helped and eased my mind a little bit. I now knew what kind of place I would be going to and knew where it was located. Even this small bit of familiarity made the whole episode less daunting. This was the only part of the situation I could have some control over in my mind and it did comfort me. My mind was racing about the thoughts of counselling; what questions I would be asked, would this help me and so on. I really hadn't a clue what to expect. And the unknown always scared the hell out of me. That morning is a bit of a blur to me. I was so nervous that I find it hard to recollect the first session. I remember waiting in the counselling room. I liked the atmosphere in the room, but I was shaking with nerves. I was watching the door anxiously for the counsellor to appear.

I had prepared a document in the previous days that detailed my problems in college, my fear of being away from home, the struggle I had meeting strangers, how I blushed with embarrassment, my lack of confidence, problems on the playing field, my indecision and difficulty making phone calls, problems giving presentations, how long it took me to learn how to drive, my fear of travelling, my failure to go to the gym or to go swimming, my being body conscious, problems going to the doctor or the dentist, and my fear of seeking promotion, even though I had the intelligence and ability to do the work.

My counsellor and I talked about what I had written down. It was such a relief to finally let all this out. We went through every item that I had written down and explored it. There was no magic formula, we just talked, mainly me while he listened. I made me feel so good. I could have talked for hours. He kept asking me questions like 'How does this make you feel?' 'How do you feel now?' This made me delve deeper into

my problems and try rationalise them. I had
never dealt with feelings before. This was completely new to me. Feelings were something I
buried deep inside me. During the counselling
I learned different techniques for dealing with
situations that I magnified in my head and make
them into huge issues for myself.

The counselling process was difficult for Jason. Many
sessions were painful, but ultimately he banished many
demons of his childhood. It might encourage you to
see where he is at present.

Since I started counselling, the changes to my
life have been enormous. I am no longer the
person who had absolute no self-belief or confidence in myself. Fear had taken over my life
and made simple everyday things such as driving
the car or picking up the phone an excruciat-
ingly difficult task. Over a year later, I am now
enjoying life and for the first time I am happy. I
have started a new phase in my life where I am
at last living. Now I do things that I enjoy, not
to please others, I am confident to try all kinds
of new kinds and have completely changed as
a person. I have started a new career that I love
and I have moved out of home, which I never
would have thought possible. I have achieved so
many small victories also, for example, giving a
speech, getting my full driving licence, perform-

ing in front of a room of people and coaching young people. Things such as eating on my own in a restaurant, going to the gym, driving the car or making a phone call are all things that I now have the confidence to do with comfort and ease. My social skills have improved no end. Now I enjoy peoples' company, whereas before I was awkward and embarrassed easily when talking to people I didn't know. My outlook on life has gone 360 degrees. Gone are the dark days of negative thinking and crippling self-doubt. I now have a positive outlook on life and am always thinking in a positive manner. I now try and find the positives even in negative moments. I am not going to tell you that it was easy because it wasn't. It took a lot of hard work to get me from the dark place I was in. But through counselling and my own determination, I have got to a stage where I am enjoying life and looking forward to what the future brings. That is not to say that it was easy because I had many setbacks. There were incidents where I broke down crying and times were there was a cloud of depression over me. But I suppose in adversity, one finds strength. I used these dark moments to reassess where I was and this made me stronger. I still need to work hard every day to ensure that I am feeling good about myself and an in a positive mind frame. I have thought about the techniques that have helped me, it has

been a combination of many, not just one that
has got to where I am today.

Jason put into action and outlines the various
techniques mentioned throughout this book, such as
regular exercise, good diet, abdominal breathing, the
SOS technique, desensitisation, getting a positive perspective, examining his negative core beliefs, keeping a
journal, and inner childwork. He was able to do this
because of his determination and tenacity. He is now
fully qualified as a professional, and enjoys his work.

Appendix 1:
Some of the possible consequences from an insecure attachment

The False Self

FEAR OF ABANDONMENT – FEAR OF failure – social fear – toxic jealousy – envy – toxic anger/rage – depression – anxiety – panic attacks – controlling impulse – internal unease – impatience – self-loathing – separation difficulties – chronic stress – suicidal ideation – poor concentration – lack of meaning – procrastination – difficulty finishing assignments – magical thinking – body image problems – negative outlook – negative thinking – stress related illnesses – avoidance mechanisms – worry – competitiveness –aggression – lack of assertiveness – people pleasing –taking in the feelings of others – low self-esteem – emptiness – addictions – perfectionism – sadness – existential loneliness – shame – poor boundaries – relationship difficulties – parenting difficulties – possible increased fear of death – difficulty in meeting the challenges of life development stages – fear of ageing – insecurity – frozen feelings – lack of empathy – compulsive behaviours – possible promiscuity – dissociation – eating disorders – inability to self-soothe – an emotional or soul wound –feeling unloved/unwanted – feeling unlovable – uncertainty –poor judgement – warped perspective – lethargy – being driven – impaired immune system – physical illnesses from stress response systems (heart problems, diabetes, blood pressure etc.) – abusiveness – psychosomatic complaints.

Bibliography

A Catechism of Catholic Doctrine (1969)

ALLEN, R M. 2005. The Evolutionary Psychology of Jealousy in Romantic Relationships: Evidence for a Sexually Dimorphic Response Mechanism in Humans. B.A. Thesis, William's College Massachusetts, USA.

Altizer, T.J. (2002) The New Gospel of Christian Atheism. Aurora: The Davies Group.

Antony, M.M. (2004) 10 Simple Solutions to Shyness. How to Overcome Shyness, Social Anxiety & Fear of Public Speaking. Oakland: New Harbinger Publications. (Entire book is also available on the internet).

Antony, M.M. and Swinson, R.P. (2008) 2nd Ed. The Shyness & Social Anxiety Workbook. Proven, Step-by – step Techniques for Overcoming Your Fear. Oakland: New Harbinger Publications, Inc.

Antony, M.M. and Swinson, R.P. (2009) 2nd Ed. When Perfect Isn't Good Enough. Strategies for Coping with Perfectionism. Oakland: New Harbinger Publications, Inc.

Barnes, J. (2008) Nothing to be Frightened of. London: Vintage Books.

Baumgart, H. (1990) Jealousy. Experiences and Solutions. Chicago: University of Chicago Press.

Beattie, D. and Devitt, P. (2015) Suicide. A Modern Obsession. Dublin: Liberties Press.

Beck, A. (ND) Fear of Failure. A lifelong search for love and fulfilment. Great Britain: Amazon.

Bee, H. and Boyd, D (2002) Lifespan Development (Third Edition). Boston: Allyn and Bacon.

Beetz, A., Uvnäs-Mobert, K, Julius, H, and Kotrschal, K. (2012) 'Psychosocial and Psychophysiological Effects of Human-Animal Interactions: The Possible Role of Oxytocin.' Front Psychology, 3, p. 234

Bekoff, M. 'Animal Emotions: Exploring Passionate Natures.' (2000) BioScience, 50 (10), pp. 861-869

Benjamin, B.E. (ND) The Primacy of Human Touch. Available at: www.benbenjamin.net/pdfs/Issue2.pdf

Bevan, L. (2009) *Life Without Jealousy. A Practical Guide. Ann Arbor: Loving Healing Press.*

Blyth, L. (2013) *The Little Book of Hugs. A gift to Bring Comfort and Joy. London: CICO Books.*

Blyth, L. (2013) *The Little Book of Kindness. London: CICO Books*

Bohan, B. (2013) *Eat Yourself Well. Simple Changes for Better Health. Dublin: Gill & McMillan.*

Boon, S., Steele, K. and Van Der Hart, O. (2011) *Coping With Trauma-Related Dissociation. Skills Training for Patients and Their Therapists. London: W.W. Norton & Company.*

Bourke, J. (2006) *Fear. A Cultural History. London: Virago Press.*

Bourne, E.J. (2005) *The Anxiety & Phobia Workbook 4th Edition. Oakland: New Harbinger Publications, Inc.*

Bowlby, J. (1988) *A Secure Base. Parent-Child Attachment and Healthy Human Development. New York: Basic Books.*

Bradshaw, J. (1999) *Home Coming: Reclaiming & Championing Your Inner Child. London: Piatkus.*

Bradshaw, J. (1988). Healing The Shame That Binds You. Florida: Health Communications Inc.

Brannan, A. (2014) 'Separation Anxiety in Adults.' Available at: www.exploringlifesmysteries.com › Health › Mental Health.

Bretherton, I. (1992) 'The Origins of Attachment Theory: John Bowlby and Mary Ainsworth.' Developmental Psychology, 28 (5) pp.759-775.

Brown, B. (2013) Daring Greatly. How the Courage to Be Vulnerable Transforms the Way We Live, Love, Parent and Lead. London: Portfolio Penguin.

Brown, E. (2013) Happier Endings. A Meditation on Life and Death. New York: Simon & Schuster Paperbacks.

Browne, I. (2013) The Writings of Ivor Browne. Steps Along the Road – The Evolution of a Slow Learner. Cork: Atrium (Imprint of Cork University Press).

Buckman, R. (2003) 'Communication in Palliative Care' in Dickenson, D. Johnson, M. and Katz, J.M. (Eds.) Death, Dying and Bereavement. London: SAGE Publications (pp.146-173).

Bullivant, R. (2015) True Real Life Stories of Reincarnation. Self-published.

Buss, A. (1986) 'A Theory of Shyness' in Jones, W.H., Cheek, J.M. and Briggs S.R. (Eds.) Shyness. Perspectives on Research and Treatment. New York: Plenum Press. (pp.39-46)

Buss, D.M. (2004) 2nd Ed. Evolutionary Psychology. The New Science of the Mind. Upper Saddle River, Pearson Education Inc.

Buss D.M. and Malamuth N.M. (Eds.) (1996) Sex, Power, Conflict. Evolutionary and Feminist Perspectives. Oxford: Oxford University Press

Butler, G. (1999) Overcoming Social Anxiety and Shyness. London: Constable & Robinson Ltd.

Buunk, B.P., Angleitner, A., Oubaid, V., and Buss, D.V. (1996) 'Sex Differences in Jealousy in Evolutionary and Cultural Perspective: Tests from the Netherlands, Germany, and the United States.' Psychological Science 7 (6) pp. 359-363.

Cannon, M. (2011) The Gift of Anger. 7 Steps to Uncover the Meaning of Anger and Gain Awareness, True Strength and Peace. Oakland: New Harbinger Publications, Inc.

Capacchione, L. (1991) Recovery of Your Inner Child. New York: Simon &Schuster.

Carter, D. (1995-2011) Thaw. Freedom from Frozen Feelings. Missouri: Internet of the Mind.

Carter, D. (1995-2012) Thawing. Adult/Child Syndrome and other Codependent Patterns. Missouri: Internet of the Mind.

Carter, D. (1995-2012) Thawing. Childhood Abandonment Issues. Missouri: Internet of the Mind.

Chamberlain, D. (1989) 'Babies Remember Pain.' Pre-and Perinatal Psychology Journal. 3 (4). pp.297 – 310

Chamberlain, D. (2013) Windows to the Womb: Revealing the Conscious Baby from Conception to Birth. California: North Atlantic Books.

Chapman, G. (2007) Anger. Handling a Powerful Emotion in a Healthy Way. Chicago: Northfield Publishing.

Cheek, J.M, Carpentieri, A.M, Smith, T.G., Rierdan, J. and Koff. E (1986). 'Adolescent Shyness' in Jones, W.H., Cheek, J.M. and Briggs S.R. (Eds.) Shyness. Perspectives on Research and Treatment. New York: Plenum Press. (pp. 105-115).

Chödrön, P. (2002). Uncomfortable With Uncertainty. Boston: Shambhala Publications Inc.

Choi, C.Q. (2011) 'Peace of Mind: Near-Death Experiences now Found to Have Scientific Explanations'. www.scientificamerican.com/article/ peace-of-mind-near-death/

Cicirelli, V.G. (2002) 'Fear of Death in Older Adults. Predictions From Terror Management Theory.' Journal of Gerontology, Psychological Sciences. 57B (4), pp.358-366.

Clark, D.M. (2005) 'A Cognitive Perspective on Social Phobia' in Crozier, W.R. and Alden L.E (Eds.) The Essential Handbook of Social Anxiety for Clinicians. Chichester: John Wiley & Sons, Ltd. Pp.193-218

Clarkson, P. (1994) The Achilles Syndrome. Overcoming the Secret Fear of Failure. Dorset: Element Books Limited.

Cloud, H. and Townsend, J. (1992). Boundaries. When to say yes and how to say no to take control of your life. Michigan: Zondervan.

Cogley, J. (2005) Wood You Believe. The Unfolding Self. The Emerging Self. Vols. 1 and 2. Kilemore Quay: Jim Cogley.

Cogley, J. (2007) Wood You Believe. The Ancestral Self. Vol. 3. Kilemore Quay: Jim Cogley

Cogley, J. (2010) *Wood You Believe. The Twinless Self.* Vol. 4. Kilemore Quay: Jim Cogley

Colt, G. H. (1991) *The Enigma of Suicide.* New York: Summit Books.

Cooper, M. (2008). *Essential Research Findings in Counselling and Psychotherapy. The Facts are Friendly.* London: Sage Publications.

Coplan, R.J., Rubin, K.H., Fox, N.A., Calkins, S.D. and Steward, S.L. *'Being Alone, Playing Alone, and Acting Alone: Distinguishing among Reticence and Passive and Active Solitude in Young Children.'* Available at: www.ncbi.nlm.nih.gov/pubmed/8131643

Cori, J.L. (2010) *The Emotionally Absent Mother. A guide to self-healing and getting the love you missed.* New York: the Experiment.

Coyle, D. (2013) *The Green Platform.* Bray: Ballpoint Press.

Crozier, W.R. and Alden L.E (Eds.) (2005) *The Essential Handbook of Social Anxiety for Clinicians.* Chichester: John Wiley & Sons, Ltd.

Dacey, J.S. and Travers, J.F. (1999) *Human Development Across the Lifespan.* Boston: McGraw-Hill

Danison, N.L (2011) Backwards Beliefs. Revealing Eternal Truths Hidden in Religions. Columbus: AP Lee &Co. Ltd.

Dawkins, M.S. Animal Minds and Animal Emotions. American Zoologist 2000: 40(6) pp.883-888

De Becker, G. (2000) The Gift of Fear. Survival Signals that Protect us from Violence. London: Bloomsbury Publishing.

DeCesare, M. (2015) Death on Demand. Jack Kevorkian and the Right-to-Die Movement. New York: Rowman & Littlefield.

Désiré, L., Veissier, I., Després, G., and Boissy, A. 'On the way to assess emotions in animals: Do lambs (Ovis Aries) evaluate an event through its suddenness, novelty, or unpredictability?' Journal of Comparative Psychology 2004: 118 (4) pp.363-374

DiMarco, H. and DiMarco, M. (2012) The Brave. Conquering the Fears That Hold You Back. Grand Rapids: Revell.

Dutton, D. G. (2007) 2nd Ed. The Abusive Personality. Violence and Control in Intimate Relationships. New York: The Guilford Press.

Echelbarger, D. (1993) 'Spirituality and Suicide' in Doka, K.J. and Morgan J.D. (Eds.) Death and Spirituality (New York) Baywood Publishing Company Inc. (pp.217-226).

Edlund, J.E. 'Sex Differences in Jealousy in Response to Actual infidelity.' Evolutionary Psychology 2004: 4 (1). pp.462-470.

Edlund, J.E and Sagarin, B.J. (2009) 'Sex differences in Jealousy: Misinterpretation of Nonsignificant Results as Refuting the Theory.' Personal Relationships, 16 (1) pp.67-68.

Ellis, A. (2001) Overcoming Destructive Beliefs, Feelings, and Behaviors. New York: Prometheus Books.

Erikson, E.H. with Erikson J.M. (1998) The Life Cycle Completed. New York: W.W. Norton & Company.

Fields, J. (2011) Uncertainty. Turning Fear and Doubt into Fuel for Brilliance. New York: Portfolio/Penguin

Filby, C. (2014) Breast Cancer. A journey from fear to empowerment. London: Britain's Next Bestseller.

Fisher, M. (2012) Mindfulness & the Art of Managing Anger. Meditation on Clearing the Red Mist. Lewes: Leaping Hare Press.

Fisher, M. (2005) Beating Anger. The eight-point plan for coping with rage. London: Rider Books.

Fontana, D. (1992) The Meditator's Handbook. A Comprehensive Guide to Eastern and Western

Meditation Techniques. Shaftesbury: Element Books Limited.

Ford, H. *Healing Jealousy (ND) (Available at: www. drhelenford.co.uk)*

Frankl, V. E. *(1984). Man's search for meaning: An introduction to logotherapy. New York: Simon & Schuster.*

Friday, N. *(1986) Jealousy. Glasgow: William Collins Sons & Co .Ltd.*

Gielen, U.P. *(2003) 'A death on the roof of the world. The perspective of Tibetan Buddhism' in Parkes, C.M., Laungani, P. and Young, B. (Eds.) Death and Bereavement Across Cultures (Hove and New York) Brunner-Routlege (pp.73-97).*

Giles, K. *(2014) Choosing Clarity. The Path To Fearlessness. Wilmington: Thomas Noble Books.*

Glasser, N. *(1989) Control Theory in the Practice of Reality Therapy. New York: Harper & Row, Publishers.*

Glasser, W. *(1998) Choice Theory. A New Psychology of Personal Freedom. New York: HarperCollins Publishers Inc.*

Glasser, W. (2000) Reality Therapy in Action. New York: HarperCollins Publishers Inc.

Graham, L. 'The Neuroscience of Attachment' at lindagraham-mft.net

Grant, M. (2015) Pain Control with EMDR. Treatment Manual. Kew: Self-published.

Greenfield, S. (2015) Mind Change. How digital technologies are leaving their mark on our brains. London: Rider Books.

Grohol, J.M. (ND) '15 Common Defense Mechanisms.' http://psychcentral.com/lib/15-common-defense *– mechanisms.*

Haemmerlie, F.M. and Montgomery, R.L (1986). 'Self-perception Theory and the Treatment of Shyness' in

Jones, W.H., Cheek, J.M. and Briggs S.R. (Eds.) Shyness. Perspectives on Research and Treatment. New York: Plenum Press. (pp. 329-342).

Haig, M. (2016) Reasons to Stay Alive. Edinburgh: Canongate Books.

Hanafin, P. (2015) Thoughts for your Journey. Thurles: Self-published.

Hanh, T.H. (2010) Reconciliation. Healing the inner child. California: Parallax Press.

Hansson, R.O. (1986). 'Shyness and the Elderly' in Jones, W.H., Cheek, J.M. and Briggs S.R. (Eds.) Shyness. Perspectives on Research and Treatment. New York: Plenum Press. (pp. 117 – 129).

Harmon, C., (2010) 'How Important is Physical Contact with Your Infant?' Scientific American, USA.

Harper, J.M. (1993) 'Ethical and Spiritual Concerns: Sexuality and Spirituality. A Wholistic Approach for the Living-Dying Client and the Partner' in Doka, K.J. and Morgan J.D. (Eds.) Death and Spirituality (New York) Baywood Publishing Company Inc. (pp.309-322).

Harris, C.R. and Darby, R.S. (2010) 'Jealousy in Adulthood' in Hart S.L and Legerstee M. (Eds.) Handbook of Jealousy. Theory, Research and Multidisciplinary Approaches. Oxford: Blackwell Publishing Ltd. pp.547-571.

Hauck, P. (1998) Jealousy. Why it happens and how to overcome it. London: Sheldon Press.

Heller L. and LaPierre (2012) Healing developmental Trauma. How Early Trauma Affects Self-Regulation, Self-Image and the Capacity for Relationship.

Berkeley: North Atlantic Books.

Huber, C. (1995) The Fear Book. Facing Fear Once and for All. U.S.A.: Keep It Simple Books.

Hurvich, M. 'Psychic trauma, annihilation anxieties and psychodynamic treatment.' Available at: www. apadivisions.org/division-39/sections/childhood/ hurvich.pdf

Ingram R.E., Ramel, W. Chavira, D. and Scher, C. 'Social Anxiety and Depression' in Crozier, W.R. and Alden L.E (Eds.) The Essential Handbook of Social Anxiety for Clinicians. Chichester: John Wiley & Sons, Ltd. (pp. 241 – 264).

Izard, C.E. and Hyson, M.C (1986) 'Shyness as a Discrete Emotion' in Jones, W.H., Cheek, J.M. and Briggs S.R. (Eds.) Shyness. Perspectives on Research and Treatment. New York: Plenum Press, (pp.147-160)

Jones, W.H. and Carpenter, B.N. (1986) 'Shyness, Social Behaviour and Relationships' in Jones, W.H., Cheek, J.M. and Briggs S.R. (Eds.) Shyness. Perspectives on Research and Treatment. New York: Plenum Press, (pp.227 – 238).

Jones, W.H., Cheek, J.M. and Briggs S.R. (Eds.) (1986) Shyness. Perspectives on Research and Treatment. New York: Plenum Press.

Jonker, G. (2003) 'The many facets of Islam. Death, dying and disposal between orthodox rule and historical convention' in Parkes, C.M., Laungani, P. and Young, B. (Eds.) Death and Bereavement Across Cultures (Hove and New York) Brunner-Routlege, (pp. 147-165).

Karnes, B. (2008) Gone from my Sight. The Dying Experience. Vancouver: Barbara Karnes Books.

Kassinove, H. (Ed.) (1995) Anger Disorders. Definition, Diagnosis, and Treatment. Washington: Taylor & Francis.

Kelsey, R. (2012) 2nd Ed. What's Stopping You? Why Smart People Don't Always Reach Their Potential and How You Can. Chichester: Capstone Publishing Ltd.

Kershaw, I. (1999) Hitler. 1889-1936: Hubris. London: Penguin Books.

Kindes, M.V. (Ed.) (2006) Body Image. New York: Nova Biomedical Books.

Krueger, L. (Ed.) (2009). Anger Management. Farmington Hills: Greenhaven Press.

Kubler-Ross, E. (1969) On Death and Dying New York: Macmillan.

Labriola, K. (ND) 'Unmasking the green-eyed Monster. Managing Jealousy in Open Relationships.' Available at: www.cat-and-dragon.com/stef/poly/Labriola/jealousy.html

Langner, T.S. (2002) Choices for Living. Coping with Fear of Dying. New York: Kluwer Academic/Plenum Publishers.

Layton J. 'How Fear Works.' Available at: science.howstuffworks.com/life/inside-the-mind/emotions/fear.htm

Leis, J.A., Heron, J, Stuart, E.A. and Mendelson, T. (2014) 'Associations between Maternal Mental Health and Child Emotional and Behavioral Problems: Does Prenatal Mental Health Matter?' Journal of Abnormal Child Psychology, 42 (I), pp. 161-171.

Lerner, J.S., Gonzalez, R.M., Dahl, R.E., Hariri, A.R. and Taylor, S.E. (2007) 'Facial expressions of emotion reveal neuroendocrine and cardiovascular stress responses.' Biological Psychiatry, 61(15), pp.253-260.

Levy, K. N., & Kelly, K. M. (2010) 'Sex differences in jealousy: A contribution from attachment theory. Psychological Science, 21(2), pp.168-173.

Loftus, E.F. (1997) Creating False Memories. Scientific American 277 (3) pp.70-75

Lohmann, R.C. (2009) The Anger Workbook for Teens. Oakland: Instant Help Books. Imprint of New Harbinger Publications, Inc.

Logie, R.D.J. and A. De Jongh, (2014) 'The "Flashforward Procedure": Confronting the Catastrophe'. Journal of EMDR Practice and Research, 8 (1), pp. 25-32.

Lou, A. and Bettner, B.L, (1996) A Parent's Guide to Understanding and Motivating Children. Media: Connexions Press

Luminare-Rosen, C. (2000) Parenting Begins Before Conception. A Guide to Preparing Body, Mind and Spirit for You and Your Future Child. Rochester: Healing Arts Press.

Luxmore, N. (2006) Working with Anger and Young People. London: Jessica Kingsley Publishers.

McBride, K. (2013) Will I Ever be Good Enough? Healing the Daughters of Narcissistic Mothers. New York: Atria.

McDowell, A. R. (2015) Making Peace with Suicide. A Book of Hope, Understanding, and Comfort. Riverside: White Flowers Press.

Markway, B., Carmin, C., Pollard, C. and Flynn T. (1992) Dying of Embarrassment. Help for Social

Anxiety & Phobia. Oakland: New Harbinger Publications, Inc.

Marshall, J. R. (1994) Social Phobia. From Shyness to Stage Fright. New York: BasicBooks.

Milescu, S. (ND) Anger Management. Self Help Guide for Controlling Your Anger. Self-published

Miller, A. (2002) The Drama for Being a Child. The Search for the True Self. London: Virago Press.

Miller, A. (1983) For Your Own Good. The Roots of Violence in Child-rearing. London: Virago Press.

Ní Chinnéide, M. (Ed.) Peig. (Ed. Baile Átha Cliath: Comhlacht Oideachais na hÉireann.

O'Shea, J. (2011) Abuse. Domestic Violence, Workplace and School Bullying. Cork: Atrium (Imprint of Cork University Press).

O'Shea, J. (2008) When a Child Dies. Footsteps of a Grieving Family. Dublin: Veritas Publications.

Palmer, S. (2006) Toxic Childhood. How the Modern World is Damaging our Children and What we can do About it. London: Orion Books Ltd.

Parnell, L. (2007) A Therapist's Guide to EMDR. Tools and Techniques for Successful Treatment. New York: W.W. Norton & Company.

Peppermint (2003-2006) Jealousy and Control. Unpublished Manuscript. www.pepperminty.com

Phillips G.M. (1986) 'Rhetoritherapy. The Principles of Rhetoric in Training Shy People in Speech Effectiveness' in Jones, W.H., Cheek, J.M. and Briggs S.R. (Eds.) Shyness. Perspectives on Research and Treatment. New York: Plenum Press. pp. 357-374.

Pines, A.M. and Bowes, C.F. (1992) Romantic Jealousy. How to recognize where jealousy comes from and how to cope with it. Psychology Today. (Taken from Pines, A.M. (1992) Romantic Jealousy: Understanding and Conquering the Shadow of Love. St. Martin's Press).

Pratto, F. (1996) 'Sexual Politics: The Gender Gap in the Bedroom, the Cupboard, and the Cabinet' in Buss D.M. and Malamuth N.M. (Eds.) Sex, Power, Conflict. Evolutionary and Feminist Perspectives. Oxford: Oxford University Press. pp. 179-230.

Rees, L. (2012) The Dark Charisma of Adolf Hitler. London: Ebury Press.

Rogers, C.R. (1951) Client Centred Therapy. Its current practice, implications and Theory. London: Constable.

Rogers, C.R. (2001) *On Becoming a Person. A Therapist's View of Psychotherapy 25th Ed.* London: Constable.

Rose, S. (1980) *The Soul After Death.* Platina: St. Herman of Alaska Brotherhood.

Rosen, E.J. (2001) *Families Facing Death. A Guide for Healthcare Professionals and Volunteers Revised Edition* San Francisco: Jossey-Bass Publishers.

Rothschild, B. (2003) *The Body Remembers. Casebook. Unifying Methods and Models in the Treatment of Trauma and PTSD.* New York: W.W. Norton & Company.

Rubin, K.H., Coplan, R.J., and Bowker, J.C. (2009) *'Social Withdrawal in Childhood.' Annu. Rev Psycho.60 pp.141-171.*

Russell, D., Cutrona, C.E and Jones, W.H (1986). *'A Trait-Situational Analysis of Shyness' in Jones, W.H., Cheek, J.M. and Briggs S.R. (Eds.) Shyness. Perspectives on Research and Treatment.* New York: Plenum Press. pp.239-249

Ryan, M.J. (2004) *Trusting Yourself. How to Stop Feeling Overwhelmed and Live More Happily with Less Effort.* New York: Broadway Books.

Samaritans (2015) Suicide Statistics Report 2015.

Sansone, R.A and Sansone, L. A. (2006) 'Borderline Personality Disorder and Body Image' in Kindes, M.V. (Ed.) Body Image. New York: Nova Biomedical Books.

Schiraldi, G.R. (2000). The Post-Traumatic Stress Disorder Sourcebook. A Guide to Healing, Recovery, and Growth. Los Angeles: Lowell House.

Shapiro, F. (2001) Eye Movement Desensitization and Reprocessing. Basic Principles, Protocols, and Procedures. 2nd Ed. New York: The Guildford Press.

Shapiro, F., Kaslow. F.W. and Maxfield, L. (Eds.) (2007) Handbook of EMDR and Family Therapy Processes. Hoboken: John Wiley & Sons.

Shapiro, F. and Forrest, M.S. (2004) Updated Edition EMDR The Breakthrough "Eye Movement" Therapy for Overcoming Anxiety, Stress, and Trauma. New York: Basic Books.

Schore, A. (2016) Affect Regulation and the Origin of the Self. The Neurobiology of Emotional Development. Classic Edition. New York: Routledge.

Shipon-Blum, E. (ND) 'What is selective Mutism?' Available at: smartcenter@selectivemutismcenter.org

Simington, J.A. (1995) 'The Power of Expressive Touch.' Humane Medicine, 11 (4) p.162-165.

Skeen, M. (2014) Love Me. Don't Leave Me. Overcoming Fear of Abandonment & Building Lasting, Loving Relationships. California: New Harbinger Publications, Inc.

Sky, T. (2015) The Joy in Dying. Restoring Love and Peace to the Dying Process So Living Can Begin. Bloomington: Balboa Press.

Solomon, S., Greenberg, J. and Psyzczynski T. (2015) The Worm at the Core. On the Role of Death in Life. UK: Allen Lane.

Sonstegard, M. (ND) Creating Harmony in the Family. A guide for parents and other adult carers. Aylesbury: Adlerian Workshops and Publications.

Steinberg, L. (2014) 'Should the Science of Adolescent Brain Development Inform Public Policy Issues' Court Review, 50, pp.70-77.

Stevens, K.B. (2013) Death: Are You Ready For The Truth? (Self-published booklet).

Sunderland, M. (2003) Helping Children with Fear. A Guidebook. Milton Keynes: Speechmark Publishing Ltd.

Szabó, G., Holderith, N. Gulyás, A.I., Fruend, T.F, and Hájos, N. (2010) 'Distinct synaptic properties of perisomatic inhibitory cell types and their different modulation by cholinergic receptor activation in the CA3 region of the mouse hippocampus.' Eur J Neurosci 31(12) pp.2234-2246

Tanaka-Matsumi, J. ((1995) In Kassinove, H. Anger Disorders. Definition, Diagnosis, and Treatment. Washington: Taylor & Francis.

Thurston, A.F. (1996) 'In a Chinese Orphanage'. The Atlantic Monthly 277 (4) pp. 28-41.

Tolle, E. On Fear. Available at: www.beliefnet.com/inspiration/2010/07/eckhart-tolle-on-fear.aspx

Trouche, S., Sasaki, J.M., Tu, T., and Reijmers L.G. (2013) 'Fear Extinction Causes Target-Specific Remodeling of Perisomatic Inhibitory Synapse' Neuron 80, (4) pp.1054–1065,

Tuan, Y-F. (1980, reprint 2013) Landscapes of Fear. Minneapolis: University of Minnesota Press.

Tubridy, Á. (2007) When Panic Attacks. Dublin: Gill & McMillan Ltd.

Venselaar, M. (2012) 'The Physics of Near-Death Experiences: A Five-Phase Theory.' Institute *of Noetic Sciences, issue 23, also available at: psychologytomorrowmagazine.com › Consciousness*

Wallace, A. (2013) Fear of death. It's about life actually. Self-published.

Wehrenberg, M. (2008) The 10 Best-Ever Anxiety Management Techniques. New York: W.W. Norton.

White, Mandy (2012) The Jealousy Game (self-published).

Whitfield, C. L. (1993). Boundaries and Relationships. Knowing, Protecting and Enjoying the Self. Florida: Health Communications, Inc.

Wiederman, M.W and Allgeier E.R. (1993) 'Gender differences in sexual jealousy: Adaptionist or social learning explanation?' Ethology and Sociobiology 14 (2) pp.115–140.

Winch, G. (2013) 'Ten Signs You Might have a Fear of Failure.' Available at: https://www.psychologytoday. com/.../201306/10-signs-you-might-have-fear-failure

Worden, J.W. (2003) Grief Counselling and Grief Therapy. A Handbook for the Mental Health Practitioner 3rd Ed. Hove: Brunner-Rutledge

Wyatt, J. (2015) Right to Die. Euthanasia, assisted suicide and end-of-life care. Nottingham: Inter-Varsity Press.

Yalom, I.D. (2008) Staring at the Sun. Overcoming the Dread of Death. London: Piatkus

Yalom, I.D. (1989) Love's Executioner and Other Tales of Psychotherapy. London: Penguin Books.

Zong, C-B and DeVoe, S.E. (2010) 'You Are How You Eat: Fast Food and Impatience.' Psychological Science 21, pp.619-622

Index

A

abdominal Breathing 89–90, 204, 205, 308, 328

acceptance 85, 126, 211, 247, 254, 255, 256, 257, 278, 279, 309, 310

adult needs 303

aggression 29, 58, 63, 64, 66, 67, 69, 70, 71, 72, 73, 79, 85, 86, 196, 329

agnostics 212, 241, 242

Ainsworth, M. 14

Alive viii, 89, 134, 219, 234, 243, 298, 304

anger ix, x, 3, 4, 7, 16, 18, 20, 22, 39, 48, 50–64, 66, 69–75, 77, 78, 79, 80, 81, 82, 83, 84, 85, 87, 88, 89, 90, 91, 92, 93, 94, 95, 96, 97, 98, 99, 101, 102, 103, 111, 113, 114, 116, 121, 122, 125, 131, 133, 154, 155, 157, 163, 164, 172, 180, 181, 195, 202, 222, 223, 235, 249, 256, 268, 273, 275, 279, 280, 285, 286, 294, 301, 302, 311, 318, 329

  anger management 52, 80, 82, 93, 95

  passive aggressive 62–64, 68–69, 82, 85

  road rage 91–92

anxiety 12, 16, 19, 20, 21, 22, 30, 47, 48, 62, 76, 77, 80, 89, 95, 101, 119, 120, 121, 125, 133, 136, 138, 145, 148, 154, 156, 157, 165, 166, 172, 176, 177, 180, 181, 184, 188, 189, 192, 194, 196, 197, 198, 199, 203, 205, 210, 222, 228, 249, 252, 253, 262, 288, 292, 299, 306, 312, 313, 315, 329

  adult separation 119, 138

www.ingramcontent.com/pod-product-compliance
Lightning Source LLC
LaVergne TN
LVHW052013080426
835513LV00018B/2019